The Concrete Cradle

THE CONCRETE CRADLE

by
Joseph N. Sorrentino

Published by Wollstonecraft Incorporated

FIRST EDITION

Printed in the United States of America

Wollstonecraft Incorporated
6399 Wilshire Boulevard
Los Angeles, California 90048

All the events in this book are based on actual case histories. Only the names of children and parents have been changed to protect their identity. All names of parents and children are fictitious, and any resemblance to the names of living persons is wholly coincidental.

Library of Congress Cataloging in Publication Data

Sorrentino, Joseph N.
The concrete cradle.

Bibliography: p.
1. Juvenile delinquency—United States.
2. Juvenile justice, Administration of—United States. I. Title.
HV9104.S74 364.36'0973 74-15935
ISBN 0-88381-010-7

To Mary Gwynn,
who only knew
how to give to people

Contents

Rock-a-bye baby,
  On the tree top.
When the wind blows,
  The cradle will rock.
When the bough breaks,
  The cradle will fall,
And down will come baby,
  Cradle and all.
    –Mother Goose rhyme

PART ONE

The Scope of Juvenile Crime in America

1 • Kaleidoscope of Juvenile Crime

Every period of life has its peculiar temptations and dangers, but youth is the time when we are most likely to be ensnared.
–Joel Hawes,
The New Dictionary of Thoughts

To many people juvenile crime is a catch-all phrase for a mountain of impersonal statistics. To me it is an almost daily encounter with children wearing expressions of bewildered hurt and cynical hate. My perspective on juvenile crime is unique in that as a youth I was a New York City gang leader and I now serve as a juvenile court judge in California. There is nothing idealistically romantic about being a juvenile judge. You are continually exposed to a stream of tragic events that can numb your senses and your emotions. The most horrendous aspects of life become your daily reality. You only hope that you can do something to improve a bad situation.

Through my eyes

From my point of view, there is nothing intangible about juvenile crime. A young couple waiting for a bus is suddenly attacked by a teenager and senselessly slashed with a straight razor. A tall, beautiful fifteen-year-old girl is picked up for prostitution after being sold by her father. A sixteen-year-old black boy savagely attacks a confused white boy of the same age, ranting, "You kept me in slavery for two hundred years." A twelve-year-old boy who has hanged twenty-seven dogs suffers such privation he cannot utter intelligible words.

The reality of juvenile court is hearing week after week of the atrocities committed by parents against their children. The depths of parental negligence cannot even be imagined. In one fatherless home, the children survive like primitive animals—eating their own feces strewn about the apartment, eating blisters off each others bodies, catching flies and mosquitoes in the air with their tongues.

The quandary of administering juvenile justice is deciding between a middle-aged woman's story of rape and a young boy's tale of seduction—and then, nearing a verdict in favor of the youth, hearing the jolting evidence that the boy is a dangerous psychopath with a history of kidnapings and brutal rapes.

Being a juvenile judge is hearing parents say in front of their daughter, "Put her away. We don't want her." It is reading a boy's long history of criminal activity and finding at the end of the report the terse comment: "Father unknown." It is wanting to change your decision after seeing a desperately frightened black girl crying "Mama, Mama!" as a burly marshal drags her from her mother's arms and away to a detention camp.

With deep sympathy for the victims of young criminals, I see my paramount responsibility as the protection of citizens from crime. But I feel an equal compassion for the young offenders who come into my courtroom. They too are victims. Far too many people forget that juvenile delinquents are children, and that behind the mask of delinquency lives a hurt and miserable child, often a child twisted by hate, stunned by violence, bound by fear. We require conformity, but too often we do not inquire into why emotions are twisted. Many of us proceed on the naive premise that delinquent children are bad simply because they want to be, because they perversely enjoy being that way. The commonly accepted theory that only punishment can make a bad child good is a fallacy. To some extent a "get tough" attitude is necessary and disciplinary measures can be useful, but sole reliance on punishment will only beget more hardened criminals.

With the mounting incidence of juvenile crime, there is an increasing clamor for harsher laws. Pressure is building for a counterattack in which the police have repressive powers. A law-enforcement lobby is asking the California legislature to change the current juvenile age so that everyone over fifteen will be treated as an adult. Such a policy, however, would be an unconscionable return to medieval penology. The growth of juvenile crime in America is significantly due to our own failure to ameliorate social conditions. Just because in times of economic struggle these conditions are worsening, we must not "cop out" by making war on our own young. The juvenile crime problem must be attacked by more enlightened social legislation, by reformation of the juvenile justice system, by community programs of prevention, and by a restoration of moral heroism.

Statistical contours

Crime is scarcely a new concern in American society, but there is an alarming upsurge of criminal acts involving the young. According to the Federal Bureau of Investigation's Uniform Crime Reports, between 1960 and 1973 the number of "juveniles" arrested, for all types of offenses, increased by 144 per cent. In 1974 nearly half of all serious crime in this country was committed by youngsters under eighteen. The FBI study reveals that serious crime by youth in the past decade has gone up 116 per cent.

By serious crimes the FBI does not mean hubcap stealing, pot smoking, window breaking, apple-off-the-pushcart thievery, or other kinds of vandalism offenses traditionally associated with youth. The increase in youth arrests from 1960 to 1973 shows an increase of 201 per cent in murder charges, 132 per cent for rape, 299 per cent for robbery, and 206 per cent for assault. Fred Nader, of the U.S. Law Enforcement Assistance Administration, believes the expression "juvenile crime" is misleading. "I don't care about the age of the kids who mug me," he says. "It isn't juvenile crime we are talking about and trying to stop. It is serious crime committed by kids, and we cannot afford to make a mistake about that."

Not only is the upsurge of juvenile crime unprecedented in our society, but there is also something unheard of in the way it has changed the lives of Americans. In New York City I interviewed Adrien Boyce, Chief of the Brooklyn Probation Department, who told me that fear of juvenile crime in New York has swelled into an intensive vigilance, giving birth to more than four hundred burglar alarm companies and locksmiths, five hundred plate-glass dealers, and over a hundred guard and patrol services. Academies for the martial arts have sprung up everywhere, as have kennels specializing in the training of guard dogs, and gun sales are booming, while women have been draining warehouse inventories of tear-gas pens and Mace.

Armed robberies, murders, and senseless physical assaults are daily occurrences that make a great many Americans, especially the elderly, afraid to use the streets and force them to barricade themselves in their homes. At no time in the past has juvenile crime been so rampant in so many segments of society. The traditional view that serious juvenile crime is a ghetto problem is changing as more and more the courts are filled with teenagers from middle-class families. Veteran probation officer Don Van Dyke of Long Beach, California, says, "Today's youth are deteriorating from *West Side Story* to Benedict Canyon."

Schools in our big cities have been terrorized by juvenile violence to a degree unknown in history. Los Angeles school authorities reported a flurry of 306 assaults on teachers and 144 assaults on campus peace officers in 1974. The violence became so frenzied in Compton, California, that the city's entire teaching staff went on strike in protest. Detroit's junior high schools have become virtual armed camps. In 1974 Drew Junior High School had to be shut down for four days because of gang shootings. In Chicago a fourteen-year-old boy, expelled from school for disciplinary problems and transferred to a correctional school, returned to his old school "with two guns blazing," shot the principal to death, and wounded the assistant principal and a teacher.

Police blotters and probation interviews

While the statistics themselves are disturbing, the case histories recorded on police blotters are even more alarming to officials as illustrating the kinds of crimes being committed by the young today. In Paterson, New Jersey, four nineteen-year-olds were indicted in the November 1974 shooting of a seventy-one-year-old judge who was slain while presiding over night court.

In Falls Church, Virginia, a seventeen-year-old high school student was charged with killing a sixteen-year-old neighbor by shooting him three times as they stood on a tree-lined street in their middle-class neighborhood. They had resumed a quarrel that had begun earlier at school.

In Los Angeles high schools there is a gang called the Crips—short for cripples—so named because its objective is to permanently cripple its victims. It has a female auxilliary called the Cripettes and, for elementary school students, the Junior Crips. In 1974 the Crips were implicated in more than a dozen mindless slayings. Scores from the gang have appeared in my court, a number of them on murder charges, and they have all exhibited the same surliness, chanting, "Crip here, man," and the same contemptuous disrespect for the law. Unlike the average juvenile defendant who will drop his eyes submissively to avoid the judge's glance, the typical Crip will go out of his way to stare defiantly, almost threateningly, into the judge's eyes.

Charles Wiggins, Chief of Intake at Detroit's Juvenile Court, believes that many of our cities are infested with a "social cancer." He expressed distress at "the collapse of respect for authority. Guns are a lot more accessible to young, compared to ten years ago when it was a big thing to have a stabbing.

Guns in the hands of minors were unheard of a decade ago in Detroit." Wiggins tells of adults renting out guns to minors for a share of robbery spoils.

Yancy Griggs, Director of Wayne County Juvenile Hall, says Detroit in 1973 was labeled "Murder City" because of 150 juvenile killings. Head of the juvenile hall staff for twenty-five years, Griggs told me that he perceives a frightening change in young attitudes. "Kids are more casual about crime today," he said. "Twenty years ago a youngster would shy away from a killer, and the one who committed the offense would be guilt-ridden. Today the kids flock around the killer. He's regarded as a big shot, a hero, and he shows no remorse, no sense of wrong." Griggs went on to say, "There has been a breakdown in the behavior patterns of the past. Violence on the streets has become so bad that one boy asked me if he could live in juvenile hall."

Inspecting the Oakland Juvenile Hall in Pittsburgh, I heard the same mournful story of burgeoning juvenile crime in that city. In response to the growing number of juvenile offenders, Pittsburgh has constructed a mammoth new detention facility for juveniles. The city now has one of the largest confinement capacities in the nation.

Marilyn Smith, who has served for nineteen years in juvenile intake in Miami and is now Assistant District Supervisor, told me, "We are getting more serious types of offenses. Children are becoming more sophisticated in their rebellious forms. I can remember when it was a really serious thing to steal a car. Now it's nothing. Today kids rob with guns. Another difference I see is middle- and upper-class kids getting into crime. Fifteen years ago it was almost nonexistent. You would not have seen a Patty Hearst robbing a bank."

Juvenile crime is also rippling out into the small towns. The smaller the city, the larger the increase in crime; this has been the pattern in recent years. FBI statistics for the first half of 1974 clearly demonstrate the trend. Crime in cities with a population under ten thousand increased 25 per cent. Concern is voiced by rural community leaders over the growing use of drugs among their young people. Frank Hull, Chief Probation

Officer for the Fifth Court District in Montana, told me, "Sixth-graders are sniffing Pam and glue. They inhale fumes from the gas in lawn mowers. Hardware stores are doing a booming business in lock caps for lawn mowers. The kids are sniffing whatever they get their hands on. Of course, there's still a lot of beer drinking in the sticks. Our small town has thirty saloons."

The problem of juvenile crime stems in part from youth's exposure to casual violence. Raised as youngsters on a television diet of Vietnam body counts, their moral perceptions have been radically altered. Assistant Los Angeles Police Chief Daryl Gates remarked: "I can't think of a time when we've had in this city fourteen- and fifteen-year-old kids who were such cold-blooded killers. They're not concerned, because nothing happens to *them*. They have no fear any more."

In his book *Crime in America*, Ramsey Clark points out that young people are not congenitally prone to violent behavior. It is often cumulative exposure to a wide spectrum of crime and corrective institutions that eventually culminates in violent behavior. The former attorney general writes: "The deep psychosis, profound instability, sickness, and cruelty essential to premeditated murder develop slowly. Children are rarely capable of it. They start out wanting things. Later they become insensitive to human feelings. Some finally rage at society."

The trend is frighteningly in favor of graver juvenile crime. According to Professor Arnold Bennett of MIT, crime statistics in the future will be even starker: Bennett predicts that a person born in New York City in 1973 has one chance in sixty-seven of being murdered. A baby born in Washington, D.C., in 1973 stands one chance in forty of meeting the same fate. One of every thirty-five children born in Detroit in 1973 is likely to meet death at a murderer's hands by the time he or she reaches adulthood.

These projections are based on the current hemorrhaging rates of crime and population levels and assume that crime's momentum will go unchecked and that public attitudes will remain substantially the same in years to come. We can only hope for a social shift that will alter these dire predictions.

They help to highlight, however, the magnitude of the crime problem America is going to have to cope with in the future and the gross inefficiency of present methods of dealing with it. They also show that we are doing something profoundly wrong in the world we are creating for our children—a world we will have to change.

2 • Middle-Class Youth

More middle- and upper-income kids commit crimes than low-income ones.
—Council of Judges,
Los Angeles, California, 1974

The photograph of Patricia Hearst holding an automatic weapon in the course of a bank robbery stunned the sensibilities of most Americans. People will long speculate on how a young woman from one of the nation's most prominent upper-class families ended up in trouble with the law and, in the ill-chosen words of former Attorney General William Saxbe, became a "common criminal." Fading in public memory but equally confounding is former debutante Diana Oughton, a member of the Weathermen, who allegedly had been planting bombs in commercial buildings before she was blown apart by an explosion in her family's New York townhouse. Both girls justified their criminal actions with political rhetoric, naively but sincerely believing that they were undoing the enemies of the people.

Children in revolt

The sixties were a turbulent era, marked by prodigious unrest and seismic waves of youth in rebellion. A sense of exhilaration was felt by activists on campuses from Berkeley to Columbia.

The so-called generation gap was deepened by political differences between the young and their parents, with feelings running strong on both sides and symbolized by long hair versus short, jeans and T-shirts versus suits and ties, rock versus Lawrence Welk. In revolt against traditional values, the younger generation adopted a new life style and set out to achieve a new utopia, sometimes resorting to criminal violence as a means to that end.

A spontaneous flowering of idealism motivated the revolutionary spirit of the sixties. It was mainly middle-class youth who occupied administration halls, confronted police, proclaimed edicts, and demanded change. Clashes on university campuses initiated a similar trend of protest in the high schools. Crystallized in this activism was an amazing insight and awareness in young people and an uncanny ability on their part to spot hypocrisy and dishonesty. But now the so-called Age of Aquarius is over, and much of the energy that was channeled into remaking society seems to have been transferred to other less socially useful outlets.

The anti-authoritarian attitudes and anti-police chic spread by rebellious students in the sixties are now part of the social outlook of many middle-class teenagers. The campus radicals—cheered on by doting superliberals—did much to erode respect not only for the police but also for all symbols of authority. Disrespect for law creates a fertile climate for crime. Branding "the establishment" corruptly evil, many young people conveniently rationalize their thefts from merchants. Shoplifting by teenagers has risen more than 124 per cent in the past decade.

Middle-class youngsters coming into juvenile court often display an ingrained bias against the judge. Part of the blame lies with the judges themselves, as evidenced in their conduct of several trials, notably the Chicago Seven case. However, a good deal of the blame can be attributed to the radicals of that era and their indulgence in overstated tirades against anything connected with government. This is not to belittle the aspirations of the activists for a better society, but only to point out that their excesses have left stereotypes implanted in the minds of middle-class youth. The label "pig" is still widely used by many middle-class kids as a term for all policemen. Excesses may be inevitable in any idealistic crusade to reform society, but those who follow are left with the damage to repair. Respect must be restored for legal institutions. Our efforts along these lines should not be another slick public relations or shabby propaganda campaign. Restoring respect should begin with redress of valid grievances against the law.

Juvenile problems in the suburbs

A University of Michigan study shows that 90 per cent of crime is committed by thirteen- to eighteen-year-old boys, but that only 8 per cent are caught, with a mere 2 per cent winding up in juvenile court. The bulk of those who are released by the police are middle- and upper-class youth. Worried people who fled crime in the city are finding it has followed them to the suburbs. FBI statistics for the first half of 1974 show arrests in the suburbs are up 21 per cent. The biggest rise in suburban crime has been against property—larceny, burglary, and auto theft. However, violent crime was also up 10 per cent, twice the increase for big cities.

Recently a youth scandal rocked the Irvine community in Orange County in Southern California. Developed with careful attention to providing maximum privacy, isolation from disruptive influences, and idyllic scenery, the new community was assumed to be an ideal place to raise children, the quintessence of the American dream. The Irvine Company, the developers, proclaimed in its sales pitch: "In these new villages life is more peaceful and fulfilling than in a community that lacks these same planning advantages." The company was dumbfounded in its tranquil villages when nearly a hundred drug users and traders were arrested—the largest drug roundup in one suburb in American history. The police officers who made the arrests marveled at the sophistication of the teenage drug ring they broke up there.

As the police loaded more than a dozen middle-class teenagers into a paddy wagon, neighbors stood on the sidewalks and cheered. But the underlying question is how could something so tawdry happen in the midst of such a protective environment? An Irvine Company executive summed it up this way: "All the kids want to talk street talk and be tough." His analysis may be accurate as far as it goes, but it misses the root of the problem.

An article by Mike McFadden in the May 3, 1974, issue of *New Times* exposes the falsehood of the Irvine Company's claim that the planned village was a model community. In reality, the town was so homogenized, so middle-class, so "blah," that the kids really had to hunt for something exciting to do. Some turned to crime; as one teenager confessed, "It was simple. You can get the floor plan to any house you want from the sales office." Others turned to narcotics out of simple boredom. One of the arrested teenagers confessed: "It's an escape from the crap at home, there's an identification; it's status to use dope and it's an easy way to get into sex."

Middle-class teenage criminals are clearly not dogged by poverty, taking to the streets at an early age for survival. Rather, they are delinquents of affluence. They live in pleasant, even luxurious homes, lacking few material benefits. Their parents are the kind of people our society calls responsible—lawyers, teachers, businessmen. But somewhere along the way—just where is not always clear—these children find themselves in trouble. A process of withdrawal develops. Normally good students may begin doing badly in school. They may become irritable, ill-tempered, and even assaultive toward the very people they are closest to in feeling. A sullen, middle-class girl in my court repeatedly threatened to shoot her father.

For some, this alienation eventually results in car stealing, drug dealing, or robbery. It is called "acting out," the visible manifestation of unhappiness, fear, or insecurity, a sign that something is seriously wrong with the young person's life. The middle-class child "acting out" is typically suffering from emotional neglect, and it has nothing to do with whether he lives in an exquisite mansion in Beverly Hills or a modest duplex in Long Island. One counselor put it this way: "These kids are rejected. There is a lack of love and poor communications with the parents. Often it is the way the kid says, deep down, I'm in pain and I need help to relieve it. But the parents, whether too self-centered or insensitive, fail to see it."

Educational counselor Walter Brandt of Beverly Hills believes that affluence has created a personality dilemma for youth—the so-called middle-class delinquency syndrome. This commonly arises in a single-parent situation, or in a household in which both parents are ardently competitive people with little time for their children. The child, left alone for long periods of time, develops an extremely poor self-image; television tends to become a focal influence in his or her life. At the now earthquake-rubbled Sylmar Juvenile Hall near Los Angeles, a large percentage of the offenders were girls from fashionable middle-class homes in nearby Van Nuys; their ambitious fathers worked in perpetual motion twelve hours a day and their socializing mothers were away from home a good deal of the time. Children from such homes receive appallingly little training in carrying out responsibilities.

Derailed from their plans for the day, many middle-class parents come grudgingly into juvenile court with a resentful attitude. I find myself getting rankled with such people, although I try not to let it affect my disposition of the case. In one instance a mother who was having a great deal of difficulty communicating with her son told me, "Frankly, I think it's normal to hate your son." Not allowing her to get away with that remark in front of the boy, I replied, "No, I think it's more normal to love your own child. If you could start showing love for him, maybe he might begin to obey you."

In another case a Beverly Hills father acted as though the whole matter was an embarrassment to him, an annoying distraction. He was extremely impatient to get the trial over with. I ruled that his fifteen-year-old daughter was an "incorrigible child" on the grounds that she was beyond the control of her parents. The father stiffened upon hearing these words. I ordered the girl removed from her home and placed in an institution under a program of intensive therapy. Putting one arm affectionately around his daughter, the father jabbed his free hand at me and loudly disputed my decision. He insisted that he could control his child and he wanted her at home. Part of his act was to belatedly show his daughter how much he cared for her, but she was not impressed by his eleventh-hour outburst of concern. A pretty green-eyed blond, she sat silently, her eyes glazed, her skin sallow, her mind in an LSD stupor. I reminded the man of the facts in the case, that his daughter had a long history of drug use, that at one time or another she had been involved with marijuana, mescaline, cocaine, heroin, DMT, STP, PCP, Seconal, Nembutal, Tuinal, Demerol, Toluene. "Unless we remove her, sir," I said, "your daughter is on her way to dying."

A recurring problem for suburban kids is gnawing boredom. Picture a quiet suburban community on a weekday afternoon. School is over for the day. Television offers an untantalizing array of soap operas. Baseball and football have been played so many times there is nothing alluring about them, and tinkering with model airplanes has grown stale. Fundamentally interesting things remain to be done, but young people are tempted to try adventurous experiences that to them are extraordinary. Add to this situation a shifting sense of morality, changes in the family structure, and an entertainment medium that continually glorifies violence, and we have a fermenting recipe for juvenile crime.

Jack Kerouac's character Dean Moriarty claimed to have stolen hundreds of cars when he was a teenager in Denver, racing them into sublime breezes in the mountains on lost summer afternoons. Such heady escapades offer an irresistible excitement when stacked up against hours of suburban tameness. Cars represent a potent, masculine force, identified with "successful" people in a society that emphasizes speed and strength. The rash of car stealing ought not come as a surprise since it is an inverted reflection of American values. The middle-class youth who blazes along the highway in somebody else's car is out for thrills to compensate for the sanitized dullness of suburbia.

A teenage boy may steal a car on a dare, or because he wants some luxury—a luxury that his parents would probably pay for—but he feels independent and manly if he can get it himself in a way that flouts the establishment. Jerry Rubin's *Do It!*, a book whose errant philosophy infatuates certain segments of America's youth, advocates among other things "liberating the contents of department stores." The appeal of this "yippie" spirit to high school kids is not that it represents a serious political ideology but that it is enticingly novel, attractively out of the ordinary, and pungently contrary to what parents say to young people on the subject of personal property.

Imagine a young woman with a large shopping bag, pausing before a perfume or cosmetics counter, casually placing some item in her bag, and, with this exciting secret information, continuing her rounds in the store. In San Francisco, for example, a young woman from a wealthy family carried on a spirited and successful shoplifting operation at the stores of only the most exclusive designers. She would appear in a boutique in an expensive, well-tailored full-length beaver coat that covered only undergarments; then, ostensibly selecting a dress for purchase, she would take it into the dressing room and, once having put on the garment, nonchalantly make her exit from the store. The frequency with which she played this game eventually led to her detection. The shoplifting had obviously been only a lark for her because her family could easily afford to retrieve her from jail and pay the costs of defending her in court. Shoplifting, arrest, trial, attention—were all titillating novelties for someone with a comfortable background.

Runaways

Charles Dickens wrote movingly of children running away from home as a way of solving a desperate situation. Today running away is diagnosed as a child's way of calling attention to his problems, not solving them. The runaway is trying to tell emotionally deaf parents: "I've run away. Don't you want me back? Show that you love me by trying to find me!" It is not uncommon for children of six or seven to "run away" by skirting around the block. Suburban youngsters often run away only to call home to tell their parents in tearful voices why they left. But these are not the young people who make it into the endless runaway statistics. Legions of young people who leave home are never heard of again by their parents. Teen vagabonds who leave home for the big city, with a knapsack of clothes and a pocketful of savings, have no clear goal in mind. They are erratic children, impulsively fleeing to an unknown world lurking with perils. These young people find it necessary, because of family problems real or imagined, to take drastic action and to enter a way of life swarming with hardships and risks.

Of the flocks of young people who make it into police files as runaways every year, a certain number will end up as prostitutes, addicts, suicides, and murder victims. Runaways so careful to avoid the police for fear they will be returned home are easy prey to offers of false protection and security. Paranoically concealing their identities, they are among the most vulnerable members of society.

The problem of runaways is vividly highlighted by the infamous homosexual torture-murder spree that was revealed in Dallas in the summer of 1973. No more graphic example can be found of how missing children can be lumped into a swamp of runaway statistics, making it virtually impossible for parents to obtain assistance in locating them. It was discovered after the horrible story of Dallas kidnapings and murders came to light that all but one family had reported their children missing. In almost every case the police gave vague promises of action, but failed to delve into the disappearances. The authorities assumed each time that yet another child had joined the ranks of the "twentieth-century children's crusade." And yet, had the police recognized the pattern that was being established over a year by the repeated disappearances in one Dallas suburb, perhaps they could have put a stop to one of the century's most depraved series of crimes. The grisly murders of these teenagers were buried in the massive statistics.

The experimental generation

According to FBI figures from the years 1960 to 1973, youth arrests for violation of narcotics laws increased a colossal 4,673 per cent. Among the major reasons for this steep rise was the entry of middle-class youth into drug use and dealing. In his book *The Pleasure Seekers*, Dr. Joel Fort estimates that up to twelve million youngsters flirt with marijuana in America today. "Far more significant than the number of millions involved," says Dr. Fort, "is the fact that marijuana use now pervades all socioeconomic, occupational, and age groups in American society."

In a recent study conducted at a high school in West Los Angeles, a middle-class area, Dr. Thomas Ungerleider, a drug expert at UCLA's Center for the Health Sciences, found that 80 per cent of the student body had tried marijuana. Dr. Ungerleider states: "I'm convinced that I can tell the extent of the drug-abuse problem at any high school just by going to the parking lot and counting the number of cars. The problem will be proportionate, whether in Beverly Hills, Cocoanut Grove, Westchester County, or Highland Park. It doesn't mean that they aren't using drugs in Watts, but that they're using them for different reasons."

Contemporary evidence fails to show that marijuana use leads to an increase in serious crime. Since marijuana is not addictive, moderate use does not create a burdensome habit. Respected researchers and law-enforcement personnel as well recognize it as a relatively innocuous substance *if* used sparingly. This point is valid as far as it goes—but it does not tell the whole story. Research on marijuana is inconclusive. Although the body of hard facts is still incomplete, one can say with certainty that marijuana use is widespread in nearly all segments of the community. One can also say definitely that a great deal of browbeating and hectoring rages on both sides of the issue. Marijuana may cause withdrawal from ordinary levels of reality, or incline users toward social irresponsibility, but its use does not lead to a rise in juvenile crime—except in one way: marijuana use itself is defined as a crime.

A large percentage of those counted as juvenile offenders are arrested for simple possession or use of marijuana. Court calendars are clogged every day, to a large extent, because of middle-class kids up on drug charges. In 1973 California processed ninety-five thousand marijuana cases, mostly juveniles, at a cost to the taxpayers of $100 million in court time. The drug scene is to juvenile justice what war was to the economy.

The fact is inescapable that while marijuana remains illegal, its use adds to the juvenile crime problem. The solution may well be a modified decriminalization of the drug. Criminalization has failed to deter youth's use of marijuana, and has instead bred disrespect for the law, caused enormous waste of taxpayers' money, and created criminal records for otherwise law-abiding young people. It is time to re-examine our position on outlawing the "social grasser," who poses no more threat to society than does the social drinker.

Of more concern to society should be the problem of hard-drug usage. In December 1974 over two hundred student drug pushers were arrested at twenty-four high schools in Los Angeles. Police involved in the roundup indicated that many of the students were from middle-class communities and, alarmingly, peddling a wide variety of narcotics, including barbiturates and "angel dust," the street term for a pharmaceutical substance known as PCP, whose proper use is as a horse tranquilizer.

Robert DuPont, Director of the President's Special Action Office on Drug Abuse Prevention, claims that as 1975 began all indicators of hard-drug use were ominously up. The recent heroic epidemic battled in this country at a drain of millions of dollars and inestimable human misery, threats to erupt anew, recapturing old victims and savaging a new generation of American youth. Minnesota Senator Walter Mondale says that an outbreak could claim a hundred thousand new addicts a year and soon equal or exceed the worst devastation of the previous epidemic. One measure of the worsening situation is the number of heroin-related deaths. Between 1971 and 1973 that figure fell from 1,726 to 1,017. For the first half of 1974 alone, the death toll was 691. Applicants at treatment centers are also rising. From July to September of 1974, hospitals reported a 66 per cent increase in overdose cases compared with the same period in the previous year.

In the past heroin was concentrated in the nation's urban

ghettos. Today arrests, evidence of addiction, and heroin-related crimes are showing up in the suburbs and small towns. For example, addiction is rising in Des Moines, Iowa; Eugene, Oregon; and Jackson, Mississippi.

Jerome Hornblass, head of the Addiction Services Agency in New York City, where half the nation's addicts live, says the old drug epidemic never really abated; rather, large numbers of heroin addicts switched to other drugs when critical shortages developed in the heroin supply due to the discontinued opium crop in Turkey. Hornblass contends that heroin is the drug choice for thousands not now using it. Other experts agree.

The chief reason for fears about an upsurge in the heroin traffic and use in the United States was Turkey's decision last July to remove its ban on the growing of opium poppies. The decision has been assailed as a declaration of war against our children. Even without Turkish heroin returning to American streets, there would still be a threat of an epidemic because of supplies from other sources. According to John Bartels, Jr., of the Justice Department, the biggest volume of heroin supply now comes from Mexico. When Turkish law prohibited opium manufacture, Mexican "brown" heroin–a more cheaply produced variety–was put under extensive cultivation. The Drug Enforcement Agency reports that Mexican "brown," which once amounted to less than 10 per cent of the heroin used in the United States, now provides over 60 per cent of the present consumption. A blizzard of brown has hit the streets in such a pure state that dealers are staining white heroin brown to make it more salable. Mexican poppy production, concentrated in the mountainous Sinaloa State on the Pacific Coast, has proliferated by quantum leaps with no sign of leveling off. No precise production figures are available because of the many groups and connections involved, but State Department officials say that anyone with a few thousand dollars who is willing to take the personal risks can play the Mexican game.

More heroin supplies from Southeast Asia's Golden Triangle–the border region of Thailand, Burma, and Laos–have also been reaching U.S. cities. With the sharp reduction of American troops in Vietnam, substitute markets are being sought in America for the twelve-hundred-ton annual Asian crop. Together, the Mexican and Far East reservoirs can quench the approximately sixty-ton annual heroin thirst in America.

Experts agree that the U.S. epidemic could be regenerated without any new Turkish production, but with it the ravage would be nightmarishly worse. The Drug Enforcement Agency reasonably speculates that only fifteen square miles of opium fields in any of more than forty countries with the right soil and climate could supply half a million U.S. addicts. During the last epidemic, up to 80 per cent of the heroin supply came from Turkey. Through U.S. payments of $35 million in compensatory aid, in 1971 Ankara agreed to halt opium production, which galvanized a dramatic shrinkage in the American addict population. Now the first seeds of a new crop are being planted in Turkey and U.S. intelligence forecasts that the 1975 harvest will reap two hundred tons of opium, the largest crop ever.

With more heroin in circulation, teenagers who were not caught up in the earlier outbreak will begin using the drug. Dr. Mark Greene, a chemical scientist with the President's Special Action Office, says most youngsters are convinced they can stop or pull back before there is any real danger of addiction. First-time users are usually divinely ecstatic over heroin.

Undaunted by the warning wrecks of known addicts, they tend to eagerly turn on their friends to heroin. It is estimated that one middle-class user, through the pyramid process, can induce more than a thousand persons to use heroin in one year. Normally the first use does not involve a back-alley pusher, but occurs in a social setting in someone's home. After the first year, those on heroin stop trying to bring others into their circle. By this time they have seen the dismaying evidence of their own helpless degradation.

"For a long time, I just lied to myself," said fifteen-year-old Cindy Blatt, just one of countless kids who have turned to robbery and prostitution to support their habits. Cindy thought it could never happen to her, but she became so hooked that she had to have a fix in the morning before she could even brush her teeth.

If a new heroin epidemic hits America, middle-class youth will be among its victims, quite possibly its major victims. In addition to heroin, middle-class youngsters are dabbling with a milky way of other dangerous drugs. Sedatives, stimulants, and tranquilizers are prescribed by doctors at a fantastic rate. About a half million drug users are judged abusers, and many of these are middle-class youngsters who began in the medicine cabinet.

The daily life of a heroin addict can be a hellishly debased ordeal. Robert Masser, a bright, educated youth from a middle-class home who was once an inmate at California's Corona Rehabilitation Center, tells what being an addict is like for him. "Life leads from the crest of one delightful thrill," he says, "to the trough of one disheartening illusion." He lives in an apartment amuck with slop; his belongings are in disarray; his clothes are putrid; his body is filthy. He is unwilling to take a bath because hot water on the skin while under the influence of heroin adulterates the strength of the drug. He suffers from abnormal bowel movements, a condition known as "yen-shee baby," a solid mass of excretion that is formed by the accumulation of food wastes stored in the bowel tract, which, Robert says, "are roughly the size of two baseballs." The exit of the "yen-shee" is extremely painful because it tears the opening of the rectum as it forces its way from the body, causing copious bleeding. For a long time Robert had gonorrhea but didn't know it because heroin prevents the visible symptoms of an inflammatory disease. Shadows of prison follow him everywhere because being locked up is a way of life for him. He dreads most going to prison because of the abruptly forced abstinence from heroin, which cannibalizes his body in the exploding agony of cold turkey. No matter how ungodly excruciating the pain and sweating from this crucible however, predictably upon his release Robert will compulsively go searching out heroin again. Totally enslaved by the drug, he will stalk the streets, obsessed with stealing the sixty dollars he needs for "the buy," and he will break into an automobile, shatter a store window, or beat a woman to the ground until he gets it.

While heroin remains the number-one drug enemy because of its criminalizing power, the indiscriminate use of other illicit chemicals for thrills must also be checked. No one knows what delayed after-effects will surface in ensuing years. As one ex-addict who plunged into LSD, speed, valium, mescaline, marijuana, angel dust, rainbows, and reds told me, "We are uncertain about the future. The real effects of taking drugs, even for those of us who have stopped, are not going to be known for a long time. For example, I felt very safe, doctors told me there would be no permanent effects, but now they're saying I have definite scar tissue on the brain. My generation has no idea how we're going to turn out. We are an experimental generation."

3 • Girls in Trouble

Scientists noted that America's greatest source of unused brain-power was women.
—Betty Friedan,
The Feminine Mystique

On a darkened side street in Long Beach, California, Mrs. Margaret Collier, a fifty-seven-year-old bookkeeper, steps into a phone booth in front of a closed gas station as two young miniskirted girls move out of an alley into the faint light from apartment windows. Together they walk toward the phone booth, two teenagers, chattering on their way home. Mrs. Collier, finding trouble getting a dial tone, calls out, "Does this phone work?"

The girls' mood suddenly changes. "Who cares, bitch?" one of them sneers as they rush the older woman.

"What's going on?" The woman cringes back into the booth.

"Let go of that fuckin' purse!"

"Go away." Mrs. Collier clings tenaciously to her purse. The girls grab for it but she has it clutched in her arms.

"You gonna get it, bitch!"

"Help, someone! Help!"

As the three struggle in the tight space, one of the girls picks up the phone receiver and smashes Mrs. Collier in the face.

She screams in pain as blood spurts from her nose. She sags in the booth, but she is still conscious, and she squeezes her purse as if her life depends on retaining possession. One of the girls whips the phone receiver down against her head with thudding force, bashing her once, twice, three times. Finally, the woman collapses in a faint, releasing the grip on her purse. The two girls pick it up but don't immediately run off. They remain to kick the victim repeatedly with their chunk-heeled shoes, opening cuts and bruises across her face; then they run off laughing. Mrs. Collier was found ten minutes later by an off-duty fireman, who rushed her to Harbor General Hospital where she was treated for a severe concussion.

Rising female juvenile crime

The most shockingly dramatic change in youth crime has been the swift rise of female juvenile felonies. FBI statistics show that young female crime climbed a staggering 358 per cent between 1960 and 1973. At the Norwalk Court, where I have served as a juvenile judge, we processed 495 female offenders in the first half of 1974. Among these were twenty charged with strong-arm robberies, forty-two with theft, twenty-one with assault with a deadly weapon, thirty-two with burglary, two with homicide, thirty-eight with battery, ten with prostitution, one with arson, eighteen with violating warrants, ten with resisting arrest, fifty with drug offenses, and one with rape. The Norwalk Court has a tough urban ghetto in its jurisdiction, but even for this area the statistics represent an outlandish metamorphosis in female behavior.

At the outset of 1974 three young females—Bernardine Dohrn, Katherine Power, and Susan Saxe—were among the FBI's ten most-wanted fugitives. After making headlines with their bold crimes, later in the same year the female leaders of the SLA made the list. Marilyn Smith, a veteran of nearly two decades in Florida corrections, told me: "The role of the female has changed. She has become more aggressive, more emancipated, no longer just wife and mother. There is a new genre of women gangsters as heroine models." The same observation was echoed three thousand miles away. Ruth Bryan, director of the female wing of Los Angeles Central Juvenile Hall noted that ten years ago her problems with girls were sexual promiscuity, incorrigibility, and truancy. Today, girls are coming in for serious crimes as heads of burglary rings, accessories to gun robberies, and principals in homicides. Mrs. Bryan questioned the two girls who committed the strong-arm robbery against Mrs. Collier and found their implacable attitude summed up in the remark, "We'll get what we can get." Recalling her early days in juvenile work, Mrs. Bryan said, "When I first started this work, girls were more concerned about their fellow man. Our whole world is in the same 'dog eat dog' boat now. It's a predatory business. The microcosm in here reflects an ugly trend out there."

At a time when women are matching men stride for stride in legitimate endeavors once considered the exclusive domain of men, young women are beginning, unfortunately, to emulate men in the areas of crime and violence. The FBI's survey shows an astounding escalation of female participation in murders, muggings, assaults. They are the primary maimers of infants. They rob stores, steal cars, shoplift jewelry, and embezzle from banks. They sway the radical revolutionary movement today, and the FBI considers women terrorists the deadliest of all its wanted criminals. Half a century ago, women were told that the hand that rocked the cradle ruled the world. Today, that hand may be wielding a knife, brandishing a gun, or throwing a stick of dynamite. The liberation of women, which recently unshackled their energies in all directions, may have also indirectly contributed to an era of previously unknown female aggression. "Liberated women," says anthropologist Ashley Montagu, "have the aspiration and gumption to outdo men in crime. They can be better criminals than men. They are smarter. They will closely approximate men in crimes of violence, and as mob and racket leaders they will be judged not as women but on the basis of what they can deliver."

Dr. Leon Salzman, clinical professor of psychiatry at the Albert Einstein College of Medicine, claims: "There is no biological reason for the female to be less aggressive than the male. It's just that being aggressive had no meaning in a woman's life until she had the possibility a man does. Violence for women is simply no longer a positively unacceptable form of behavior. Women will move into all areas of living—including crime."

Feminism and crime

It would be extremely unfair to place the onus for rising female crime on the women's movement. Certainly the intent of the feminists is not to enlarge the criminal population. Their very legitimate aspiration is to achieve full equality as human beings. Acceptance, in business, the arts, athletics, and politics—not in prison—is what they ask. As one woman told me, "I want to be a complete person." In their struggle to secure complete personhood, they have become exposed to the same cultural factors which attract males to crime. The explanation for rising female crime lies in these factors, not in the condition of or efforts to secure equality.

Without indicting the entire feminist movement one can single out highly publicized extremist groups who do directly incite women to aggressively hostile acts, violence, and rancor between the sexes. The Society for Cutting Up Men (SCUM), founded by fanatical firebrand Valerie Solanas, sees the solution to female oppression in terms of castration and sexual murder. To prove her organization meant business, Valerie shot and wounded artist Andy Warhol. The Ballbreakers Intent on Totally Castrating and Humiliating Men (BITCH), led by Vassar graduate Carol Hennessey, scoffs at the notion that female progress is going to be made through legalistic, evolutionary efforts. Ms. Hennessey says, "Legislatures, courts, and all the other power institutions are male-controlled and manipulated by men steeped in the folklore of penis-politics. Petitions for the redress of grievances are useful only for ass-wiping." Her strategy for overthrowing male domination is a doctrine of sinister sexual sabotage: "We already have men by the balls. We need only flex the appropriate muscles and squeeze and twist."

At the 1969 national convention of Students for a Democratic Society, a group of belligerent, organized women formed their own caucus and made demands that were startling at the time. They demanded the removal of gender from language, the abolition of marriage, and recompense for past sexist oppression. Some of these same women were members of the Weatherwomen faction of the SDS, which in October 1969 made its debut in the streets of Chicago. Young feminists, during the so-called "Days of Rage," dressed in helmets, Levis, and biker-boots, roared through the Loop shouting slogans, smashing windows, and terrorizing the public. When the police arrived, many of the girls did not retreat, but instead remained to do battle, charging into the police to batter them with their pipes and chains, and at closer range to kick them in the groin. In the seventies the Weatherwomen moved underground, not abandoning their insurrectionist aims but pursuing them more clandestinely, popping up in the news only sporadically as suspects in a bomb blast.

For anthropologist Margaret Mead, women as revolutionaries may be far more vicious and ruthless than men ever thought of being. "Females," Dr. Mead says, "have been accustomed over the centuries to fight only to save their young, and so they fight to kill. They will actually be fiercer than males, less amenable to rules, more likely to carry the fighting to deadlier lengths."

Drawing my own conclusions from historical evidence, I doubt that women will ever eclipse men in deadly ruthlessness. The diabolical "final solution" of the Nazis—the cold cremation of millions of human lives, including infants—was conceived and engineered almost exclusively by males. The Boston Strangler, Jack the Ripper, Bluebeard, and most of the other fiends in history's hall of infamy are men. Common sense tells us that savagery is a potential of the human animal without regard to gender. No inherent trait can be traced to sex that would predispose a male or female to greater viciousness.

But as more and more teenage girls take part in activities that were previously engaged in only by boys, as they move away from having tea parties with their dolls and playing house and grow up less fettered by rigid concepts of what is masculine and what is feminine, exposed to the same pressures and influences as boys are, we can expect to see more females fall into the role of criminal. The proper response is not to condemn feminism but to make society a morally healthier place for all people.

Teen prostitutes

On Crenshaw Boulevard in Los Angeles around eleven o'clock at night, it is not uncommon to see attractive, highly made-up seventeen-year-old girls wearing skimpy hot pants, tight sweaters, and glossy boots, waving at passing motorists, winking at male strollers, and flouncing down the boulevard in a nocturnal promenade. Of course, streetwalking is nothing new; what is novel is that these teenagers have independently set up their own illegal enterprise without the benefit of pimps who traditionally launch young prostitutes. In the past a young streetwalker felt vulnerable without a man to protect her. Today's generation of prostitutes are not only more confident of their ability to protect themselves, but there are growing incidents in which they have been the aggressors, attacking and mugging their male customers.

According to FBI statistics, prostitution by teenagers between 1960 and 1973 increased 286 per cent. In 1974 Detroit police reported that 65 per cent of arrested prostitutes were under eighteen. A steadily bulging number of our six hundred thousand youthful runaways are entering the "oldest profession." Still more distressing is an article by Joyce Greller, "The Child Hustler," describing a growing sex market for precocious pubescent children who have not yet even reached their teens. "In most cities," she says, "this 'baby pro' action is practiced with a certain amount of discretion. But in major cities like New York, Los Angeles, Dallas, and Chicago picking up a child hustler is as easy as finding a stud or a seasoned hooker."

The splintering of America's monolithic morality into a loose pluralism has facilitated the rise of prostitution. Changed social attitudes help explain why legalized prostitution has become one of the biggest industries in the state of Nevada. Automobile and jet mobility also give restless children an easier exit from the orbit of family control. Eighteen-year-old streetwalker Bonnie Jones traces the rising demand for prostitutes to the American housewife: "She keeps us in business," Bonnie says. "God bless her. Those overfed, overdressed smug little bitches help buy my clothes and car every year. If all the wives woke up at once, and gave husbands what they wanted, I'd be waiting on tables in a beer joint. But I'm not worried. Business is getting better every month. As long as the average woman thinks she has a golden vagina I'll be in good shape."

Why do teenagers become prostitutes? Today it is not only poverty-stricken girls who need to walk the streets in order to make a living. Teen prostitutes come from every strata of society, including many middle-class runaways. Reluctant to return home, and unable to land a satisfying job, a girl may decide to sell her body. Often she starts out with the "ball for bed" rule—she gets lodging in exchange for sexual favors. Later these girls graduate to full-fledged prostitution—for the money, or the clothes, or the chance to meet older men (father figures), or just because they like the life style.

Melrose Shelby, a high school dropout, says of her entry into prostitution: "I don't like regular hours on a job. I like to mingle with people. The money doubles what I made in an insurance office. It's a terrific challenge. Every dude is different. Mostly, they're lonely. I have pride. I'm a good prostitute. Everybody's satisfied when he leaves, and not just physically. I talk to them. Dudes need compliments. They get bored with the same thing."

In 1972 females accounted for 50 per cent of all the juvenile arrests in San Bernardino County, California, a large number of them on charges of prostitution. As to the nature of the girls, an officer of the San Bernardino County Probation Department gave the following description: "The typical female offender is a dependent individual. She flounders around. She is lost. She identifies with criminally prone males and is usually involved with drugs. These are the kinds of girls who repeatedly offend. They're hard to keep track of, they're liars, and they make excuses. They are completely lost in terms of our society."

A popular notion is that girls turn to prostitution because of some major dissatisfaction with the usual male-female relationship. Kate Millet writes in *Sexual Politics:* "Prostitution, when unmotivated by need, might well be defined as a species of psychological addiction built on self-hatred." Others speculate that these girls have weak fathers, and that they are responding to the early feelings they had when they first began to resent their fathers. In *Sisters of the Night,* Jess Stearn depicts prostitutes as sick, bent on self-destruction: "They first destroy what males prize about everything else in a girl—female virtue." Psychologists Benjamin and Masters discredit the pathological labels pinned on prostitutes as no longer valid. They maintain that frigidity is higher among nonprostitutes and find that the majority of prostitutes are quite free of neurotic involvements and experience frequent orgasms. Based on my own nonscientific observations from the bench, I would say that the teen prostitutes coming into court from the ghetto do not appear to be suffering from psychiatric disorders. On the other hand, I perceive flagrant emotional turmoil in many of the middle-class prostitutes, especially the runaways. This distraught breed shows symptoms of inner chaos—isolated, insecure, filled with illusions.

Whatever the reasons, the courts are faced with an increasing number of tender-aged girls selling flesh. The antediluvian answer is articulated by moralist J. G. Mancini, who calls for scourging retribution. He says this "sinful crime" should never be punished as a misdemeanor, and urges a long imprisonment to cure any desire to start again. "The guilty girls must be tracked down by the police," he insists, "driven out of public places, watched in their homes, and then they will be dissuaded from vice." Fortunately for civilized society, this rack mentality is growing extinct.

Contemporary judges vary radically in their attitudes toward prostitution. The Honorable Morris Schwalb of New York City Criminal Court does not advocate long imprisonment but he does believe in locking prostitutes in jail for a spell to curb venereal disease. His assessment of a health hazard from prostitution is based on a limited survey done in New York in 1966, when forty-seven hundred women arrested for prostitution were carefully examined for venereal disease. Of the group, more than thirteen hundred had positive blood tests for syphilis. When the story hit the papers it was emphasized that 28 per cent were infected with venereal disease. Actually, only four women had syphilis. The others had biologically spurious positive tests. Gonorrhea, however, was actually found in over six hundred girls, a serious incidence of 13 per cent.

Judge Schwalb was also concerned with the crimes associated with solicitation. In New York a man was murdered outside the Hilton Hotel when he shunned the advances of a prostitute. Another was robbed. A growing number of businessmen, tourists, and residents are complaining of being physically jostled by brash young streetwalkers. By clamping down on solicitation, Judge Schwalb hopes to curb the accompanying abuses.

Enforcement of the law against solicitation is troublesome, even with minors, because most are knowledgeable about police tactics. It is difficult to gather evidence of solicitation without entrapping the girl. The law in numerous jurisdictions dictates that the prostitute be the first one who mentions price, which the police are finding increasingly difficult to get them to do. As one officer complained, "The broads are wisening up. One of them told me she can always spot a cop because we never say, 'Hey, baby, how would you like to turn a trick for ten bucks?'—which is what a lot of these trollers say." If the policeman quotes a price, the case will automatically be dismissed. The frustrating problem created for the officer in the field is illustrated by the following account:

"I was trolling one night and a broad walked over to the car and said, 'Mister, I'm in trouble, I could use a little money.'

"I said, 'Well, I might be able to help you out provided I get something for my money.'

"She said, 'You'll get something; how much you giving?'

"I said, 'How much you asking?'

"She said, 'How much you offering to pay?'

"I said, 'How's about a dollar?'

" 'Oh, mister,' she said, 'you must be a policeman,' and walked off.

"You see, we got to get them to set the price. Otherwise we're doing the soliciting."

Instead of tougher laws, legalization of prostitution has been proposed by some authorities. The California legislature wisely rejected this solution. Prostitution deeply exploits both female and male. Legalization implies society's stamp of approval. It would be better to modify current laws. Margaret Mead denounces existing laws on prostitution as "cruel, barbarous, and discriminatory against females. They punish, exploit, and blackmail women." I believe it would be better to concentrate on laws protecting the minor. The young runaway prostitute—helpless, dependent, desperate to stay away from home, naively gullible—is vulnerable to gross exploitation. Weaned on the "new morality," these girls are eagerly willing to have recreational sex, and therefore prostitution does not seem like a bad life. As one fourteen-year-old said, "Sex is fun—why not get paid for it?" This same teenager was being used by a commercial wholesaler to promote business with his buyers. She was set up in a Hollywood apartment, provided with a false I.D., and paid a hundred dollars to "entertain" planeloads of buyers coming to the west coast. Respectable and established businessmen, they would have trembled had they known the girl was well under the age limit for statutory rape. In no way was her age belied by her appearance. This girl had a more mature figure than the thirty-year-old police woman standing next to her in court.

Freelance writer Joyce Greller reports of brothels in America specializing in the pre-teen trade where the customers intentionally seek out very young girls. Despicably exploited, many of these girls are saturated with mind-hazing drugs and spend their adolescent years as slaves. In one brothel, Greller reports, "the majority of callers were expected between noon and two in the afternoon with the others staggered throughout the day.

Five-thirty to six-thirty in the evening was another heavy period for married business executives. Most preferred to have their little girls during proper daytime play periods." She tells of an eleven-year-old named Tierre who was pacified on her first night with heroin to prepare her for the client. Before the man arrived she was ordered "to put on a demure little pinafore, lace blouse, white knee socks, and patent leather Mary Janes. Her pubis also had to be shaved. Being eleven was too old. Tierre had to look seven for her customers."

Obviously, to punish any of these adolescent girls would be a gross travesty. The brunt of jolting sanctions should be directed against their exploiters. These girls are tragic victims who have been coerced into a way of life they cannot even comprehend. As for the older girls, the seventeen- and eighteen-year-olds who freely make their own choices, what we need for them is more counseling facilities. Treatment, not punishment, will sway these young girls from prostitution.

Female gangs

Female gangs are making an appearance in the seventies. White Fence and Big Bassette are territorial female gangs in southcentral Los Angeles, where virtually every teenager belongs to a gang. Members are either on active "combat" duty or play a noncombatant role by dint of financial support and loyalty. Any girl caught dating a male from another section is beaten and expelled. The Big Bassette gang, identified by blue satinette jackets with the Day-Glo inscription "Los Night Owls," puts each new girl through a bloody ritual of initiation.

A case was reported in which police units responding to an emergency call sped to a location to rescue a young girl who was being scratched, punched, kicked, and undressed by a mob of girls. The police thought they were preventing a killing, but the victim protested angrily at their intervention, saying she was undergoing her initiation into Big Bassette.

It takes a bit of adjusting for me to accept the language of female gang members. I do a double-take when one young black girl in court snaps at another, "You're gonna get your ass kicked," and then hear the other reply, "Right here, baby. Want some, got some. Crip here, motherfucker."

At public schools female gangs are engaging in the same extortion practices as their male counterparts. One case before my court concerned an encounter at a Los Angeles high school between Carol, a Big Bassette member, and Lillian, a freshman. Carol, accosting Lillian at knifepoint, forced her to give up her lunch money, her notebook, her shoes, her sweater and blouse—leaving her standing exposed, frightened, and vulnerable at the gate of the campus. Before the trial Carol threatened to cut the other girl's throat if she testified against her. I found Carol guilty and remanded her to juvenile hall pending a probation report.

The mothers of gang girls who appear in my court usually either sit passively through the proceedings or become very emotionally protective of their daughters. Carol's mother, in tears, pleaded with me not to send Carol to juvenile hall, pledging her word that her daughter would stay out of trouble.

"I promise to control her, your honor."

"It's a little late now," I answered.

"But I won't let her out of my sight. I'll be with her every hour. Don't put her away. I promise."

"I'm sorry, but your promise isn't too reassuring. I must think about the other girl. I have to worry about her safety. Your daughter will have to stay in juvenile hall."

In another case involving a female gang member, Christina Gomez, fourteen, was brought into juvenile hall with her clothes splattered with blood, drunk, and in an ugly mood, charged with having killed her father. The counselors in the intensive care unit were familiar with this Mexican-American girl. She had been in juvenile hall several times before. Christina was a known "butch" who liked to play the tough male part with other females. Despite the butch role, Christina was not a lesbian. She liked to brag to other girls that she would "never take nothing from no dude."

As one of the counselors removed her blood-stained blouse, Christina limply bent over to make it easier for her. She showed no outward sign of emotion and would not say why she had pulled a knife except that no dude was going to call her a "puta" (whore)—not even her father. Maybe it was years of being mocked by her brothers, or tough indoctrination from her gang; no one really knows why she stabbed her father to death.

I try to find the causes for this girl's tragedy. I hear young males bluster with bravado as if violence affirmed their manliness. Are girls now striking out in crime to prove their toughness? When I addressed the United States Job Center for Women in Excelsior Springs, Missouri, I asked five hundred girls what it was they wanted most in life. Almost all of them shouted, "To be seen."

To condone Christina's crime is wrong, but I can feel compassion for her. A few days after her confinement, Christina broke down in heaving convulsions. We can barely imagine the pain she felt. Even when she is released seven years from now, no matter how outwardly tough she is, she will never lose the agonizing scar from murdering her father.

Today's young female gang members are vastly different from Hellcat Maggie, a thief who roamed the streets of New York a hundred years ago, her teeth filed to points for ripping throats, her nails tipped with brass for gouging eyes. They are less likely today to play role of gun moll or ladies' auxiliary, and more likely to be equal partners—or, increasingly, leaders—in crime.

The rise of female crime is not unique to the United States. A British jurist, Justice Gerald Sparrow, says that he notes a sharp increase in female crime all over Europe. Today there is a tremendous release of pent-up aggressions. It seems that young women are rejecting the passive role they have held for so long, and are releasing their aggressions in negative as well as positive ways.

4 • Street Gangs

New York Police Department officials recently estimated that fifty youth gangs are involved in criminal activity in Brooklyn alone.
–U.S. News & World Report, *December 16, 1974*

During the fifties I belonged to several New York City street gangs. At fourteen, my first gang was the Lancers, which had forty members, and a girls' auxiliary composed of forty Lancerettes. Our first rumble was a fast, sloppy affair. We planned a confrontation with the 66th Street Boys, who were playing cards in their storefront club. I had never "japped" (sneak punched) anyone before, but my nerves were juicing with eagerness. We strutted down the block, brimming with boisterous confidence, flaunting our dazzling colors, mouthing cocky boasts, feeling invincible, but when we entered the club everyone froze.

As I learned over the years, it takes a lot of desire to throw the first punch. That triggers the rumble. All attention focuses on you. All pressure builds around you. The brunt of the retaliation is aimed at the first aggressor. You have to stand eyeball to eyeball with the toughest guy on the other side. Acting out of fear, most of the gang moved into the background.

For long seconds an awkward silence engulfed the room. Finally, I stepped forward to throw the first punch. To do it I had to break out of a hard shell of fear but the urge to stand out overpowered restraint. At the next rumble I again threw the first punch—and went on to repeat it a hundred times, all for the dizzying glory of recognition. I craved the neighborhood spotlight. I wanted impressed girls to say, "Hey, there's Joe Sarry," when I passed. I wanted a "rep."

You might say I was strongly motivated to succeed. In the middle-class society I live in now the same competitive drive prods me except that I now am going after a "rep" by using brains instead of fists, and I understand the shallowness of simply pursuing flash and self-glory. Human beings need to play ego games to make life stimulating, they need to invent plumage of status to feel superior, but in the street world these ego trips take their toll in life and limb.

The first wave of publicized gang activity reached its familiar height in the early to middle fifties. According to Stephen Kennedy, then New York City's Police Commissioner, the city had an estimated five thousand street warriors. But gangs were scarcely new or unfamiliar to history. Violent confrontations between groups of youthful contemporaries have a long and illustrious past, from those staged annually by the Spartans through the rampages of that notorious medieval hellion, the European university student.

In modern America street gangs reportedly began to emerge distinctly on New York's Lower East Side in the 1920s. Immigrant minorities hostile to one another lived in close, crowded quarters. If a Jewish boy walked around the corner by himself there was a good chance he would be beaten up by the Irish, or the Italians, or the Polish. An Irish boy rounding the same corner was just as likely to receive the same treatment. So boys formed ethnic bands to protect themselves. During World War II, when blacks migrated to New York in large numbers to find jobs, gang activity in the city swiftly escalated. Racial antagonisms fueled the growth of the gangs, although other invisible inner needs were fulfilled by gang unity and fraternity.

These trends continued until the tumultuous gang wildness of the fifties laid siege to zones of our cities. Then as the fifties drew to a close, economic prosperity dealt a blow to the gangs, as more and better job opportunities opened up and poverty was mitigated. In regions where improved economic conditions were slower to penetrate—the black and hispanic ghettos—police crackdowns, internecine casualties, and debilitating drugs helped to wipe out the gangs. A youth in desperate need of a fix has no inclination for rumbles. When the sixties began, sociologists looked back at the street gangs as a species of social dinosaur, convinced they were gone forever. But they were wrong.

Street gangs are back again

Now, in several of America's largest cities, the gangs are flaring up again, but with some frightening differences. In 1973 New York City was averaging one gang-related death every ten days. Street gangs in New York are larger and better-armed than ever before, and drugs are suspect. "I saw what they did—lots of guys ripped off, strung out, or dead," says Eddie Cueyas, president of the Reapers, a tough two-hundred-member Bronx gang. The Majestic Warlocks are spread over ten blocks of city territory. The Black Spades can muster fifteen hundred rumblers.

In only a very short time, Philadelphia has witnessed the resurrection of an estimated two hundred gangs at war in the streets. A gang is called a "corner," and a rumble is "warrin' time." Although turf trespass remains the chief provocation to combat, some gangs seem to be natural aggressors. The Norris Avenue "corner" for instance, is known as a bunch of "crazies" because each member is reputed to have two or three "bodies" under his belt. "Getting a body"—shooting someone—is the surest way a gang member can get a rep, and "blowing somebody away"—killing a rival—is the ultimate act of macho.

In the seventies in Los Angeles, a typical headline read, "Gangs Roam in Packs, Terrifying Residents." A reign of terror that would have been unimaginable in the America of the sixties now exists in Los Angeles. The gangs of Chicago have graduated to big-time crime as profiteers in guns, extortion, and gambling. Not only is there a resurgence of gangs, but contemporary gang behavior differs from that of the fifties. Today's gangs are more sophisticated, more brutal, and far more willing to splash into murder on a whim. Zip guns have been replaced with militaristic arsenals of sawed-off shotguns, M-1 rifles, .38-caliber handguns, and even automatic weapons. A gun is more easily obtained than hitching a ride. Twenty-five dollars buys a .38 with no questions asked.

In the past few years the litany of gang-linked violence stuns our consciousness and our conscience. Joyce Ann Huff, a four-year-old child, was walking out to shut the gate of a neighbor's home in Hawaiian Gardens, near Los Angeles, when she was slain by a shotgun blast from a passing car, the innocent victim of a gang retaliation that went wrong. Eighteen-year-old Robert Ballou and two friends were leaving the Hollywood Palladium after a rock concert when they were approached by twenty youths who demanded their leather jackets and then beat them up when they refused. Ballou died later that night. A forty-eight-year-old epileptic, John Haynes, was shot to death by a juvenile gang while watering the flowers in his front yard. The killers said they were looking for kicks.

Gang culture

The gangs have built a rigid, almost stifling social structure for themselves that stands in odd contrast to their rejection of social institutions. School doesn't interest them—at least half of Philadelphia's gang population are either total or partial school dropouts. The great majority live at home, but many easily manage to keep their gang ties secret from their parents, and a home life scarcely exists. Gang members often spend days, weeks, or months on end living in basement gang headquarters. Eddie Cueyas, whose family lives in one of the endless rows of decaying buildings in the South Bronx, speaks of his plans to marry: "Me and my old lady are reaching out for something. We don't know what it is yet, but we're going to make it." His instincts tell him of the lack of hope in the ghetto, but no one there dwells on it. They move too fast. Action blocks out thought.

Emptiness can be buried behind colorful exteriors. Wearing your "colors" (gang jackets) is a morale-booster, magically giving the gang an enchanting charisma and an image of comic book heroics. On the negative side, colors can provoke carping stops from the police, as members of the Royal Dutchman gang can attest. After frequently being frisked without cause, their jackets were confiscated by the police, who told them not to be seen wearing colors again. In 1973 I scoured the South Bronx to shoot a film of teen gangs flashing their colors, but I couldn't find anyone wearing them. The gangs told me they had stopped wearing the jackets because it makes them an obvious target for the police.

Initiation into a gang is typically harsh. A Mexican-American boy in Los Angeles described his initiation this way: "You hang around and sort of get to know the guys and then you ask to join. They take you someplace and you got to get jumped. Everybody beats on you and maybe they cut you up for about a minute, and then you're in. They do it to show you that it's not going to be an easy life." From that point on a member builds a reputation on more brash acts of aggression. A member of Los Vatos Locos—Spanish for crazy guys—will do anything from killing a policeman to burning down a school to prove his macho. Violence brings with it the satisfaction of creating concrete change in the world. By beating, stabbing, and shooting, one leaves a mark in the world, like initials carved on a tree. The gang itself, just by force of numbers, inflates the individual's sense of power.

Sociologist Lewis Yablonsky refers to the gang as "a separate, distinct, and often irresistible force of loyalty and solidarity," creating a strong group identity where only a weak sense of individuality may have existed before. The "sociopathic" youth—one who is severely disturbed or even a borderline psychotic—often finds a comfortable niche in gang society. The gang battlefield allows the unstable person to "do his thing" without censure and even with commendation. Professor Yablonsky estimates that 25 per cent of gang membership may be made up of this sort of marginal person.

Not only is the gang a convenient excuse for violent behavior, but some disturbed youths find this behavior rewarded by representatives of society. Police officers and social workers may construe an individual act by one youth as part of a "gang war" because to them it is a logical explanation for a senseless act. Acting out violence may stem from emotional aberration, but most gang members rumble to enjoy a "feeling of belonging" and to elevate their self-image.

Violence is the key to moving up in the gang. The more aggressive one is, the bigger one's rep. Senior members sometimes step down to allow younger toughs to make names for themselves. They also use the younger members to beat the system, making them do the shooting because they know the courts won't come down so hard on a twelve-year-old. Since a term in jail is a signal of upward prestige, young members will take a rap even when it does not legitimately belong to them. Hence an extraordinary number of twelve- and thirteen-year-olds are arrested for serious crimes. In such cases the boy is often back out on the street in a matter of days.

The numbing insensitivity of the macho ideal of the gang is borne out in chilling ways. Police Captain Frank De Leon of Los Angeles recounts his experience: "Bring in one of these kids and ask him 'How do you feel about this guy you killed, his family, the fact he just got married and wasn't even a gang member?' Maybe he'll say 'So what's to feel?' or maybe 'It ain't no big thing,' like one kid we had in here. Maybe he'll just look at you with a smirk and describe how he and his gang go around blowing away people with no feelings, no emotions at all." This is a truly terrifying comment on the depersonalization of gang violence.

Two gang members

Martin and Jesus Estrada are two members of a typical Los Angeles street gang. Fast-talking Martin, at eighteen, is the elder statesman of the streets. He doesn't need to prove his machismo as much as the younger members; his toughness and "balls" in street fighting—and street bargaining—are already well known. Jesus, like Martin, was born and raised in the isolated world of the East Los Angeles barrio. He shares Martin's sometimes rigid views of the world, especially on the subject of the street gang. While most of the country has moved into the sixties and out again, much of the Mexican-American community continues to embrace out-of-date styles. Pendleton wool shirts, pointed French-toed shoes, and long overcoats are still what's happening. A Chevy with a fire-engine shine, tinseled with chrome and tailed by a hot muffler remains the grooviest "wheels." Short hair, a Pancho Villa mustache, and a tough-guy walk right out of the movies are all inflexible characteristics. Oddly, "coming out" parties, "debutante" balls, and formal receptions—activities long ago laid to rest in most of California—still find followers in this community. Styles are transformed into rigid uniforms, and any variation is viewed with suspicion. "I don't like to see a Chicano with hair way down or dancing real fast," says Martin. "It doesn't look right to me."

Martin's baptism by fire came when he was barely fourteen. Since that time violent clashes have become far more common. He tells of a brutal murder to which he was witness in a pedestrian underpass in his part of town.

> I was with some friends—members of a gang called Los Vatos Locos. This tunnel that goes under the street is between their territory and the other gang's. For many years it has been this way, too. My friends were waiting for someone to come into the tunnel. They were hiding in the shadows. They broke the lights, except for one. It was very dark. They were just waiting for some guy from the other gang to come down into the tunnel. We waited for maybe an hour, until we heard footsteps coming down the stairs. I knew what was going to happen. I could see the boy coming—maybe fourteen or fifteen—from the other gang. I could not see his face until he was under the light, and then the light was behind him. He didn't see anyone else. Maybe he knew he should be careful and was taking a chance. When he is almost to

> the other side—on the territory of my friends—they jump him and start knifing him. He didn't make very much noise. They just kept kicking him and stomping him until he didn't move anymore. Maybe the police found him later the next day.

Martin and his friends, like their fathers, and perhaps even their grandfathers, carry on an ancient tradition—defending the turf. In Philadelphia and New York, families grow up perpetuating gang vendettas whose origins are distantly obscure. New gang members embrace the traditional quarrels with all the enthusiasm and fervor of the young.

Martin is quite sophisticated in his self-knowledge. He realizes the part that his family has played in his being a gang leader. He has emulated his father and his uncles. His life style is the most obvious and rewarding for anyone in his position. A splendid gymnast, he is a young man of considerable athletic talent, and insightful enough that he might have helped to bring about changes for the better had he grown up under other circumstances. "When I was a little kid my father would come home with a bottle of tequila in one hand and a blade in the other. He was tough and I wanted to be like him. He didn't pay much attention to my mother. Maybe he never licked my ass enough when he should have, but it doesn't matter because now whenever I see him he says 'Hey, son, let's go get fucked up' and we have a good time together." Martin has seen his father only a few times in the last few years. He was around more often when Martin was younger.

Jesus has been in trouble with school authorities for a variety of reasons during the last year—since he started junior high school. It is unlikely, in spite of pressure from his mother, that he'll stay in school until he's sixteen. School doesn't interest him very much; social life outside is more fulfilling, and he has something of a language problem anyway. There's very little inducement for him to stay in school. The fact that he was suspended recently for making a telephone call during class makes him feel school is very inflexible, very disinterested in him.

One thing that Martin and Jesus agree on is that there is

a sense of terror in the street. Ultimately the reason that they belong to a gang—leader and future leader—is self-protection. Martin says: "Any time I walk down the street I know that some dude can come up and beat my ass. They can rip me off, beat me in the head, or shoot me. But if I'm in a gang and I'm wearing my colors they know they better watch out. Because then we're gonna stomp them. They know my gang is gonna back me up and come down mean on them." In a sense he has merely taken initiative in a battle that rages around him and that is not of his making. Born into a turbulent and fierce society, he is simply protecting himself.

If you live in the ghetto and are not a gang member, life can be a habitual flight from harassment and ambush. Paul Ling, a seventeen-year-old Japanese-American, lives in a black neighborhood of Detroit, surrounded by hostile and potentially lethal enemies. He tells of the dread a walk to school instills in him:

> My mother can't drive me to school every day. She has to work and she can't be a chauffeur. But she doesn't know how really frightening the streets can be. Police make rounds every quarter of an hour in the neighborhood, but they're ignorant of what's happening. A fight can melt into the shadows in a split second. A mugger can disappear at the approach of a car. When I hear footsteps coming down the sidewalk I move across the street. I never know when some gang is out to cop my jacket or lunch money. Every time I've been beaten by gangs I've been left bleeding. Sometimes I would call from school, begging my mother to come and pick me up. I remember looking through the school fence, watching for my mother, feeling as if I was on a safe island surrounded by a stormy sea.

Why the resurgence of gangs?

The world of the seventies is an acutely difficult one to grow up in. Dishonesty at the highest level of government, immense and impersonal corporations, crowded and numbing cities, and a generally unresponsive world create and augment feelings of powerlessness and smallness. There was a time when democracy seemed far more participatory, when the individual in charge was accessible, and the "complaint window" was open for suggestions. That time is becoming a relic of the past.

The typical American image of the successful male compounds the problem. The disparity between such larger-than-life screen superstars as Charles Bronson, John Wayne, Jim Brown, Isaac Hayes and a youngster who on some level views himself as a powerless little boy is quite overwhelming. American machismo—strength, temerity, and brashness—is a goal that is continually broadcast by the media. A counterculture once seemed to offer new goals to the American male. Perhaps it still does. But the grandeur of the macho male is more powerfully persuasive than ever. Macho goals are blatant in the behavior of gang members. Souped-up cars, shotguns, switchblades, threatening talk, swaggering walk, and group sex all are obvious symbols of a desire to master James Bond potency.

PART TWO
Causes of Juvenile Crime

5 • The Moral Temper of America

Morality depends on images of excellence. Every society tends to fall to lower levels unless these images are present.
—Samuel Miller, Dean, Harvard Divinity School

At five-thirty one afternoon in the spring of 1973 a UCLA student was seen tied to a telephone pole on a busy thoroughfare near the UCLA campus. It was the height of the rush hour in Los Angeles; traffic moved in a slow but steady stream toward the freeway. The woman tied to the pole was almost nude because her dress had been ripped to shreds, and she screamed for help from the passing motorists. But no one helped her; they merely stared at her curiously. In the bushes nearby, two graduate students in sociology carefully noted the results of their experiment.

In July 1974 twenty-five-year-old Judy Widmer, blood gushing from her head, ran into crowded Lincoln Park in Chicago, pointing to a youth who had just whipped her with a chain. She screamed for help, but the pedestrians, joggers, and bicyclists that summer afternoon only gaped and then continued about their business. She ran from the youth past a man reading a newspaper, past guards taking the flag down at the nearby Academy of Sciences, and past a bus stopped at a busy intersection. "For God's sake, won't somebody help me?" she cried. The man went on reading his newspaper; the guards continued taking down the flag; the bus proceeded along its route. Judy left a trail of blood. This time there were no nearby graduate students taking notes. This was no experiment.

At 3:20 A.M. in a comfortable middle-class neighborhood in Queens, New York, twenty-eight-year-old Catherine (Kitty) Genovese returned home from her job as manager of a tavern in New York. As she was leaving the parking lot for her apartment building about a hundred feet away, she noticed a man skulking at the far end of the lot. She stopped momentarily, looked over at him nervously, and then headed down the street toward a call box to the 102nd Precinct in nearby Richmond Hill. But before she got to the streetlight in front of a bookstore, the stranger was swooping down on her. She screamed. Lights flickered on in the ten-story apartment house across the street, windows opened, and people called out in the dark morning. Kitty screamed, "Oh, my God, he stabbed me! Please help me! Please help me!"

From an upper-story window someone shouted, "Leave that girl alone."

The attacker looked up, shrugged, and walked down the street toward a white car parked nearby. Kitty struggled to her feet.

The lights went out again. Within minutes the stranger was back. Once again he shoved her down and again he stabbed her.

"I'm dying!" she shrieked. "I'm dying!"

Windows opened again, and lights clicked on in many of the facing apartments. The attacker got into his car and drove away. Kitty staggered to her feet. A city bus on its way to Kennedy International Airport passed on the nearby boulevard. It was 3:35 A.M.

The attacker returned again. By this time, Kitty had crawled to the back of the building, and her assailant found her slumped at the foot of a stairway. He stabbed her for a third time. This time he killed her.

The police received their first call at 4:00 A.M. and arrived at the scene in two minutes. The neighbor who had called and two women—one of them seventy years old—were the only people on the street. Nobody else had come out.

For over half an hour thirty-eight upright citizens in the Kew Gardens area of Queens had watched and listened to a murderer hound and fatally stab their neighbor. The man who had finally called the police—at least some twenty minutes too late—explained that he had decided to call only after phoning a friend in Nassau County for advice and then crossing the roof of the building to the apartment of the elderly woman to get her to make the call.

"I didn't want to get involved," he told the police.

Density dulls

The sheer size of our cities has a smothering impact on public morality. Taking a ten-mile radius as the yardstick, the average central city in the United States would permit over 2.5 million contacts between people in a year, in Chicago over 5.3 million contacts, and in Manhattan, a staggering 23.5 million. According to Professor Philip Hauser of the University of Chicago, this tremendous density has a bomb-shelter effect on city dwellers: they quickly learn to build an impenetrable shell around themselves, a barrier that absorbs at least some of the impact of the hordes of people they encounter day after day.

Overwhelming numbers of people can extinguish our natural tendency to be concerned about one another. When a teenager steals ten dollars from a liquor store and then almost as an afterthought shoots the owner dead, it may be that the boy sees the man as just another object in a vast sea of impersonal objects. William Sloan Coffin has said: "There are people and things in this world, and people are to be loved and things to be used. But in American society I think we are using people and loving things more and more." The sheer size and massiveness of our society is doubtless one cause of the growing incidence of callous crime.

Lack of moral leadership

"There is a persistent vein of violence and cruelty in human nature. Man has often striven to rid himself of what he recognizes as being a hideous moral blemish, unworthy of human nature's better side. Sometimes man has fancied that he has succeeded in civilizing himself." These incisive words are from the eminent historian Arnold Toynbee. For most of human history, moral standards have been clear. Someone taught or told the individual what to do, what was right or wrong; someone was held up as a model of moral excellence and inspired imitation. But the role of the church, so long the dominant institution in the field of moral leadership, has diminished, and industrialization and urbanization have abolished the traditional elite who served as secular superiors. We in America live in a society without a shared moral authority. No church lays down the moral laws for all. No tribal customs or taboos define the limits of our thoughts or actions. We are free to be prejudiced or promiscuous, to cheat or to chisel.

Every society needs recognized heroes, brilliant spirits to whom people can look up, unselfish servants to venerate, noble navigators to serve as models. A John F. Kennedy will be briefly idolized after his death, but a man like Kennedy comes along seldom indeed. America needs a revival of heroes—moral heroes. Novelist Anton Myrer defines a moral hero as a soul greater than the rest of us who succeeds where we have failed and who can touch all our losses with nobility. "What is disheartening," he finds, "is that so many contemporary [literary] protagonists are so much less than most of us are, even in our bad moments."

The American hero has been replaced, in our time, with something else, something less. How many people in the country actually undertake something courageous, venturous, or sacrificial? One critical factor is our affluence and the premium we place on security. America no longer really offers us anything truly heroic. Life is too sedentary, too cushioned, too vicarious. Our adrenalin surges while we watch sports on television and stuff ourselves with junk food. We look up to football players who desert their teams for more money elsewhere, to basketball players who brawl in nightclubs.

To fill the vacuum we venerate glittery actresses who have acquired a parade of rich husbands and opulent homes. We seem to have replaced the moral hero with the neon celebrity. This may explain the attraction of a James Bond, that mythical hero who combines the glamorous risks of sex and violence with ultra-heroic efforts for the common good. These contemporary hero surrogates are not what America needs in the seventies. According to Dr. David R. Mace, executive director of the American Association of Marriage Counselors, "It is the people who can act, entertain, who become the rallying point of the people's need for heroes. They are essentially shallow, irresponsible people. Our young people must be very hungry for heroes."

Tragically, in the age of Watergate, not only are youth left without exemplars of excellence but through the media they are constantly exposed to shabby moral models. A West Covina, California, high school teacher writes: "Over the past year I have noticed that it is the brightest and most aware students who have reacted most negatively to Watergate. They appear to move further and further from confidence in any political leader or system. It was to them that Gordon Strachan was speaking when he told the Senate Watergate Committee that his advice to young people was to 'stay away' from politics. . . . Watergate is teaching them not to care."

The effect of political events can even be seen in children of elementary school age. Susan Kramer, an elementary school teacher in Los Angeles, systematically sampled the effect of Watergate on her students. The discouraging result was that a majority of the children were "consistently bitter, convinced that government officials and powerful corporations have tainted our social system. These students view the former President of the United States as 'a robber who gypped the government.' The students seem to be saying that if illegal activities were sanctioned at the government level, such conduct is permissible at a personal level. One boy said that Nixon's tax evasions were unfair, yet most maintained that cheating on one's taxes is all right as long as you get away with it. They expected to cheat on their taxes when they grew up. The general feeling was that if you're caught, it's not so bad because the punishment is not that drastic. One student summed up the sentiment: 'If I were President I wouldn't pay my taxes. None of those politicians do, so I should be able to get away with it.' "

Incremental moral damage was done by the privileged treatment given the Watergate defendants. Men in positions of the highest trust in the federal government who committed the most solemn crimes against the U.S. Constitution were given judicial taps on the knuckles. Spiro Agnew, deposed from the vice-presidency for bribery and graft, a "law and order" zealot who shrilly shouted for truncheoning of ghetto offenders, was awarded a probationary sentence and thus the opportunity to become a millionaire through lectures, literary projects, and business ventures. Former President Nixon was granted a premature pardon with no legal sanction for his high misconduct and now enjoys the benefits of a presidential pension and other privileges at the taxpayers' expense. His book reportedly earned an unparalleled advance of $3 million. Granted commutation, John Dean was out of prison in a few months, and received an advance of $300,000 for his upcoming Watergate book. National lecture bureaus are scrambling like ambulance chasers to sign up Kalmbach, Dean, Magruder, and Liddy for appearances on the college circuit, where they will earn lucrative fees of $2,000 to $4,000 for each lecture. Kids in the ghetto—and elsewhere—see no justice in these events.

The macho tradition

"Hey man, why did we kill that dude?"

The fourteen-year-old boy shifted nervously in the hard, straight-backed chair as he asked the question; his eyes scanned the floor, as if he expected to find the answer etched in the stained tiles.

His partner, older and more streetwise, knew the answer.

"Hell, man, we killed him to make an example outa him. That was real cool the way the blood came outa his mouth and that gargling sound he made. He just laid there and jerked."

"What's gonna happen to us now?" the younger boy asked, hoping for assurances from his experienced companion.

"The police might take us to juve hall, but we won't be there very long. We'll be home before tomorrow morning." He reconsidered. "Hell, if they can find our folks to come and get us, they might send us home tonight."

There was not an inch of fear or remorse in his words. He fully expected to be home even before the police pieced together the details of the murder they were talking about—the killing of a sixteen-year-old acquaintance, shot through the chest at a neighborhood birthday party.

"What'll happen after that?" the younger boy asked. He seemed to be trying to keep the talk alive, afraid to listen to his own thoughts.

"If they can prove you killed the dude, maybe they'll send you to a camp for a few months," the older boy answered. "But when you get out, you'll be a big man on the street."

They sat in the empty interrogation room, talking about the taking of a life in the same casual, offhand way they might talk about a stickball game—self-confessed killers, ages fourteen and fifteen. There was no simple motive for the crime; not robbery, or the passion of jealousy, or even revenge. To them, murder was a means of gaining stature on the streets, a badge of prowess, the ultimate macho achievement. For this status symbol a life could be traded as easily as a bubble-gum card.

In September 1872 three mounted bandits rode up to the gate of the Kansas City Fair, where a crowd of ten thousand had gathered. The bandits shot at the ticket seller, hit a small girl in the leg by mistake, and made off for the woods with their spoils—less than a thousand dollars. In reporting the crime, the *Kansas City Times* characterized the robbery as "so diabolically daring and so utterly in contempt of fear that we are bound to admire it and revere its perpetrators." Two days later the *Times* was even more enthralled: "It was as though three bandits had come to us from storied Odenwald, with the halo of medieval chivalry upon their garments, and shown us how the things were done that poets sang of. Nowhere else in the United States or in the civilized world, probably, could this thing have been done."

In September 1974 more than twenty-five thousand out-of-state visitors, most of them young people, descended on a small town near the Snake River in Idaho. Down river there was not a motel room to be had for fifty miles around, but the sprawling packs of youths were not fazed. Thousands more were camping on the rim of the canyon, still more near the edge of the cliff, and another crowd was on the outskirts near Shoshone Falls. A million had paid ten dollars admission to view the upcoming event on closed-circuit television in movie theaters across the nation. All these Americans were breathlessly eager to behold just one thing: Evel Knievel risking death by rocketing across the Snake River Canyon on a steam-powered "spacecycle."

The flamboyant daredevil who calls himself the "Last Gladiator" had previously gained fame by breaking virtually every bone in his body during motorcycle stunts. This time Knievel would either be propelled almost five thousand feet across the canyon and thereby earn $10 million, or he would plunge 540 feet to his death on the canyon floor. Clusters of young people interviewed before the event expressed adulation for Knievel: "He's got guts," "He's a real man," "He's my hero," "He's not afraid of nothing," and "He can beat the mountain." As it turned out, Knievel did not "beat the mountain," nor did he kill himself. Although his machine failed to span the gulf, he made a safe and soft landing by parachute, and was millions of dollars ahead of the game.

The promoters of the American closed-circuit television showing of the 1974 World Cup Soccer matches went for the viewing public's jugular with a hard-hitting home television advertising campaign featuring film clips of the most rugged bump-and-tumble scrimmages of soccer—a sport which, while rough at times, is nowhere near as violent as hockey—featuring voice-over commentary about how the narrator had never seen such brutal scrapes in any sports arena anywhere, at any time.

Entranced by TV football, Americans idolize jumbo-sized pro football stars and deify the victors of the superbowl. We spend millions of dollars on the swashbuckling dash of auto racing. The gruesome sight of females clobbering females in roller derbies has made the sport one of the top attendance draws in the nation. Promoters of sports that are ostensibly nonviolent do not sit idly by. In commenting on a basketball game, for example, Bill Russell said, "Of course basketball's a *contact* sport—football, now there's a *collision* sport." Americans flock to movies thirsting for action and the sight of larger-than-life men doing bigger-than-life deeds. Monumental John Wayne is still a magnetic box-office draw, even if he is over sixty. Sam Peckinpah's *The Wild Bunch*—one of the bloodiest screen epics ever—attracts sellout crowds.

This represents a sampling, a drop of the torrents of evidence that demonstrate how deeply ingrained the mystique of machismo, or aggressive masculinity, is in American life. Yet many of the same people who worship the macho ideal sit over drinks in the evening and express shock and anger over juvenile crime and urban riots. They see no connection. Nothing they learned in their schools or home prepared them for the view that domestic violence in the sixties and seventies is not a mere aberration in American history or a sign of the disintegration of American institutions, but rather a trait long rooted in America's historical psyche.

"Crime is not caused by lack of bread alone"

The President's Commission on the Causes and Prevention of Violence said that the roots of crime are low incomes, bad schools, unemployment, and other economically related conditions. Partially in response to this theory, a vast welfare bureaucracy has been developed over the past generation to upgrade the economic status of the poor. But some analysts, weighing historical evidence, repudiate the view that poverty is an overriding cause of crime and that a welfare approach is the cure. They point out that we are, after all, now living in the most prosperous society on earth. A smaller percentage of the total population is poor in America today than in any previous period or place known to history. Yet at the same time we are confronted by an ever-mounting wave of juvenile crime. If the poverty argument is correct, there should be more crime during years of oppressive depression, but the reverse is true. Virtually every type of crime statistic relating prosperity to depression runs counter to the poverty-as-cause thesis. Judge David Pine recalls that during the thirties there was abject poverty, distress, and misery, but he says, "I do not recall at that time there was an upsurge in crime."

During the Depression years, the delinquency rate for American children was twenty-one per thousand. By 1957 it was up to thirty-five per thousand, a rise of 70 per cent. In 1940, fairly tough times, two hundred thousand cases of juvenile delinquency were handled by the courts. By 1960 the number of juvenile crimes had skyrocketed to over a half a million, an increase of more than 150 per cent, far greater than the increase in the juvenile population in the same twenty-year period. Congressional records reveal that rates for juvenile delinquency increased during the twenties, when some features of our society resembled those of today, and declined during the Depression years of the thirties.

Those who stand behind the poverty thesis rest their argument on the mammoth crime problem found in the slums and ethnic ghettos. But some poverty-ridden areas—those with "proper moral foundations"—are more law-abiding than many middle-class neighborhoods. Researchers have discovered that crime rates in Chinese and Jewish enclaves are markedly lower than society's average. Lawlessness in San Francisco's Chinatown was found to be less than half that for the community as a whole.

These assertions are reinforced by reports from outside the United States. A 1960 United Nations report concluded: "The existing data suggest that the improvement of living conditions—what is called a better standard of living—does not necessarily reduce juvenile delinquency. Although statistical data are incomplete, it would seem that juvenile delinquency is not caused by poverty or poor economic conditions alone." Juvenile authority Roul Tunley found that progress was recognized as a major factor in delinquency in almost every country he had visited, and cites a government official in India as saying that relative poverty and backwardness are actually deterrents to juvenile crime. In making the same point in regard to England Tunley said, "Twenty years ago people in Great Britain said that if you could do away with poverty and slums, it would help do away with delinquency. But we've done away with lots of poverty and we've improved housing, and it's worse than ever." In Sweden, too, the juvenile crime rate continues to soar in spite of the fact that every welfare measure imaginable has been launched to alleviate poverty and the fear of it. In fact, according to Tunley, Sweden has "one of the highest [juvenile crime] rates, if not the highest in the world."

So apparent is the lack of correlation between poverty and crime to Katherine B. Ottinger of the U.S. Children's Bureau that she believes that juvenile delinquency is "more likely to increase in a time of prosperity than in a time of depression." Persuasive statistics inform us that juvenile crime in America has indeed followed affluence. By 1971 America's well-heeled teenagers were spending an aggregate $21 billion a year on an endless variety of consumer goods. Thus, by the logic of the poverty thesis, suburban children ought not to be part of rising juvenile crime, yet it is in the suburbs that we see the most feverish upturn in the juvenile crime temperature. Car thefts, burglaries, and drug addiction are now common scandals in the "very best" American communities. Harrison Salisbury of *The New York Times* concludes that "split-level delinquency in the quiet suburban communities is just as deadly a menace to the younger generation as are the festering conflicts of the housing projects and the old slums."

I do not mean to imply that poverty plays no part in juvenile crime statistics. Unquestionably it does play a significant role in crime, a role that cannot be overlooked. My point is that we must reject the simplistic equation that makes poverty the only, or even the overriding, cause of juvenile crime.

But if poverty is not the basis for delinquency, then what is? We Americans are members of a huge, impersonal, materially driven, sex-obsessed, violence-fascinated society. Conditions in our world are changing so swiftly that many people's adaptive mechanisms, suffering from future shock, have ceased to function. Our moral values are about as solid as quicksand. We live in what many consider an age of moral crisis, one of the most intensely discussed subjects in the United States. When I offered a course at UCLA called "Morality: Twilight Zone of the Law," fifteen hundred university extension students were attracted, the second largest enrollment since a course on space engineering was offered shortly after the launching of Sputnik. People are passionately interested in morality because morals in America are in a state of flux. Old values have broken down and we do not know what will replace them, and in the meantime, without a moral anchor, we are drifting.

What are some of the mystifying changes that have taken place in our moral structure in the recent past? Divorce on demand or by mutual assent is one example. Not long ago divorce was considered scandalous, conjuring up visions of fallen women, brutish men, and unseemly conduct. Today, however, there is no stigma attached to divorce, and the rate of dissolution is soaring. This is not to imply that easier divorce, or terminating an incompatible marriage, is wrong or morally reprehensible. It is merely another symptom of the dismantling of our traditional moral code.

The tearing down of the barriers of censorship is another indication of change. Over the past thirty years or so traditional "under the counter" materials have been placed on top of the counter, where they are freely available and freely distributed.

The effect of this on juvenile crime is questionable and fiercely debated, but it is certainly an influence on our moral values. The legalization of abortion is another example of something that is changing our moral structure, for better or for worse. So is the growing acceptance of homosexuality; as homosexuals come out of the closet and become integrated into society, our ideas of morality must change to accommodate them. The widening availability of contraceptives is still another sign of change, as is the growing acceptance of loosely improvised ethical canons such as "Do your own thing" and "It's right if it feels good."

The changes are myriad and—whether we like them or not—affect us all because they symbolize the breakdown of our orthodox Judao-Christian moral system. In terms of juvenile crime the net effect is that the young, like the rest of us, are cast adrift in a sea where there are fewer universal truths on which they can rely. Presumably the juvenile crime rate remains low in Chinatown because youth are provided the mooring point of a traditionally stable moral code. But in society at large the charts are still in the fragile process of being redrawn, and until the boundaries are once more delineated in some precise form—no matter what it is—we will continue to see an increase in juvenile crime.

Only time will tell what the eventual results of this moral upheaval will be. But while morals remain in a state of flux, people—the young included—will be hard pressed to know what to do, and this will continue to manifest itself in a rising rate of criminal activity.

6 • The Family in Upheaval

There are no bad children, only bad parents.
—Italian proverb

As the Los Angeles sky darkened toward dusk, Willie Jones, age thirty-nine, pulled on a pair of black leather gloves and picked up a pile of folded mail sacks from the floor of his bedroom. His son Bobby, fifteen, also put on a pair of gloves before he picked up a metal box containing an assortment of drills, screwdrivers, and other tools. Marge Jones looked on disapprovingly, knowing where her husband would be taking her oldest boy, but she didn't protest. As they drove west on Manchester Boulevard, father and son talked about the location of the watch collection in a particular house in Westwood. On Kiowa Street, the elder Jones slowed his late-model Dodge to a stop, and he and his son walked the hundred yards to a corner house, the Spanish-style residence of Mr. and Mrs. Paul Kelson and their four children.

A light burned in the parlor of the house, but Willie Jones knew, from a gardener, that the Kelson family was on a camping trip. Unlatching the backyard gate, he and young Bobby stepped across the carefully tended lawn to a huge avocado tree nestled against the house. By climbing the tree they were able to jump onto the lower side of the roof, a flat area with a skylight. Willie Jones sifted through his metal box for the right tool, and he skillfully began prying open the corner of the skylight. As he worked he spoke softly to his son, giving him pointers on roof entries, tutoring him in the art of breaking and entering, preparing him to go it alone someday—apprenticing him to the trade of burglary.

The pair were caught that evening, however, through the inadvertent visit of Larry Potts, Mrs. Kelton's brother, who—remembering the camping trip—noticed people moving in the darkened rooms. He immediately notified the police. Willie Jones was dealt with by the adult authorities, and—copping a plea—he was released on formal probation. His son Bobby came into my courtroom for trial. He expressed admiration for his father, seeing him as a street hero. Over strenuous protests from Bobby's attorney, I ordered Bobby to be sent to a group house for rehabilitation.

"Give him a chance to change," his lawyer reasoned. "This is his first offense, and after all, he's only fifteen."

"I don't see how he *can* change in that family environment," I answered.

Criminal parents

The Jones case is an extreme, yet factual, example of a parent's being responsible for his child's criminal behavior. It is rare that I see parents who actually tutor their children in crime. More often, parents influence their children's criminal behavior in more insidious psychological ways. Criminologists agree on the crucial importance of the family as a factor in juvenile crime. A strong family relationship is one of the major defenses against the outbreak of youthful criminality, while a weak or otherwise deficient family relationship is often a root cause of delinquency and juvenile disorder.

The "decline of the family" in American life is frequently cited as a contributing factor in delinquency and crime. While the ebb of the extended family is a reality, the notion of a decline of the basic family unit is not universally accepted.

Despite scattered groups of hippies and other independent-minded people who make attempts at communal living, and despite some young middle-class couples who live together outside of marriage, there is no compelling indication that the basic family system is about to be scrapped in American society.

But it is true that the family is no longer a self-sustaining economic unit, that the institution of permanent monogamy is finding competition in serial monogamy, and that many of the family's former socialization functions have been taken over by other institutions. The unity of the family is not as strong as it once was. But Edwin M. Schur, author of *Our Criminal Society*, contends that "loss of reverence for family and marriage ties as ends in themselves may have been offset by the accompanying increases in freedom and independence of family members. If the child does not always unquestioningly obey the parents, at the same time he may be learning to think for himself in a way that formerly was less often nurtured."

High divorce rates tell us nothing about the quality of the marriages that do *not* break up. An absence of divorce does not necessarily imply marital health; the term "emotional divorce," adopted by one observer to describe turmoil-plagued marriages that nonetheless survive, points up the danger of assuming that the absence of an open break signifies an underlying stability. Worth bearing in mind, too, is that while America has nagging divorce rates, the nation has high remarriage rates as well. Americans are a long way from being disillusioned about marriage and the family, and although average family size has declined, there is hardly a glimmer of a trend that Americans no longer want children.

The New York Times reported recently that 1 per cent of New York's families produces 74 per cent of the city's delinquency. From my own day-to-day observations in the courtroom, it is clear to me that a large majority of young offenders come from unhealthy family situations, whether the family is "broken" or not. Perhaps society should more consistently acknowledge that juvenile delinquency is a symptom of family, rather than individual, illness. A step in this direction has been taken in Los Angeles with the introduction of the innovative Family Treatment Unit, which seeks to rehabilitate delinquent children by treating everyone living in a child's home, including grandparents.

Poor family relationships

In examining the huge number of cases in which parents influence their children toward criminality, one can detect patterns of family arrangements that contribute to delinquency.

A father's shirking of responsibility in child rearing is a common cause of delinquency. A vivid example of paternal abdication is evident in the case of Robert Collins, a middle-class youth with a long history of arrests for theft. Robert's father, an attorney, was the typical nonfather, wavering on questions of discipline, jealously self-oriented with his free time, fanatically engrossed in his career, a weak pal who is fitfully affectionate and away most of the time. He does not serve as a model for his children. He delegates the task of teaching values to his wife. He grumbles irritably when the children demand his attention. Mr. Collins unequivocally fits the model of "nonparent" in every particular.

When Mrs. Collins divorced her husband, Robert remained in his father's custody, while his mother took the two younger children to live with her. Testimony showed that Robert would often go to his mother's house, several miles away, to steal money from her purse, but that when Mr. Collins was informed of his son's actions he did nothing. A great deal of animosity had festered from the divorce, and it appeared that Mr. Collins was using his son's thefts as a form of malicious revenge against his former wife, although he would probably have never admitted it.

Family counselor Eda Le Shan, reviewing the implications of the television series *An American Family,* says, "I think the program demonstrates how desperate young people are for standards and directions from parents—and that this lack for children accounts for the breakdown of the family in America. We have gone from father as autocrat to the father as nothing."

Where have all the middle-class fathers gone? In many cases, to cold spires of glass and steel to concentrate on making money. A fourteen-year-old burglar from a wealthy Beverly Hills family, for example, felt anguished because he could never manage to capture his father's interest. He painfully recalled his father's response to an invitation to watch his son play Little League baseball on a Sunday afternoon: "If you like this big house we live in you'll understand that Daddy has to work today." I was not surprised that this rich boy was out committing burglaries. Finally his father was paying attention.

Early signs of dishonesty or criminal tendencies are usually ignored by the nonfather. He is either too busy, or feels too guilty, to punish the child. Jean Vermeer was a girl whose father knew she had been stealing from him, but he never took her to task for it. He would give her a dollar to buy the newspaper, and she would fail to return the change. She filched money from his dresser in the morning, but he never mentioned it to her. Divorced from his wife—mainly as a consequence of his consuming ambition—and wishing to make amends for the mother's absence and desperately needing to be loved by someone himself, this man allowed his daughter to make a regular habit of her petty larcenies at home. It came as no surprise, then, that she should indulge in her larcenous habits at school. Had her father taken just one firm step, her criminal pattern might have been averted, but he, like all too many others, was a morally feeble nonparent. The "emancipated" women who is unbudgeably riveted to her career can become a nonparent as well.

The nonparent and the overpermissive or easy-going parent are virtually synonymous. In my own childhood, I frequently heard my mother criticize my father for being "too easy-going with the kids." She would urge him, almost daily, to put his foot down, but he let things slide, allowing me to get deeper and deeper into trouble. Volatile, he then would explode when it was too late.

Being a good parent requires consistency and firmness tempered with reason and flexibility. My father's favorite theory was that children "grow up good or bad themselves; it's what they're made of inside that counts." To support his view, he drew a comparison between my older brother and me: "Your brother never gets into trouble, and I don't have to yell at him." Perhaps it is true that some children are more inclined to misbehavior than others, but that does not mean a parent should not attempt to discipline rebellious children.

The parents of the criminal Caryl Chessman can be categorized as easy-going. The executed murderer's biography reveals that his parents were loving, that he did not suffer poverty, and that he was not exposed to drunkenness or other gross behavior that can so often be traumatic to a child. His parents always urged him to "do the right thing," to return to reform school after he had escaped, and so on, but they were never strong, firm, or commanding with him. They were, in fact, weak and trusting people, incompetent to deal with their delinquent son. Whatever excuses he gave they accepted docilely without question, allowing themselves to be manipulated by him, and ultimately became like children to their own son. They never exercised any authority over Caryl, giving him only an easy-going and benign love that in the end proved unmistakably fatal to him.

The popularity of permissive child-rearing theories has waned in recent years, but they remain a subject of controversy in juvenile sociology. The theory holds that the child is basically "good," and parents must prevent him or her from being corrupted by external pressures by minimizing stifling restraints, fostering natural impulses and providing opportunities for the spontaneous creativity of one's inner nature. Unfortunately, human instincts are not unswervingly attracted to benevolence. Anyone who has watched infants at play knows they can be ruthlessly self-centered. Since the fracturing of value systems by unbridled impulse is, to one degree or another, a factor in crime, extreme and dogmatic permissiveness often does more to damage a child by loosening impulses on society in the form of criminality than to help in his or her creative molding.

Every child requires a wholesome measure of discipline in the home, in the classroom, and in society at large. Unless general restraints are built into the character of children, the result is social chaos. Floyd Simpson, one of the most effective counselors at a Los Angeles camp for hard-core delinquents, stresses a child's needs for limits, and comes down hard on permissiveness: "The kid is suffering from an inferiority complex to begin with, or he feels unloved, and he will take your indulging him as a sign that you don't give a damn. You have to be steadily firm, but caring. The kid has to know you care about him, and you show it by disciplining him and rewarding him when he makes a special effort for you."

These conclusions are vigorously endorsed by many law-enforcement officers who have to deal with delinquents. A midwestern district attorney, for example, impugned the widespread opinion that if a person gets into trouble he needs treatment. "They start in nursery schools these days," he said. " 'Don't stunt the child's personality.' When he gets older and gets into more serious trouble, they say, 'Let's not be hasty.' These kids know this. They trade on it. Everybody wants to rush in and salvage the wrongdoer." This may be an overstatement, coming as it does from a prosecutor, but there is some measure of truth in it.

Jess Rupon, sixteen, was recently in my court for trial on his seventeenth offense, and his attorney zealously argued that the boy should not be placed in a detention camp. The youth indicated that he had a job, a fact stressed by his lawyer as a hopeful sign of rehabilitation. As the proceedings continued, a check on his employment showed it to be nonexistent. When I informed the defense attorney, he still refused to budge from his position. My decision to send the boy to a detention camp was not grounded in malice; rather, as I asked his attorney, "How many chances do we give this kid at the expense of the community?" If the same case had come up in an adult courtroom, the lawyer's request would have been plainly out of line. Yet the view persists that juveniles should be given as many chances as they need, or want. This, to my mind, is permissiveness carried to an absurd degree.

We would certainly be shocked and revolted by a father who wantonly led his own daughter into prostitution and other sexual crimes. Ironically, by going to the opposite extreme and attempting to shackle a child with the strictest controls, tyrannical parents can produce the same results.

In a recent case before my court, for example, the middle-class southern parents of petite fourteen-year-old Barbara Totter were asking for the release of their daughter from a reformatory. Barbara had a chronic history of running away from home. Her parents were fervently devout Jehovah's Witnesses, a religious denomination whose moral rules are iron-clad in their stringency, and sexual promiscuity is thundered against with somber threats of fire and brimstone. The girl's mother, especially, constantly checked on everything she did. If she failed to come home promptly after school, Barbara could expect a sharp tongue-lashing. Dating was absolutely prohibited. Parties were taboo, and talking to blacks was forbidden, although the family lived in a neighborhood where there were many black people.

Resentment is bound to mount in a girl who, in her own eyes, is unreasonably denied the freedom enjoyed by her friends and when she is constantly belittled and berated for minor mistakes in conduct. The explosive result in the case of this fourteen-year-old was that she ran away from her oppressive mother and, possibly out of revenge, became the sexual pawn of a clique of black pimps. When her mother learned of Barbara's whereabouts and life style, she heaped insults and vilification upon the girl. The police took Barbara home, but the situation was hopeless—Mrs. Totter slapped at her daughter in an attempt to exorcise Satan—and so she ran away again. The cycle repeated itself a half dozen times. Each time she was retrieved from the pimps the scene with her mother was repeated.

Tragically, the mother apparently could not live with her

daughter, but she couldn't live without her either, nor could she even dimly comprehend the motivations prompting Barbara's behavior. Her monomaniacal attitude throughout the tribulation was that her daughter had been possessed by evil. My decision as judge was to order psychiatric counseling for the family as a whole. I am not sure, though, given the mother's extreme religious zeal, that she will be able to give Barbara that small latitude of personal freedom she needs to grow spiritually and emotionally in a normal way.

An example of a different kind of parental incompetence can be seen in the case of Louis Preston, a lanky fourteen-year-old honor student whose mother showed up at trial in my court festooned with diamond cocktail jewelry, an ermine coat, and a Gucci handbag. His father, educated at an eastern prep school, had an air of supercilious pomp. Louis was accused of a weird form of sexual perversion. Reconnoitering from a hill on his four-speed bicycle, he waited until he saw a girl walking alone and then descended at streaking speed, slowing up as he approached the girl, reaching out and squeezing her breast, and then, coming around full circle, making another pass, grabbing under her dress. Designated by police as "The Strafer," he was identified by four different victims, yet his parents, hiring one of the highest-paid attorneys in the city, attempted by obvious perjury to establish an alibi for him. A long procession of character witnesses, including teachers, were also presented to rebut the prosecution's case. "With all due deference to the minor's fine school record and comfortable home," I said, "these elements, while probative, are not determinative. The court must assess the facts on a scale of probabilities, and I cannot blink at the eye witness testimony of four objective witnesses. Leopold and Loeb were also model students."

The most disturbing aspect of the case was that the boy's parents seemed more concerned about hushing up the incident than in finding the cause for their child's strange behavior. In fraudulently testifying that he was at home at all times, they were trying to keep up their image in their own eyes and the eyes of their neighbors. As Bertrand Russell once observed: "The trouble with parents is that they want their children to be a credit to them."

Then there are those parents whose only relationship with their child is a purely biological one. David Roden, sixteen, had been in the custody of the California Youth Authority from the time he was nine. He came into my courtroom charged with escape from detention and theft, destruction, and abandonment of a motorcycle. A nice-looking, slender boy with brown hair and blue eyes, his manner was languid and his speech sarcastically flip, yet I detected a deeper mood of hurtful despair. His attorney saw little point in putting up a defense and was ready to plead the boy guilty, which added to David's depression. Although he had been in the state correctional facility intermittently for seven years, his parents had never visited him, never written him, never appeared at his trials. They were connected to him only by biological accident.

David was anticipating another stinging sentence of three years or more, but I wanted to show him that somebody cared about him. In open court I told him that if during the next five months in detention he demonstrated a good attitude and stayed out of trouble, I would order his release from detention and placement in a suitable foster home. "You can get out of that place if you show me these next five months that you want to be a good citizen," I said. "I want you to know that there *are* people who care about you. If at any time you need to get in touch with someone for a problem you can call me."

The boy's cheeks reddened and he seemed genuinely touched. I called him up to the bench and gave him a warm handshake, though I really wanted to hug him. He didn't call me during the period of his detention, and five months later he reappeared, looking healthy and happy, and in the status of an honor ward. He was released for good conduct and placed in a foster home where he is now getting the love and attention he never got from his real parents.

These cases are only a few of the many thousands that could be found in any large city's juvenile court records. Nor is the list of categories complete; there are many other ways in which parents influence their children toward delinquency and criminality.

Probably the most appalling category of parents is that which might be called "perverted parents": those who send their daughters out into prostitution. I have seen this on several occasions, the most unsavory case involving an attractive fifteen-year-old eighth-grade student in a Catholic school for girls. Her father took photographs of her in the nude and then placed them in the photo-ad section of a pornographic newspaper, asking for an exchange. Both men and lesbians responded to the ad and, for a fee, the father obliged all applicants. It was the complaints of neighbors who observed the father photographing his daughter that provoked police action.

Another, less repugnant, example is that of parental favoritism, in which parents show love and affection to one child to the exclusion of another with often devastating results. Still another example is that of parents who abuse their children either physically or verbally. Most children cannot defend themselves—and what recourse do they have? Out of the several possibilities, the route chosen by some youngsters is that of crime and delinquency.

Emotional starvation

Psychologists say that for human beings to be happy they must fulfill their need for emotionally rich experiences. Many, however, are forced to conclude that modern life, both within the family and in society at large, leaves a large segment of youth emotionally neglected in important ways. Or, putting the matter even more bluntly, it may be that young people today typically suffer from some degree of emotional starvation.

Frederick Trasher writes that "the adolescent finds in the gang the desired escape from, or compensation for, monotony." Slum kids who do increasingly reckless things keep "raising the ante," to convince themselves that they are really alive. This phenomenon can be seen just as clearly among affluent delinquents, and, as noted by a Michigan prosecutor who put three young middle-class murderers behind bars, it leads to similar results. Kids go bad, he says, when they continually try to outdo one another. "For lack of anything better to do, they'd throw rocks at the windows in the high school. They hang around together, they brag, they talk about doing things and there's always one guy in the crowd who will actually do it. It may be a filling-station stickup, it may be murder."

Emotional starvation can spin a young person around in a spiral of tight distrust and fear. Drifting young people meander around public parks in our cities taking solace in the warmth of the sunshine and the friendliness of the trees.

Take the example of fourteen-year-old Linda McDermott, who was found wandering in Elysian Park in Los Angeles. The police officer who picked her up had seen her several times that Saturday, and finally decided, late in the afternoon, to ask her why she had spent the day aimlessly in the park. She seemed to be in a daze, but there were no needle scars, no dilated pupils, no evidence of drug usage. In any case, Linda refused to tell the officers where she lived, and—in keeping with the department's policy on runaways—the officers took her to Juvenile Hall so that her parents could be located and notified of their daughter's whereabouts.

I saw her for the first time the following Tuesday when she was brought into my courtroom. Don Miller, the social worker assigned to her case, came up to the bench as she sat, unmoving, next to a small table at the front of the courtroom. "Not too much to tell you about this one, your honor," Don told me, and filled me in on the few facts that he knew. Then he added, "She opened up a little over at the Hall, after she got over being scared."

"Where's her family?" I asked.

"Well, her mother lives out in the valley, in Encino," Don said, "but she doesn't seem very interested in Linda."

"What do you mean?"

"I talked to her yesterday, and explained where Linda was, that she was all right, and why she'd been picked up. But I'm not sure that Mrs. McDermott understood everything I was telling her. She sounded pretty well gone, even at three in the afternoon."

I asked him to bring Linda up to the bench. When she came closer I was able to see her eyes for the first time—they were a deep sea blue.

"We want to be able to help you, Linda, but you know that you'll have to cooperate with us here, just the way you co-operated with the people at Juvenile Hall." She nodded, uncertainly and shyly. "Where are your parents?" I asked.

"My mom's probably at home in Encino, but I don't think she's going to help you." Linda looked directly at me for the first time. "Sometimes she drinks some."

"How about your dad? Is he there too?"

"No, he's in Iowa or someplace like that. I don't know for sure. I haven't seen him in a long time."

When Don and Linda sat back down again, I tried calling Linda's mother myself. The phone rang six times before she answered. She sounded sleepy.

I told her who I was, and that her daughter was in my courtroom, waiting—waiting to be taken home, as she had been since the previous Saturday evening. I asked Mrs. McDermott when it would be convenient for her to come and pick Linda up.

"I don't know," she told me. "I'll try to make it down there sometime, I guess."

"I'm not sure whether you understand the situation, Mrs. McDermott," I said. "Linda has been here several days. She was picked up after she spent a whole day wandering around in a park here in Los Angeles. Don't you want her home, where she belongs?"

"Why don't you keep her?" She sounded as if this was a new idea, one that had just come into her head. "She's probably pretty well off there. You can have her, Judge. I don't want her here. Yeah, why don't you keep her?"

Mrs. McDermott's mind was made up, it seemed. Perhaps after years of frustration, she was abandoning her daughter. When she hung up, I asked Linda to come up to the bench again.

"Linda, I've just been talking to your mother on the phone. It looks like you're going to be staying at the Hall for a while, until we can find a new home for you." She took this news without any show of emotion, gazing vacantly at the wall.

Linda stayed at Juvenile Hall for seven months—it is not easy to find a foster home for an abandoned fourteen-year-old girl. Don Miller kept me informed about her case by giving me some news of her progress occasionally. While Juvenile Hall is not the most comfortable or attractive place to live, I was happy to hear that Linda was doing well there: going to school and making above-average grades, following the procedures without complaint, and even making friends among the other girls in the Hall. "As a matter of fact," Don told me one afternoon, "she's very popular over there. It seems that she's found a neighborhood—if you can call it that—that finally seems like home to her. I've even caught her smiling these last few weeks."

Seven months is not a very long time when you balance it against a whole lifetime, but that's how long it took to find a home for Linda. She was placed with a middle-aged couple in Westwood, not far from the UCLA campus. The couple's own two children had grown up and moved out, and they were only too pleased to have a younger person in their home again. I was pleased too; it seemed to me that Linda was going to be able to grow up in a happy environment and realize the potential I had seen in her eyes that day in the courtroom.

My job doesn't let me follow up very closely on the cases I hear; sometimes, though, when I'm interested in a youngster's progress, I try to keep tabs by asking the probation officers and social workers what the current status of the case is when I see them. Don Miller knew how interested I was in Linda, and usually I didn't even have to ask him about her—he'd give me a little progress report without any prompting on my part whenever I saw him.

Linda, he told me, wasn't having the easiest of times in adjusting to her new home. Her foster parents reported that she sometimes seemed depressed and withdrawn, sometimes would sit in her room for hours on end, just staring out the window. She was going to school and doing moderately well, but she didn't seem to be enjoying herself—she was a loner on the campus, without any friends to speak of. Don's opinion was that she was going through adjustment pangs. "I've seen a hundred cases like it," he told me. "It just takes them a while to get used to the kind of life they never had before." I was inclined to agree. It might take a while for Linda to become accustomed to her new environment, but at least I was fairly sure that Linda was not going to return to Juvenile Hall.

But she did return to Juvenile Hall.

This time she didn't come in by the normal route of arrest and detention, though. She was apprehended, four months after she had been placed in the foster home, trying to climb over the Juvenile Hall fence: she was trying to get back *in*. When the police officer lifted her down from the fence, she begged him, sobbing, "Let me go in there! Please! It's the only family I ever had! Please!"

As a juvenile court judge I encounter human catastrophe on a regular basis. Recalcitrant young criminals pour into juvenile court like stockyard cattle. Social scientists are forever scrutinizing these delinquents, searching for profound, complicated explanations for their deviation, but the answer often is relatively simple. Many of these children are suffering from emotional undernourishment, never having received the love every person needs for a healthy social development. Many of today's pop songs tell about a famine of warmth in today's infinitely dense, insanely discordant, impersonally anonymous inner cities. They are truly concrete cradles holding our youths in embalming coldness.

To fill the emotional void many children turn to escapes that are self-destructive. They seek deliverance from emptiness through the synthetic heaven of drugs. An estimated five hundred thousand U.S. teenagers are alcoholics. More and more young persons are coming into juvenile court for sniffing the toxic fumes of paint or inhaling the chemicals in glue. These kids are looking for ways to thrill their minds, to experience an intense feeling, because they are starving for emotional satisfaction.

Beyond the family, society itself may fail to provide the

emotionally gratifying activities needed by youth. The swing to hard drugs in the suburbs has been interpreted as an artificial hunt for excitement. Emotional starvation, the driving need for a dimension of emotional stimulation that is not furnished by the family or society, may be one of the major causes of juvenile crime in America today.

7 • Electronic Media: Hall of Freak Mirrors

No man's model of reality is a purely personal product. While some of his images are based on first-hand observation, an increasing proportion of them today are based on messages beamed to us by the mass media.
—Alvin Toffler, Future Shock

Today's youngsters are highly susceptible to the influence of mass media, with television as their major source of information and entertainment. All surveys indicate that both young children and adolescents are television's most constant audience. According to the National Commission on the Causes and Prevention of Violence, children in low-income families spend an average of a fourth to a half of their time in front of a television screen—more time than they spend in school. On Sundays, middle-class youngsters watch television for an average of four hours, while youngsters from low-income families watch it for as much as six hours. In that thirty to sixty hours a week, those children are bombarded with two phenomena: increasingly sophisticated messages urging them to buy products, and increasingly unsophisticated maelstroms of violence.

Television violence

Televised law and order has turned into a bloody orgy—all those bodies crashing through windows and being stuffed into car trunks must make some penetration into young minds. In one two-week period in 1974, television's heroes and heroines braved a wild mix of uncaged mayhem: Mannix went off a cliff in a flaming car, Kojak fought off a knifer, one of the Rookies took a bullet in the neck, McMillan was wrapped around a tree, Banacek fell from a bridge, Ironside was dumped rudely from his wheelchair, and Cannon was clubbed on the skull with a shovel. Columnist Erma Bombeck tells, only half in jest, how she had planned a vacation in Hawaii but canceled it because during a three-month period she saw "no less than thirty-eight bodies washed up on the beach in *Hawaii Five-O.*"

Sandra Haggerty of *The Los Angeles Times* voices similar concern, decrying the images of blacks on the movie screen as "glorified potheads, pimps, whores, superbad bucks, and supersexy women." She fears that such images are "contaminating" black youth. Academy Award director George Seaton worries about the effect of the new ultra-realism in movie violence: "Pouches of fake blood are exploded by small charges of powder, raw meat and bits of lamb bone are used to demonstrate how a man's chest can be blown to bits by a dum-dum bullet."

The excessive violence on television is apparent to any reasonable watcher. The Senate Subcommittee to Investigate Juvenile Delinquency in 1968 documented the number of violent acts on television: in one week in New York City, youngsters were exposed to an average of six acts or threats of violence per one-hour program. Between the fifties and sixties, a period when juvenile crime rose more than 50 per cent, the number of "action and adventure" programs tripled; they now constitute nearly two-thirds of all programs on prime-time television.

It is abundantly clear that children are being exposed to a high level of television violence—but what is the moral nature of this violence? Is it offset by redeeming social values explicit or implicit in the context? The answer is a loud "no." Most encounters are between clearly identified "good guys" and "bad guys," but the violence is initiated equally by each, so that the distinction between "good" and "bad" is not determined by violence. Those who commit acts of violence more often do it in their own self-interest than in the service of some other cause. Nearly half of all the leading characters who kill achieve a clearly happy ending. Lawful arrests and trial are rarely shown as a consequence of violent acts, and physical pain is shown in only one out of every four violent acts. Peculiarly, in television drama, violence does not seem to hurt.

How influential is media violence?

A San Francisco woman is suing NBC for $11 million on the charge that her nine-year-old daughter was "raped" by a boy and three girls, ages ten to fourteen, in a fashion similar to the broomstick assault portrayed in *Born Innocent,* a made-for-TV movie about juvenile detention homes.

The controversy over the effects of media violence on children has raged for years. Victor E. Cline, a professor of psychology at the University of Utah, insists that the latest evidence compiled by social science researchers leaves no room for doubt that "media violence does affect us, and potentially adversely." But, when attacked for peddling violence, filmmakers argue that the screen merely reflects already established public behavior patterns. Defenders of television violence go even further, claiming, for instance, that tips gleaned from crime programs might save our lives someday.

Aristotle's ancient concept of catharsis—dramatizations arousing pity or fear that help purge the viewer's emotions—survives as the prime argument in favor of theatrical violence. Proponents of televised violence contend that these fictional dramas perform a service to the community by providing viewers tension release through harmless identification with the actors. Far from leading to real violence, they say, fabricated blood and guts has the beneficial effect of siphoning off the viewers' hostile impulses. By watching electronic images of wild gun duels and combative sports such as boxing, football, hockey, and the roller derby, young people can vicariously vent their aggression and adrenalin without hurting anyone.

The dominant effect of the media, according to some psychologists, is the refinement of pre-existing viewpoints. People tend to watch programs that jibe with their personal attitudes and tastes. The preponderance of these findings are derived studies with adults, however, and their validity seems considerably weaker with respect to children.

Children between the ages of three and eight are particularly susceptible to visual learning when the material portrayed is new to them and easy to grasp. What younger children see on television is "real" because they are still in the process of learning to discriminate between fantasy and fact. They have no ingrained, preconceived versions of reality, no established tastes or attitudes, a fresh mental slate. What children see on television may substitute for—or overwhelm—parental guidance in coloring their perceptions of conduct and their choice of solutions to personal problems.

As they grow older, children begin to bring somewhat more purposeful motives to their television interests. Adolescents consciously rely on mass-media models in learning how to play real-life roles, using these models as sources of ideas and advice about dating and behavior toward the opposite sex. For teenagers who lack strong family ties, television becomes a readily available substitute for real-life experiences. When a group of teenagers asked whether they agreed or disagreed with such statements as "The programs I see on TV programs are just like the people I meet in real life," 40 per cent of the poor black adolescents and 30 per cent of the poor whites strongly believed in the true-to-life nature of television content. In short, most young children and a large proportion of teenagers from poor families believe that real people behave the way they do in the artificial world of television.

Film director George Seaton has no doubts that the mass media, particularly film, touch and shape the habits and attitudes of viewers. He recalls that "when Clark Gable revealed his uncovered upper torso in *It Happened One Night*, undershirts became as outdated as buggy whips; when leading men appeared bare-headed, the sale of hats took a mighty plunge; when Marlene Dietrich introduced slacks, pants for women became the style; and when the late James Dean hit the screen the dress habits of the young changed overnight." More recent concern has been expressed by various animal-protection agencies that appeared on the set of the movie *Willard* to make certain that the rats were not ill treated. These groups do not approve of even the simulated mistreatment of animals, convinced that an actor kicking a dog, tying a can to a cat's tail, or stepping on a rat too often inspires children to follow suit.

The mother of one problem child told me: "I hate what this kid stands for. He's impressed with the trashiest of plastic values. None of what I teach him matters. The boob tube has replaced me as his parent. Even though I got rid of it, he still gets indoctrinated through his friends who still watch. All he cares about is this team beating that one, cars that speed and shine, nothing about people or nature. I tell you, I hate my own son!"

Top police authorities throughout the nation interviewed in 1974 almost unanimously charge that television and movies give youth ideas for crime. An overwhelming 87.5 per cent of these officials condemned crime shows for "advertising criminal acts and how to commit them." Typical of the comments was that of Boston Police Commissioner Robert D. Grazia, who said: "People definitely do get ideas for crime from watching TV. We had a horrible murder here where a group of boys doused a girl with gasoline and set her on fire. Only one day earlier they had seen a movie on TV called *Fuzz* in which the same crime was shown." Denver Police Chief Arthur Dill similarly reported: "A bank in this area was robbed by some guys in stolen police uniforms—after the same thing had appeared on TV."

Perhaps the most potent argument for television's sizable influence is the money spent on advertising. As Bishop Fulton J. Sheen points out, "If violence does not suggest violence, then why do the TV stations accept millions from soap manufacturers in the belief that the advertising will suggest the buying of that product? Why is it that TV believes the picture of a

Dodge will induce buyers to buy a Dodge but that the picture of burning the feet of a girl bound with rope will not tempt youths to do the same?" A TV writer interviewed in a study for the 1971 Surgeon General's report said, "We aren't going to get rid of violence until we get rid of advertising. The advertisers want something with which to get an audience. Violence equals excitement equals ratings."

Exploitation of violence

New York Times TV critic John O'Connor says, "The problem with American television is less the inclusion of violence than the exploitation of violence, an exploitation rooted either in gross stupidity or arrogant cynicism." People do imitate styles, copy mannerisms, whistle jingles, and go out and buy products, and, most importantly, learn ideas about the world from watching commercials. The Surgeon General's office noted that "the greater the level of TV violence, the more the child is willing to use violence as a solution to conflict and to perceive it as effective." In California, a high school honor student's murder of his father, mother, and three sisters was ascribed in part to a latent hatred for his family, but the boy confessed that this bloodbath was triggered by a similar incident he had seen in a movie. One of the first skyjackings, which precipitated a rash of imitations, was copied from a TV episode on *Night Gallery* in which a skyjacker parachuted away with a million dollars.

Professor Lewis Yablonsky of California State University indicts the media's exploitation of violence as a kind of fertilizer that helps gangs to flourish. "If guys go to a football game they go out and hunch their shoulders. If they are consistently exposed to media vigilantes and outlaws, they will absorb these modes of behavior. Many youngsters are not astute at delineating between the real world and fantasy. Instead of ball games on television, you had a whole generation raised on '383 dead in Vietnam today.' " A daily diet of media machismo has numbed a generation to violence. The leading purveyor of violent sensationalism has been the visual media, but even the press has capitalized on electrifying bloodshed and has thereby contributed to the growing cult of machismo. Uplifting self-affirmation is felt upon seeing one's exploits reported to millions of people. Gang members cheer with vanity reading newspaper accounts of their crimes. It is another way of finding some concrete self-importance in an impersonal, indifferent world.

Dr. Morris Janowitz, a sociologist at the University of Chicago, wrote, in 1970, "Recent research employing rigorous experimental methods has strengthened the conclusion that high exposure to violent content in the mass media weakens personal and social controls." These new findings are based on probing fantasies and psychological responses of young people after exposure to violent content. Dr. Janowitz's judgment is that the towering evidence collected by social scientists over the past thirty years decisively points to a discernible negative impact of the media on social values and on the personal controls required to inhibit individual aggressiveness. No one has yet concluded that television programing is the principal cause of juvenile violence, but it is a large part of the external universe that influences an impressionable young mind.

In my courtroom shortly after I convicted a young black boy for armed robbery he was ushered by a guard down to the courtroom lockup to await delivery to a detention camp. Within minutes after the steel door closed behind him, he tore into a white youth without provocation, pounding him with both fists and yelling, "You kept me in slavery for two hundred years!" What relationship does this incident have to media violence? In my judgment, if black exploitation movies such as *Blackula, Hit Man, The Mack, Black Gun, Shaft, Superfly,* and *Trick Baby* portray blacks using violence against whites in a spirit of vengeance, then black youth will be more prone to act out these scenes in reality. In a more direct case of media influence, a youth accused of brutally assaulting another boy with karate sticks admitted to the court that he became interested in the mastery of this oriental weapon from watching a show on television.

Perhaps even more ominous was the comment by a fourteen-year-old girl in juvenile hall who wrote home about what a great man was portrayed in the film *The Godfather*.

Statistics seem to establish the credibility of the juvenile's receptivity to the media. As the analysis continues, the central issue is not whether the media can influence a juvenile, but to what extent they do actually shape American youth. How does the juvenile react to violence in the media and why do these reactions occur? Once this transference of identity is understood, perhaps the media can be developed into effective social tools in helping to curb, retard, and extinguish crime.

8 • Saturday Night Specials

More than anything else, the availability of guns has contributed to rising youth violence. Americans own more guns than any other people on earth.
–Brian Aimer, Chief Juvenile Prosecutor, Compton, California

A bright fluorescent lamp illuminated the living room of the apartment of a young married couple in the southcentral area of Los Angeles. Eighteen-year-old Vivian Clemens, an early riser, playfully cradled her baby, preparing to take her to Marineland for the day. Vivian's husband Jimmy, also eighteen, came into the room and, glancing at the baby, said, "I don't think you ought to take Vickie to Marineland today."

"Why not?" Vivian asked.

"The air's too cold out for her today."

"Come on, Jimmy, don't be silly."

"I'm serious. I been outside."

"I can dress her warm."

"You're not taking her. The kid just got over a cold, and I don't want her catching pneumonia."

Vivian's voice rose. "I'm telling you, I can put warm clothes on her!"

"No. You're not taking her."

"Listen, Jimmy, this kid is mine as much as she's yours. You're not giving me any orders." The baby, Victoria, looked on without understanding her parents' words, but feeling the rising tension between them.

"You go out the door with that kid and you're asking for trouble!" Jimmy was shouting now.

"Oh, what's the big man going to do, beat me up?"

"I'm getting pissed off now, Vivian!"

"Come on, man, get out of my way."

"Look, all I want you to do is forget about taking the kid today."

"Hey, I'm not forgetting anything. You can just fuck off!"

"I'm warning you for the last time!"

"Why don't you shoot me, then, big man?" Vivian shouted.

"I will if you try to take that kid out the door!"

"Well, shoot me then, motherfucker!"

With that last taunt, Jimmy stormed into the bedroom and over to the dresser, where a .22 revolver lay in the top drawer. Vivian raced in after him. As Jimmy pulled the gun from the drawer, she grabbed for it as well. They tussled for the weapon, and Vivian's finger closed around the trigger. A round exploded from the chamber, and Jimmy suddenly dropped to the floor, clutching his right side. For a moment the room was charged with a shocked silence after the deafening gun blast, and then Vivian fell to her knees and embraced her husband. "Oh, baby, I love you—I love you! You know I wouldn't do that to you! I didn't mean to do it!"

Less than three hours after an argument with his young wife—a quarrel over whether their infant daughter might catch a cold during a planned trip to Marineland—eighteen-year-old Jimmy Clemens was pronounced dead in the hospital emergency room. At 0957 hours, at precinct headquarters, young Vivian Clemens was arraigned for the gunshot murder of her husband.

"Everybody seems to have a gun nowadays"

Since the urban riots of the sixties, the possession of firearms has proliferated at an alarming rate among the general American public. In the decade from 1964 to 1974, nearly thirty million guns were added to the civilian stockpile, and the sale of handguns quadrupled. Police experts estimate that for every hundred thousand Americans there are fifteen thousand handguns. By contrast, for every hundred thousand people in England, Finland, the Netherlands, Greece, and Switzerland there are fewer than five hundred handguns.

Firearms are a primary instrument of violent death in America. In the past ten years gun homicides have doubled, and in 1973 alone twenty-five thousand Americans were killed by guns. Of the 150 juvenile killings in Detroit in 1973, 90 per cent were committed with handguns. In the same year the Los Angeles police confiscated over two hundred guns from school children. A correlation *does* exist between the rising murder rate and the increasing number of guns owned by Americans.

The growing need of private citizens to own guns, particularly handguns, must be attributed to a rising fear of violence. Studies by the Senate Subcommittee on Juvenile Delinquency disclose that gun sales in a particular area tend to increase sharply during and after a period of disorder. After the 1967 Detroit riot, for example, gun sales skyrocketed, with four times as many handgun permits being issued in the central city and five times as many in the nearby predominantly white suburbs than had been issued two years earlier. And a great number of the guns purchased by adults to protect home and family end up in the hands of minors who use them for criminal violence.

In 1974 I tried a case in which three members of the Los Angeles Crips gang forced a youth to take them into his home so they could steal his father's handguns. Numerous other weapons thefts were reported on that day in southcentral Los Angeles, and the police learned that the Crips were planning a massive ambush on a rival gang, the Brims. The attack was set for the time the Brims would be leaving school, with a fusillade of bullets spraying the students as they surged into the streets. The Crips were not deterred by the fact that innocent bystanders would probably be killed; they were thwarted only by the fortunate foreknowledge of the police.

Lending impetus to the arms buildup are the exhortations of extremist groups, whether black, white, or hispanic, who in their speeches and publications incite their members to buy firearms and to be prepared to use them against "the enemy." Neighborhood protective associations have multiplied and have sometimes come to share the fears of the right-wing paramilitary groups, with the result that firearms are now being stockpiled in the home as well as "in the hills." Extremist organizations urge their members to obtain firearms for neighborhood and home defense, and sometimes for guerilla warfare and terrorist activity as well. The Zebra murder cases in San Francisco in 1974—in which blacks were randomly shooting whites on the streets of that city—are horrifying examples of guns being wantonly used in extremist madness. Ironically, extremist groups, regardless of race, are remarkably alike in their attitudes toward firearms and in their opposition to gun control.

Firearms, particularly handguns, facilitate the commission and increase the danger of the most violent of crimes—murder, armed robbery, assault, and rape. It is easier and less risky for a rapist to keep his victim silent by threatening her with a gun than by simply telling her to be quiet. "Half of our murders occur," says a New York City detective, "because so many people have guns in their pockets. Two kids get into an argument, one of them reaches into his pocket for a gun, and bang, a murder. If there wasn't a gun in his pocket, who knows? Maybe they could have talked it out and parted friends, there wouldn't have been any violence at all. But the fact is everybody seems to have a gun nowadays."

While personal injury and death stemming from criminal acts occur more often in the United States than in any other industrial nation, the circumstances of most homicides suggest that a person without ready access to a gun would not invariably kill with another weapon. Studies show that most people who commit homicides are not relentless, determined, cold-blooded killers, but rather are likely to act on impulse in a moment of rage or passion without a determined plan or intent to kill. There is no compelling evidence to prove or disprove the contention that, lacking a gun, an enraged person will resort to a knife or other weapon. But there is evidence demonstrating that the fatality rate in firearm attacks is more than four times greater than it is in knife attacks. Thus even if the number of violent attacks did not decrease, the number of fatalities would be substantially reduced if the attackers did not have guns.

Guns and kids

Almost daily in the Los Angeles Juvenile Court we encounter tragic cases of shooting violence. Three boys drive through the streets of Compton randomly practicing marksmanship and kill six innocent people. A man tries to usher a friend away from an argument with gang toughs and he is shot point-blank with a shotgun. A fifteen-year-old boy leaves his house after arguing with his father; he returns minutes later with a handgun and shoots his father through the neck. A young black decides he wants to kill a Mexican—"any Mexican"; he walks the streets with a gun snug under his shirt, spots an unsuspecting Mexican, the father of four, sitting in a garden, walks up behind him, and blasts away part of his head. If the guns had not been so easily available, would all these people be uninjured, or at least alive?

During the fifties, when five thousand street gang members were rumbling in New York's streets, the only firearm was the zip gun. This homemade handpiece was fashioned from a snippet of pipe about the length of a stogie cigar, cut from a curtain rod, car radio antenna, or pipe ripped out from a street light. This crude barrel was fastened with wire and tape to a whittled block of wood that served as the stock. The square metal rod ordinarily used to connect door knobs was filed to a point and used for the hammer, and the trigger mechanism consisted of rubber bands. Releasing the heavy rubber bands stretched across the stock forced the firing pin into the cartridge and exploded the bullet out. The gun had a very limited range, was inaccurate, and lasted only perhaps three firings before it fell apart or exploded in the user's hand. Few gang members actually used these weapons in rumbles, and when they did they were not very effective. At that time, only six or seven shooting deaths occurred in juvenile gang action in the course of a year in New York.

Street gangs in the seventies, however, are armed with an assortment of weapons that gives today's rumbles the aura of military campaigns. Factory-made handpieces, rifles, shotguns, machine guns, and walkie-talkies have been confiscated from South Bronx gangs. In Los Angeles, a popular weapon is the "zip" shotgun, made by sawing off a 12-gauge shotgun at both ends and carving the stock into a curved handle, thus turning the shotgun into a handgun. At close range these revolverlike shotguns are extremely deadly. The main gang weapon, however, remains the ordinary handgun, factory-made .22's, .32's, and .38's, all of which are readily available in the "Saturday night special supermarkets." A ghetto youth has no trouble finding a gun peddler in the local schoolyard or in a neighborhood bar. Sellers of guns are as well known as drug pushers, and are an equal menace to society. The guns they sell are stolen, usually from gun stores, with their serial numbers filed off. Recently a number of .45-caliber pistols have appeared, stolen from the Army in Vietnam. Perhaps the most ominous was the July 5, 1974, theft of more than 150 M-16 military rifles, M-60 machine guns, .45-caliber pistols, and M-79 grenade launchers, plus thousands of rounds of ammunition, from the Compton, California, National Guard Armory. That much ordnance at large in the community touched off a mild panic among police officials. The amount of ammunition stolen was relatively small considering the number of weapons, but any sporting-goods store or gun shop stocks such ammunition—and in our society it is no problem for anyone to legitimately buy ammunition for stolen weapons.

A ban on firearms would not be a panacea to juvenile crime, but it would help de-escalate the problem. In England, where weapons have been effectively controlled, fewer people were killed in a year by gunshot than are in little more than a day in the United States. In Tokyo, with a population of eleven million, there was only one shooting homicide in 1971, thanks primarily to a ban on handgun sales.

The presence—fast becoming an omnipresence—of guns in

society is incontrovertibly a major factor contributing to both juvenile violence and juvenile crime. It isn't the only factor, but in this particular parade of horribles, it is near the top of the list.

9 • Life in the Ghetto

Three out of four arrests and four out of five serious crimes take place in the ghetto. The ghetto is the incubator of crime.
—Commissioner,
New York City Police Department, 1972

"When you're born in the ghetto, odds are ten to one you'll never get out. What's worse, you know it. So what do you do? Well, you look down the street at the corner and you see a guy with a beautiful girl on each arm, a three-hundred-dollar custom-tailored suit, and you say, 'Man, I'm gonna be just like him. He was born here. He lives here. And he's beaten it. I'm gonna be just like him.' Not like O. J. Simpson. Not like Willie Mays. Not like Bill Russell. Because nobody's really like them. At least, nobody you know. So right there you decide. Eleven years old and you decide on your future. You're going to be a pimp."

This advertisement, placed by Direction Sports in California, an organization dedicated to helping ghetto youth find a constructive way of life, points out one of the major problems in the ghetto. Street heroes are often bejeweled gamblers, elaborately preened pimps, and flashy mob murderers. They are the only local people who visibly display the conspicuous trappings of success. In the neighborhood where I lived as a boy, it was the local Mafia capo driving his Fleetwood Cadillac who was looked up to as a success symbol by the local kids.

The trap of poverty

The ghetto is a serpentine trap of hopelessness. Slum dwellers are unable to share in the benefits of their affluent nation. Despite our cherished beliefs in equality of opportunity and the equality of all people, in many areas of this country generations of families have subsisted in conditions of deprivation and poverty which are beyond the comprehension of the rest of the nation. Poverty is not limited to any particular region of the country, or to color of skin or ethnic background. It exists in urban ghettos and barrios among people whose skins are black and brown, in the countryside of Appalachia among people whose skins are white, in dusty reservations among people whose skins are red. Not all Indian reservations are intolerably stultifying, not all of Appalachia is untillable, not all of California's migrant farmworkers live in squalor and hunger, and not all residents of any ghetto or barrio depend for their lives on welfare, or are even poor. But over ten million American families are.

During my years as a young gang leader in New York City, my father was a street sweeper. His take-home pay was forty-four dollars a week, and he had a wife and seven children to support. The month's rent wiped out one full week's salary. The icebox was often empty by the middle of the week, except for some leftover pasta. My mother seldom paid cash for anything. Instead, she traded with the door-to-door salesmen who gave her credit—and charged her double for the privilege. To pay the bills, Dad borrowed from loan companies that soaked him 30 per cent interest, tacked on late fees, and sent collectors to threaten him. Once a loan company even sued him to get at his paycheck. His only defense was that he had missed his payments because he had had to pay for an operation to remove his son's ruptured appendix. Dad promised to pay the loan company as soon as he could, and asked the judge not to "garnishee" his salary. Cavalierly, the judge, unimpressed, explained that he was under oath to administer justice according to the law, which meant looking at the terms of the contract and ordering garnishment. No wonder a deprived youth learns early to regard the law, and those who represent it, as his enemies.

The sad truth is that most people simply cannot understand the blistering emotional effects that poverty has on a young person's development. Deprivation for most means postponing a planned vacation, or waiting another year for a new car, but imagine for a moment the feeling of confused hurt a young boy feels at the sight of his mother being punched unconscious by his father during an argument over money for a birthday dress for his baby sister. My parents were decent people, and seeing them claw at each other because of money was enough to make me bitter, and to make me view society as a rotten, merciless place. Since the fifties, conditions haven't appreciably changed in the ghetto.

America's wasteland

"Sal es puedes," they say in the South Bronx—"leave if you can." Garbage is thrown out of windows and gets stacked so high that it seems to creep back into the same windows. Almost every roof is a "shooting gallery"—a place where kids take their heroin injections. Inside the cold-water apartments, shivering people are sleeping on top of each other in close quarters. I've seen a family of fourteen living—if you call it that—in a two-room flat. The place was overrun with cockroaches, swarms of them crawling on the bread box, but the family went right on eating, moving only to swat the insects away from their food. Hallways were splattered with week-old dog droppings, and the basements smelled even worse, reeking from the stench of backed-up toilets. Nobody ever bothered to fix the plumbing.

Over 80 per cent of the buildings in the South Bronx violate the New York City Health Code. A study by the Kings County Health Center reveals that 50 per cent of low-income housing is without heat over half of the time. "There is a rapid deterioration of the body in many people after the age of twenty-five," says Dr. Harold Wise. "Something happens to your body when you spend the entire winter without heat." Darker, if less tangible, damage is done to the mind and soul.

The South Bronx is a scar on the American conscience—rawly violent, drug-ridden, burned-out, graffiti-swashed, and cruelly abandoned. Forty per cent of its four hundred thousand residents are on welfare, and 30 per cent of the employable are out of work. Latin rhythms dance in the air, pulsating from radios or from makeshift garbage-can conga drums, the anguished beat of a forgotten land in the heart of America's largest city. On a typical day, a drug pusher is fatally struck by six bullets that graft a cross on his body, the victim of a youth gang carrying out a thirty-dollar contract from a rival pusher. A youngster is stomped nearly to death outside his school in an argument over a soda bottle, valuable for its nickel deposit. A runaway girl is crippled after being beaten with belts and chains.

Uniqueness is not a label that can be placed on the South Bronx. It by no means has a monopoly on decaying destitution. All of America's ghettos are wastelands where only hatred and violence flourish. Former New York Mayor John Lindsay called Brownsville—a sprawling Brooklyn slum—bombsville, because it has over five hundred abandoned buildings, hundreds of vacant lots, and rows of empty stores. Lots are heaped with vermin-infested rags, broken bricks, shattered glass, and reeking garbage. Half of all the tenements in Harlem were built in the late nineteenth century and are now crumbling. Riot-racked Bedford-Stuyvesant, in Brooklyn, covers a few square miles and registers 90 per cent of its residents as black or Puerto Rican, and with five hundred thousand inhabitants has a population density thirty times that of the average suburb. In Detroit, ghetto schools are the oldest and most crowded, and are staffed by teachers with the poorest qualifications of any in the city. Life expectancy is the shortest in the slums, and more children die there at birth than anywhere else. Compared to the average suburb, the incidence of spinal meningitis in Watts is 20 per cent higher, of rheumatic fever 40 per cent higher, of whooping cough 60 per cent higher, of polio 80 per cent higher, of food poisoning 100 per cent higher. The unemployment rate in Watts is three times the national average, and the rate is higher now than it was at the time of the riots.

Resentment breeds violence

It is common knowledge, confirmed by countless studies and statistics, that the low-income, overcrowded areas of our cities are also the zones of highest crime, and that the poorer segment of our population–which usually means our racial and ethnic minorities–contribute disproportionately to our crime rate. The National Commission on the Causes and Prevention of Violence stated, "Violent crimes are chiefly a problem of the cities of the nation, and there violent crimes are committed mainly by the young, poor male inhabitants of the ghetto slum."

If slum life offers nothing more than cankerous tenements, ruptured sidewalks, empty food shelves, debilitating maladies, and abysmal squalor, while its young are constantly being reminded by television that the America "outside" pampers itself with an ostentatious standard of affluence, an aching sense of injustice begins to smolder. It is difficult for these kids to understand why they cannot share in these advantages. Even now, when the rest of the world looks less rosy every day–when more than six and a half million were jobless at the beginning of 1975 with that number threatening to balloon to eight million by midyear, when layoffs are reverberating through industry in ever-widening circles, when inflation plagues the rest of the nation and appears to be with us for the foreseeable future–life in the ghetto remains an economic dungeon compared with the rest of the country. It is even more of an inferno for ghetto youth, who at 18.9 per cent have the highest unemployment rate in the nation.

Children in the ghetto begin to view life as clearly divided between the "haves" and the "have-nots," and a dull ache of injustice throbs near the surface, always ready to boil over. This combined with the feeling of futility, of cynical rejection of hope, adds a recklessness to their mood of resentment. A number of ghetto youths who have come into my courtroom shrug at the prospect of jail. A penal institution is not intimidating because for some it will provide the best food and shelter they have ever known. The ghetto streets where they grew up have been just another form of prison.

Smouldering resentment eventually detonates violence. More than eight hundred grisly crimes were reported in just one year in the South Bronx, most of them linked to the youth gangs that have been breeding like locusts. What kind of grotesque environment is it that can warp the innocence of youth into such blind and unfeeling cruelty? What makes a thirteen-year-old boy kick an old man to death for a vague and blurred reason? Scorching hatred born of resentment is directed at everyone and everything when a young man is made to feel that he is part of the dregs of society. Escape grows into an obsession—escape at any cost, escape from the slow death of the ghetto. Voracious rage can explode into riots, rape, robbery, and murder, or it can be forged into a creative determination to succeed, to somehow transcend the fate of ghetto youth—drugs, frustration, prison, and even death.

When you grow up in the ghetto the odds on achieving a decent life are stacked against you. An individual may be able to overcome these odds through his or her own tenacity, but I also believe that society has an obligation to improve conditions, to give ghetto youth a fairer chance. Juvenile crime will not abate as long as millions of Americans are living in slums. Equality of material comforts is an unattainable goal for any society, but we can reach a standard of decency and dignity for every American. We can strive to fulfill the promise of equal opportunity. We can try to implement the aims of democracy as they were expressed by Lincoln when he said the nation must continue "the struggle for maintaining that form of government whose leading object is to elevate the conditions of men, to afford an unfettered start and a fair chance for all in the race of life."

10 • Education Is a Failure

Your typical juvenile offender is four to eight grades behind in his reading skills. If a person is going to function in society he must at least know how to read.
—James Hayes, Supervisor, Los Angeles County

Attorney Lois Forer, with the Office of Juveniles in Philadelphia, is convinced that the most severe problems confronting delinquent children are not in the home but in the school. Her office analyzed one hundred consecutive cases in their files and found that school problems had become part of the record in ninety-four instances. Many of these children could not even read a simple letter. A second-grade geography text was beyond the reading comprehension of many youths of fifteen to eighteen.

I have frequently seen sixteen-year-old offenders who could not even read the printed form directing them to the court building. Judge Charles Wright of the Philadelphia Juvenile Court finds that at least 78 per cent of juvenile delinquents are functional illiterates. The city of Compton, California, which posted the highest crime rate in America in 1974, also has the nation's lowest reading level for its children. A child who stammers and falters with basic reading develops into a teenager and adult who cannot function normally in society, and who may turn to crime to earn a living. The blame for this social deficiency must be placed on the schools, which have simply failed to respond to the needs of their students in today's world.

Conformity to what?

The major problem with the school system today is that it is a mass institution which cannot effectively deal with the needs of the individual student. The system demands conformity from the student, but the conformity demanded often disregards cultural and social disadvantages. The whole operation revolves around arbitrary standards that tend to stultify minority and lower-income children.

This is clear in the results of standardized intelligence tests used for class placement. Ignoring linguistic and cultural differences, these tests are tilted unfairly against ghetto children. They are generally based on the values and home environments found in the white, middle-class mainstream. One such IQ test, for example, asks youngsters to decide what they would do if they discovered that they had been given too much change from a purchase. The "correct" answer, the one that most clearly reflected middle-class values, was to return the money. But the other three choices could be equally "correct," or at least plausible, to youngsters from different sociocultural backgrounds. Moreover, these tests usually emphasize verbal aptitude, which is only one of the many measures of intelligence, but is more highly regarded in middle-class society than in lower-class communities, where manual skills are more esteemed.

In reality, such IQ tests measure only a specific segment of the population and are valid only for a portion of all students. That this portion constitutes the majority is beside the point, for the cultural bias of the tests deprives a significant number of children of the chance to develop to their full potential.

Arbitrary standards are also responsible for the disproportionate number of minority-group students in classes for the Educable Mentally Retarded (EMR). Lloyd Dunn wrote the first major work urging regular class placement for socioculturally deprived students who had been labeled EMR. He observed that 60 to 80 per cent of all the pupils in these classes were from low-income backgrounds and broken, inadequate homes, and all had had behavior problems in their regular classes. Fred Krause, executive director of the President's Committee for Mental Retardation, agrees that sociocultural deprivation is the main cause for what appears to be retardation. Children who are ignored, neglected, abandoned, and shunted aside are growing up in an intellectual vacuum; it should come as no shock that they seem to be handicapped intellectually. A 1960 study by Blatt demonstrated that low IQ does not play an important role in causing delinquency and criminality unless it is combined with deprivation and with a home environment in which psychological problems exist: "Mentally subnormal children do not have to become delinquent; nor can we explain delinquency as a manifestation of subnormality. It is not surprising that some of these children become delinquents; it is amazing that more do not. Society must recognize the need for . . . realistic education, and vocational counseling for all its citizens. More important, we must cease looking with derision at those in a different cultural milieu." Yet it is precisely this "different cultural milieu" which alienates lower-income and minority students in the classroom and which often keeps them out of the very classrooms in which they belong.

Role of the teacher

Sociocultural differences tend to alienate students from their teachers as well as their schoolmates. Complaints are lodged against inner-city teachers for being insensitive to the needs underlying aggressive behavior. Granted, the unruly ghetto youth can strain patience and jangle nerves, but the answer is not retaliation. The teacher who reacts to misconduct by lowering grades and inflicting punishment is aggravating the errant student's already negative view of the educational system.

As the "authority" figure in a student's eyes, the teacher holds the spotlight in communicating the attitudes of the society at large. Mistreatment by their teachers arouses skepticism and hostility in students. Mrs. Dot Stalvey, a Los Angeles mother, writes of her own children's experiences in inner-city schools, describing the tensions between teachers and students. Her children expected teachers to slap, hit, and kick certain children—usually lower-income minority children whose speech, dress, and attitudes seemed to upset their middle-class teachers. These children were constantly humiliated, labeled slow or stupid, and physically abused. According to Mrs. Stalvey's son, one black child was made to stand in a waste basket all afternoon because she wouldn't say, "Yes, ma'am" to her white teacher. Her teacher's degrading treatment only heightened the hostility in this child, whose mother was a drug addict and whose father was a convicted murderer.

With another child, a boy named Josh, Mrs. Stalvey found that he used his aggression to mask his embarrassment in not knowing how to read. One teacher felt "guilty" about Josh because she was allowed to teach reading for only one hour a day in a class in which seventeen of the thirty children—one of whom was Josh—had severe reading problems. The stubborn pride of Josh and the school's indifference hindered any progress in his reading. At his teacher's request he was later transferred to an all-black school known for its gang fights and low level of academic achievement.

Mrs. Stalvey was a substitute teacher for a ruffled and disillusioned Peace Corps dropout who virtually abandoned his eighth-grade class when he was unable to reach his students. Disharmony was sounded in the twilight signs of body language—that is, a number of teachers projected stupidity and inferiority onto their students without ever expressing their feelings verbally. With few exceptions, they glossed over slower pupils, focusing their energies on favorites and being patronizing when they did relate to ghetto children. It is an empty gesture to move students to other schools if they cannot escape from teachers with segregating eyes.

Curriculum problems

According to sociologist James Coleman, the typical curriculum is too narrow and constricted since it is oriented toward information rather than experience. During a national TV interview in 1974, leaders from a spectrum of junior high schools complained that the biggest problem in education was "the dullness and lack of relevance of the classes." Schools offer youths the basic academic skills but overlook the more practical aspects of life such as managing one's own affairs, training for and finding a job, taking responsibility for other people, and working for and with others. From time immemorial, such "extracurricular" skills were learned at home from the family, but as modern society evolved and the home stopped serving this function, the school was expected to fill the need. Lamentably, the schools have failed miserably in this function.

The irrelevance of instructional material to an "underprivileged" environment produces discontent and boredom for the inner-city youth. The student must either tolerate these dragging hours or forfeit schooling in search of a job. But the ghetto youth's lack of experience and the difficulty of acquiring job-market information deepen the futility of pursuing a "straight" life. An ironic failure in our school system, for instance, is the strange fact that automotive shop classes abound in the affluent suburbs, where middle-class teenagers tinker with their late-model cars, but are seldom found in ghetto schools, where they could be used for job-training programs. Auto mechanics is a field badly in need of new practitioners, but as the situation exists today, the schools are not creating craftsmen, only hobbyists.

Moreover, text materials used in the schools seem to be chosen without sufficient regard for students' needs or heterogeneous backgrounds. The extent to which textbooks critically influence children has not been determined with precision, but because they serve as the springboard for both teachers and students their effects must be carefully weighed. Imagination tempered with discretion should be the key in selecting textbooks. Learning materials chosen with misguided judgment often bring negative results to the students who must use them.

It is neither practical nor wise, for example, to present students with textbooks that offer theories, or even assumptions, about racial traits that are barely more than unproven hypotheses, and might certainly have a detrimental psychological effect on some readers. The same holds true, in this era of greater emphasis on women's rights, for texts which promulgate sexual stereotypes. Yet primary-grade readers often depict little boys in traditional masculine roles and little girls in weaker, feminine roles. This sort of socialization is difficult to counteract, but its impact on children as they grow up must not be discounted. At the same time, texts need not be "laundered," as is the case now in many school districts, to remove from their pages any shred of controversy. Students of all ages can deal with controversial material, and indeed they do so every day, on the streets and at home. When texts are too bland, and too insipid, their effect can be as harmful as when they openly propound prejudice and bias. Both extremes can turn students off the learning process, leaving too many children adrift among low-paying, unchallenging jobs (or none at all) and faced with the temptation to turn to crime not only to relieve frustration and boredom, but to earn a living.

PART THREE

The Juvenile Justice System

11 • Police and Youth

The bosses don't want us to do our job any more. This whole law business has become a political thing.
—Detective Anthony Miniciello, New York City Police Department

The police play a critical role in America's juvenile justice system. When a young offender first comes into contact with the system—when he is stopped or arrested—it is through contact with a police officer. Policemen are visible to youth on the streets, in the news and entertainment media, and in school and community programs. Young people are more likely to see the men in blue going about their business than they are to see judges, jailers, or other members of the justice system. Juveniles probably have more day-to-day contact with police than with any other municipal officers. Yet it is safe to say that the young do not understand the police, nor do the police understand the young.

A question of mutual antagonism

In the most basic terms, kids don't trust cops and cops don't trust kids. The question of which comes first, lack of understanding or lack of trust, is moot. The city youth might be taught in school that policemen are his friends, but when he leaves the schoolyard (and even, in many cases, while he is still on school grounds) what he sees doesn't square with what he has been told and when policemen walk their beats or cruise their streets in squad cars, their observations of what *is* happening is often colored by their anticipation of what *might* happen. This, coupled with their training, can make them overly suspicious and distrustful of any situation involving teenagers. New York City Patrolman Joe Buscetti talks about interaction between youth and police on his beat: "These kids know that they're going to get off easy. They take advantage. They dare you to hit them."

Mutual uneasiness probably stems from the different conceptions of "the street" held by each side. The inner-city juvenile, especially the lower-class gang member, sees the street as his second home. His perception of city blocks as "hangouts," "territories," or "turfs" invests the street with a special meaning for him. Drinking, smoking pot, and gambling—activities that suburbanites might think best confined to the home, if done at all—are done by the inner-city kid on the street, in social company. When a policeman invades this "home," a gang member feels that his personal privacy has been violated, and he wants to retaliate. Gang toughs taunt the police with jibes of "pig" and "motherfucker," as if to dare the officer to become a bigot and bully to defend his own honor.

To the policeman, on the other hand, the street is his office, his shop, his place of work. His job there is to maintain order, to keep things running smoothly, and he has a vested interest in imposing his own rules. He does not want his "office" cluttered with dirty and unproductive people. Policemen on the beat, like gang teens, tend to view the street as their possession. The Chicago police, for example, are heard to use the phrase "Gimme that corner!" when ordering young people to move on.

Although police behavior on the streets of America's large cities tends to reflect their conception of how "their" streets should be used—a conception much at odds with that of juveniles—the police do not routinely move to stop all undesirable behavior. To do so would not only be unnecessary, but it might well be suicidal. A certain amount of "offensive" behavior is tolerated, but an attempt is made to keep the people on the street "in line."

In urban areas the police stage periodic "shakedowns" to remind the neighborhood youth that they, the police, are the ultimate authority. Such a confrontation is described by a New York City teenager: "One time me and a couple of friends, we came down to the corner on Monday night because we was supposed to have our meeting. And we was standing there on the corner bullshitting like usual, only four of us. Then this motorcycle cop pulled over and walked up to us. I seen him before. He cruises the neighborhood a lot. He didn't say nothing. He just zipped down his jacket and there was his big old billy club. And then he started asking questions, what we were doing, and all that. And he searched us and got our names. We wasn't doing nothing 'cept bullshitting. They do anything to get our names down on that book. They want us to know they in charge."

Police discrimination against youth and ethnic minorities

Shakedowns by the police are viewed by teenagers as another form of harassing discrimination against them because of age. Unable to vote, unorganized, unrecognized by the media, street kids are a powerless group, vulnerable to police excesses. Perhaps the police use them as an outlet for their own tensions, but whatever the reason, the facts are that police do seem to discriminate against young people.

When rookie Arnold Guyn joined the Los Angeles Police Department he was teamed up with a thick-necked, street-wise veteran who told him, "Don't sweat search-and-seizure rules or any of that Bill of Rights bullshit when it comes to juveniles. They ain't got no rights anyway." Patrolman Guyn discovered subsequently that the oldtimer's observation—as far as police conduct was concerned—was essentially correct. The district to which they were assigned contained several public parks, in theory available to anyone who wanted to use them. But the daily police log designated these parks as a "Police Hazard," and instructions were to clear them out.

"Let's check the park to see if the little bastards are hanging around plotting something," the oldtimer would say to Guyn. "If we keep the heat on they'll stay the hell out of the park so decent people can use it. And since there ain't any decent people in this district, we just got to discourage anybody from using the park."

Juveniles protest to the juvenile court that the police see them as threats to society simply because they are young, and they resent police surveillance. To young blacks, especially, the police are seen as alien soldiers patrolling occupied territory. And from the front seat of a moving patrol car, street life in a typical ghetto is a succession of suspicious scenes. Every flamboyantly dressed young man or woman standing aimlessly on the street is scanned for criminal intent. Every boy wearing a club jacket or who has long hair is potentially responsible for some unsolved burglary, mugging, assault, or rape. Every hostile look directed at a passing patrolman is read as a sign of possible guilt.

While it is true that middle-class teenagers are not immune to what they, at least, see as police harassment, the phenomenon is much more noticeable in inner-city areas. And if resentment against such tactics is bred in affluent youth, it is much more pronounced—and far-reaching—in ghetto youth. Most officers are white, even in cities where a high percentage of the population is black and even where the police have made sincere efforts to recruit members of minority groups. This is also true, of course, in communities with large Mexican-American or Puerto Rican populations. And because of their general distrust of authority, minorities often see minority police officers as Uncle Toms, as having sold out to the white power structure. James Baldwin once said of the police in the ghetto, "Their very presence is an insult and it would be even if they spent their entire day feeding gumdrops to children. They represent the force of the white world, and that world's criminal profit, and its wish to keep the black man corralled here in his place."

Professor Francis Heussenstamn, of California State University, carried out an experiment in 1969 that tends to show police discrimination against minorities. Using fifteen students—five black, five Mexican-American, and five white—he demonstrated that a Black Panther bumper sticker on the rear of one's car was enough to turn many a cop against the vehicle's driver. All students in the study were daily drivers, and none had received a moving violation for at least a year. Each participant taped a Black Panther sticker on his car and proceeded with his daily routine. Within two days the participants had received six tickets for such infractions as incorrect lane changes, following too closely, and driving too slowly in the fast lane of the freeway. At the end of the seventeenth day, thirty-three citations had been received, and the study had to be terminated because all experiment funds had been exhausted to pay fines. While the experiment has been construed as demonstrating racial discrimination, it should be noted that the Black Panthers represent a militant group with a history of sizzling clashes with the police. To hate the Black Panthers is not to hate all blacks. The fact that the five black students had not previously been cited shows there was no bias against them merely because of race. Nevertheless, it is this sort of overt discrimination against political activists, and those who tend to support such groups as the Panthers, that leads to the reciprocal lack of trust between youth and police.

Further examples of invidious bias are amply documented. The police are granted wide discretion not only in how they will enforce the law but also in what laws they will enforce. In trying to maintain order they sometimes not only fail to enforce the law evenly but resort to harassing tactics as well. Ghetto youngsters complain of being singled out for harassment, as this conversation between young ghetto dwellers indicates:

"Things don't change. Like day before yesterday, we were sitting down on the steps talking with Joe and them. So here comes the police, coming down there messing with the people.

" 'Where do you live?' they say.

" 'Up on the hill.'

"He say, 'Where do you eat at?'

" 'Up on the hill.'

"He say, 'Where do you sleep at?'

" 'Up on the hill.'

"He say, 'Where you get your mail at?'

"I say, 'Up on the hill.'

"He say, 'Well, don't you think you ought to be getting up the hill—*right now!*' "

Incidents of police brutality are subsiding, but those that do occur blemish the police image. In a study conducted by Donald Black and Albert Reiss in three major cities during the sixties, graduate students riding with policemen witnessed thirty-seven eruptions of police brutality. The following account is extracted from one of their reports:

> As the two policemen were moving across the precinct shortly after 10:00 P.M., a white man and woman in their fifties flagged them down. Since they were obviously "substantial" middle-class citizens of the district the policemen listened to their complaints that a Negro man was causing trouble inside the public transportation station from which they had emerged. The woman said that he had sworn at her. The older policeman remarked, "What's a nigger doing up here? He should be down on Franklin Road!" With that they ran into the station and grabbed the Negro man who was inside. Without questioning him, they shoved him into a phone booth and began beating him with their fists and a flashlight. He pleaded that he had just been released from a mental hospital, and, begging not to be hit again, asked them to let him return to the hospital.

Uneven enforcement of the law

The matter of the policeman's discretion in enforcing the laws is another kettle in which distrust and antagonism have been simmering. While the police may claim that their function is to enforce the laws as written and that therefore their behavior is dictated by legislators and judges, this is not how it is seen at the street level. For example, an inordinate amount of police time is spent in the investigation and arrest of marijuana users—most of them young people—in America's largest cities. There were ninety-five thousand marijuana arrests in California alone in 1973, primarily of youths, at a cost of a hundred million dollars. Although marijuana use is a criminal offense in California and the police are bound to enforce these laws, it is still true that smoking marijuana is a victimless crime in that no one other than the user is affected. Why then, ask the young people who are arrested or threatened with arrest for using marijuana, must the police, in enforcing the laws "selectively," select that specific law so often? Is it because it is an easy bust, an easy way to make points on the career scoreboard, and a quick and simple way to take youthful "offenders" off the streets for some period of time? (Not for a long period, either, as juvenile judges are loath to sentence juvenile offenders to jail terms for possessing relatively small amounts of marijuana—often as infinitesimal as one marijuana cigarette, or even one or two *seeds* found in a car or jacket pocket.)

It is no mystery why young persons distrust the police. They see around them countless brutal crimes—assault, robbery, murder, rape—yet the police crusades are directed against young marijuana users.

This criticism of bad police practices does not, of course, apply to the entire force. Most policemen are not bullies or bigots, and they have extremely difficult—at times hazardous—jobs. More than nine hundred policemen were killed from 1963 to 1973. They too often reap the abuse that would be more fairly directed at political higher-ups, and the vast majority are both good people and good citizens. Even so, discriminatory treatment is never justified. The police should be commanding and firm, but not abrasive. Those policemen who are temperamentally unfit to enforce the law fairly and impartially should be weeded out—or, better yet, not hired in the first place.

But even the good policemen—and I have no doubt that the vast majority fall into this category—may perpetuate the kinds of behavior that antagonize street youth, because of their training and the nature of their work. The police nimbly straddle a thin edge. They see the rising tide of crime but they are under pressure from many quarters to take greater care to insure that the law is enforced civilly and evenly. Many officers feel they have been stabbed in the back by civil libertarians who would tie their hands in enforcing the law. How, the policeman might ask himself, can I expect any respect from the young when their parents, and sometimes even society's leaders, no longer respect what I'm trying to do?

But the police all across the nation have a long way to go. The image of the police officer of fifty years ago—the jovial, red-faced man on the beat helping an occasional old lady across the street and chatting amiably with fruit vendor and schoolchild alike—is no more. We might well question whether anyone ever really fit this homely image, or even whether, in the face of the need for professionalism on the police force, such an image would be desirable, but that is not the crisis facing us today. Today's police officer has such a bad reputation with America's youth that it is essential to improve community relations.

Tom Tiede graphically described the problem in an article entitled "Why Do People Hate Cops?" in the *Trenton Evening Times* of July 6, 1967.

He tells of a Peoria, Illinois, grade school teacher familiarizing her class with the duties of various city agencies. The instructor held up pictures of several employees and asked the children what each man did.

The kids said the fireman "put out fires," the animal welfare man "caught stray dogs," and the sanitation worker "picked up the garbage."

"And what about the police officer?" the teacher asked.

Suddenly the mood of the students changed. "He's dumb," one child said.

"He hurts you," another commented.

"He shoots you," added a third.

The police officer? "He shoots you"—this is where the problem with police lies among America's youth, and it is this attitude toward the police that we must change, both in the minds of juveniles and in the minds of policemen.

12 • Juvenile Trial: Legal Tug of War

Almost anything we could do is better than what we have been doing.
—Jerome Miller, Commissioner, Massachusetts Youth Services

The juvenile judge is expected to perform miracles with the thousands of youths who pour into his courtroom. Most of these kids are already badly crippled by what passes for family life as well as their life in the streets. The usual assumption is that a judge will be able to arrest fifteen years of distorted development in the average of thirty minutes he has for each offender. How unrealistic to believe that one person can stand alone against the tide of poverty, drugs, crowded slum conditions, inferior schools, parental neglect, abuse, and the readily available models of crime and vice.

The battle against juvenile crime cannot possibly be won in the courts. Courts should be the place where only the worst casualties should appear, for whom perhaps, with compassionate care, there is some hope of survival in spite of scars and chronic disabilities. The main focus must be on prevention, and that is a job for the institutions in the community that can help children without the ordeal of a trial, without labeling them delinquents, and without burdening them with criminal records for the rest of their lives.

Evolution of the juvenile justice system

Until about 1900, juveniles accused of crimes were tried in adult court, sentenced to the same adult prisons and executed on the same gallows. The juvenile court movement began in a humane effort to provide special treatment for young people in trouble. Under this system the judge was expected to deal with the young defendants in an informal, fatherly manner, analyzing the needs of the accused and ordering programs of treatment. Unfortunately, the new system did not always work as envisioned. In many cases, judges or those appointed to work in juvenile court had no special training or understanding of young people. Frequently the presiding official was a probation officer with no legal training or a political appointee with limited judicial qualifications, which helped make the juvenile court the bottom of the barrel in the judicial system. As a result, the juvenile court became not the special protector of juveniles, but simply a stop on the way to detention camps and prisons.

Technically, the courts were held to be civil rather than criminal in nature, and were said to hold "delinquency hearings" rather than criminal trials. Because of this fiction, none of the protections that were available to an adult charged with a crime applied in juvenile court. Often no transcript of the hearing was kept, making an appeal almost impossible, and no attorneys were permitted, which meant that the level of proof required for conviction was far below the adult standard.

Then in 1967 in the case of *In Re Gault,* the United States Supreme Court ordered sweeping changes in juvenile court procedure. Gerry Gault, a fifteen-year-old Arizona boy, was accused of making an obscene phone call. An adult found guilty of the same crime could have been imprisoned in a county jail for a maximum of thirty days. However, Gerry Gault could have been kept in a state school for boys until he was twenty-one, the equivalent of a six-year prison sentence. As a result of *Gault,* the Supreme Court extended specific Bill of Rights guarantees to juveniles charged with delinquency in state courts. The Court granted the juvenile the right to timely notice of charges; to be represented by an attorney, court-appointed if necessary; to confront and cross-examine witnesses; to a transcript of the proceedings; and to appellate court review. Later, in 1970, in the case of *In Re Winship,* the Supreme Court held that a juvenile could be found delinquent only if the facts proved guilt "beyond a reasonable doubt." In other words, the same standard of guilt must be established in juvenile hearings by the same rules of evidence that govern proceedings in adult courts. The Court, however, refused to take the next step and order that juveniles be granted the right to trial by jury.

Not only have the juvenile courts been changed to protect young offenders, but the state may intervene in family situations to protect children. Until the last half of the nineteenth century, children were treated as chattels of the family, legally deaf and dumb possessions like furniture. The state could step in only in cases involving criminal abuse by parents, who otherwise had absolute power over their children. Today, under the theory of protecting the child, the state may take action even though the family unit may be a healthy one. The state, as *parens patriae* (benevolent legal parents), has the duty to see that every child within its borders receives proper care and treatment. Thus the state can intervene in the case of a Jehovah's Witness family to overrule parents who, because of their strict interpretation of the Bible, object to blood transfusions even if a child's life is threatened. The courts have uniformly held that an order compelling a blood transfusion when a child's life is endangered is a proper exercise of the state's power of *parens patriae* and is not an encroachment on either the parents' freedom of religion or their parental prerogatives. In another case, *Matter of Seiferth,* the Children's Court of Erie County, New York, would not overrule parental objections and order Martin Seiferth, a fourteen-year-old boy with a massive harelip, to undergo cosmetic surgery that was not essential to preserve his health. For the court to intervene, there clearly must be an abuse of parental authority which threatens the moral or health welfare of the child.

In the juvenile justice system there are different policies for male and female offenders. Meda Chesney-Lind, writing in *Psychology Today,* says, "Our juvenile court system acts as a Big Father to female delinquents. Anxious to shelter virgins and sure their crimes are largely sexual, we discriminate in the name of chivalry." If a female juvenile is caught having sexual relations with a male juvenile, the female often will be arrested for an immoral act while the male will be sent home. The so-called "morals crime" is not the only area in which the female juvenile appears to receive unequal treatment. In 1965 over half the girls picked up for waywardness, incorrigibility, and truancy were referred to juvenile court, compared to only one-fifth of the boys. Ms. Chesney-Lind states, "Obviously the system selects for punishment girls who have transgressed sexually or defied parental authority. In this manner, it defines a narrow range of acceptable behavior for girls, and the courts interpret even minor defiance as a substantial challenge to family authority." In some juvenile systems, girls still have to undergo a pelvic examination even if the crime committed is nonsexual. The rights of women are still inferior to those of men, even behind bars.

At what age are minors qualified to appear in juvenile court? Under Anglo-American common law three age classifications are recognized for purposes of criminal procedure:

1. Birth to age seven (infants)—conclusively presumed not to have the mental capacity to commit crime.

2. Age seven to fourteen (impubes)—presumed not to have the mental capacity to commit a crime; however, this presumption is not conclusive but is "rebuttable"—that is, the prosecution is permitted to overcome this presumption, and in fact must do so before guilt can be found.

3. Age fourteen to twenty-one (adolescents)—considered adult for criminal-law purposes unless special treatment is provided by statute. In most states juvenile codes have been enacted segregating all offenders under eighteen for special treatment in juvenile courts, and the terminology in juvenile court is different from that used in adult court to indicate the noncriminal nature of the proceedings. For example, the accused is not referred to as the "defendant" but rather as the

"minor." At the close of the proceedings the minor is not found "guilty"; his "petition is sustained." And he does not have a "sentencing hearing" but rather a "disposition hearing."

Notwithstanding the legislative precaution in altering nomenclature, the words defendant, guilty, and sentencing *are* heard in juvenile courts. Cases are argued by a district attorney and a public defender before a robed magistrate, with police witnesses, and the proceeding does resemble a criminal trial.

Grist mill justice

Along with the continuing rise in adult crime rates, juvenile crime in America has shot up dramatically in the past ten years. The total number of juveniles arrested in 1973 for all offenses was over 1,700,000, reports the FBI. Thousands of new offenders have come into the criminal justice system, but the adjudicative capacity of the system has remained the same. There has been little expansion of courtroom space and personnel to keep abreast of hemorrhaging urban crime. Aggravating the problem from an administrative point of view is the increasing number of trial rights being granted to accused youth by higher courts; thus, a boy accused simply of curfew violation or truancy has the right to a court trial with all the delays and technicalities inherent in the process.

The Criminal Court of the City of New York, a network of six courthouses and ninety-six judges, braces itself each morning for the human tidal wave of some fifteen thousand persons sluicing into its corridors. By 1969 felony arrests had zoomed to a yearly rate of seventy-five thousand, yet only six hundred felony trials had plodded to completion. By 1970 the backlog had inflated to a gargantuan seven hundred thousand cases. The city's juvenile courts themselves processed forty-four thousand cases.

One effect of this sheer magnitude of numbers is that the chance of going to prison for a felony is only one in two hundred in New York. Juveniles come through the court like faceless, ageless objects. The pressure of numbers places a premium on administrative speed. A juvenile judge who carefully ponders the future destiny of each minor may be evaluated as inept because he has not cleared his calendar. The judge who whips the proceedings along in quick cadence, who rushes through as many as thirty juveniles in a day, dispensing human destinies like instant coffee, will be considered proficient. One judge praised by clerks in Long Beach actually used an electric cattle prod on attorneys to accelerate their pace.

The massive load of cases also militates against proper trial preparation. A Los Angeles deputy district attorney may have thirty cases on his calendar in a single day. A substantial number will be disposed of by motions or postponements, but half a dozen may remain for trial. How can an attorney manage anything but the most cursory preparation when he must try six cases in a day? Los Angeles District Attorney Joseph Busch says that his attorneys must "try cases by the seat of their pants as a result of the many cases and inadequate time given for preparation." In New York City, the sheer weight of numbers has bent the system to the breaking point. Criminal justice has thus lost its cherished precepts of the protection of society, the presumption of innocence, a speedy trial, and a careful search for the truth. In Philadelphia, Family Court Administrator Judge Frank Montemuro, Jr., summed up the horror of our juvenile courts by saying, "We are running a feeding system for the adult criminal courts."

In Los Angeles the caseload is growing ten times faster than the population. Defense attorneys are not displeased by the crowded courts; they frankly admit that delay is their best weapon, and congestion definitely slows things down. Time will beat any case as long as you have enough of it. A prosecution is a fragile process. A case that was strong a month after the arrest may be anemic by the time it is finally called for trial. Witnesses die or simply disappear. The memories of police officers and witnesses fade, often so much that a judge has a reasonable doubt and must dismiss the case. Witnesses tire of returning again and again for continuances, until finally, even under notice of subpoena, they fail to show up and the court must dismiss for lack of prosecution. In Washington, D.C., delays between arrest and trial have been as long as a year.

In juvenile court cases appear and disappear like soup cans on an assembly line. The Los Angeles juvenile court system of thirty-four courtrooms processed forty thousand cases in 1974. Each morning the victims appear, often still wearing a blood-stained dressing over their wounds. Witnesses arrive, deprived by subpoena of their day's work. Hundreds of policemen and detectives also arrive, diverted from their precinct duties or their days off to testify. While they wait in court, it costs the Los Angeles Sheriff's Department alone more than $400,000 a year for overtime. From the city's juvenile halls come the detained offenders, the boys in white T-shirts and dungarees, their hands cuffed behind their backs, led like lemmings into a jammed waiting room. The girls in yellow or green gym-suit outfits are also squeezed into skimpy, friction-sparking quarters. Everyone else sits restlessly in the packed vestibules and hallways waiting for his or her case to be called. The father of a boy charged with possession of marijuana complained by letter that "the treatment we received was demoralizing, and shocking. Throughout the proceeding, the matter was treated with no more seriousness than a double parking violation. The lackadaisical attitude of all the court officers, the appearance of the courtroom, and the complete lack of facilities for the children and the witnesses make the whole juvenile justice process suspect."

Grappling with the problem, Judge Alfred McCourtney of Los Angeles says, "No matter how hard we try, it is a monumental task for human beings to overcome." Given the plethora of juvenile cases, the courts experience periods in which they are unable to reach all defendants. During one week, for example, fifty cases were dismissed because the prosecution had failed to bring them to trial within the statutory period (forty days in California). The egregious effect of overcrowding may reduce our courts to roulette justice. If by chance a juvenile's case gets into the courtroom within the forty-day period, he may be adjudged a delinquent and sent to security camp; if, on the other hand, his case is kept from reaching court within the forty days, the charge will be dismissed and he will go home.

In the Cook County Juvenile Court in Illinois, parents and children are first questioned by law students and recent law school graduates, who—as "investigators for the public defender"—spend about ten minutes on each case. They jot down the child's name, his school record, his past difficulties if any, and then advise the parents. To enter a juvenile courtroom, observers need the permission of the chief judge. Held necessary to protect the juvenile's anonymity, critics argue that this secrecy protects the system far more than it does the child.

In the case of Gregory Watson, his mother had complained that he stayed away from his home overnight, so he had been adjudged a "minor in need of supervision," a term by which the court differentiates noncriminal children from delinquents. For two months Gregory vegetated behind bars in the Audy Home, a high-security detention center, while a social worker told the judge that he still had not found a foster home for him, but Gregory's mother still refused to take him back. The public defender took the mother aside, and in an off-the-record huddle urged her to agree to a finding of neglect against her. This would have turned Gregory into a "neglected child," making it easier to find a place for him. The mother at first demurred, then agreed, and the judge ordered Gregory back to the lockup pending further search for a foster home.

The Chicago Citizens Committee on the Juvenile Court found that 331 children under the age of six had been dumped into the Audy Home in a recent year. Another 447 were six to twelve years old. Sometimes the bureaucracy, having dumped the child, loses or forgets him. One boy, left "temporarily" at the Audy Home when he was six, remained there on and off until he was sixteen.

Lawyers and judges

Commonly, a deputy district attorney represents the state in juvenile court, and either private counsel or a public defender represents the minor, depending upon ability to pay. In deciding financial ability, the system unwisely measures the minor's assets rather than the parents, based on the strained logic that a minor cannot be left without counsel if parents refuse to hire one for her or him. While parents are under no legal compulsion to retain a lawyer, the state is legally empowered to collect from parents after providing their child with a public defender, although enforcement is sporadic. The ludicrous result is that sometimes wealthy families will have their criminal offspring's defense subsidized by the taxpayers.

The public defender representing the minor is frequently a fresh law graduate learning his craft, quick to panic in the face of the unexpected. Naturally, he will be more apt to blunder and make fundamental mistakes than a veteran public defender. His newness may also create a need to prove himself, which will be manifested in a dogged determination to win. Although few lawyers will admit it, there is respectable opinion that the adversary nature of court proceedings can at times be detrimental to both the minor and the system. One young attorney, zealously hungry for victory, weaseled five continuances in a marijuana case, each time maneuvering the case into a new courtroom before a new judge who was unfamiliar with the prior continuances, and inexcusably was not reminded of them by the prosecutors. Each time the matter came to court, the minor's attorney disregarded the fact that several policemen and expert chemists had to be summoned away from their normal duties, all at taxpayers' expense.

Not all cases should be put on trial or fought tooth and nail every step of the way. Where the charge is petty, the evidence is overwhelming, and the minor has no defense to offer, a sound attorney realizes that he is wasting valuable court time and denying other clients preparation by proceeding to trial. For example, not long ago a fourteen-year-old boy with no prior record, whose only offense was that he was drinking beer in the street, was before my court. I let it be known to the public defender in chambers that I did not consider the charge serious, that I was prepared to dispose of the matter without a probation report, that I felt a very mild rehabilitative measure was in order, and that the matter would be dismissed after compliance.

Despite these judicial assurances, the public defender obstinately demanded that the case be litigated. The evidence against his minor was clear and compelling, with several eyewitnesses and the minor's confession both before and during the trial, but the lawyer fought to exhaustion to win the case by hair-splitting evidentiary arguments and the most far-fetched constitutional motions, consuming almost three hours of courtroom time, all to disprove that the minor had drunk a few cans of beer. As the trial sputtered and hissed with legal arguments between defense lawyer and prosecutor, the defendant seemed to shrivel and fade into the woodwork. Everyone forgot about him until the inevitable verdict of guilty was handed down.

In another case, Larry Pontius, an Indian boy from Montana, shuffled into court in a torpor, accused of inhaling toluene, a liquid chemical found in spray paint and in automobile anti-knock solutions. The defense attorney, instead of reflexively revving up for trial and attempting a burlesque defense, requested a pretrial psychiatric examination of the minor. This report indicated that Larry was one of the brightest boys ever tested and that although the toluene had not done serious damage yet, if he continued to inhale paint it would ruin his brain. The attorney, soberly assessing the minor's best interest, had him admit the charge and asked the court to order psychiatric help for Larry on a regular basis. His enlightened concern helped Larry overcome his deadly habit permanently. This minor was lucky in having a public defender who had the sense to get treatment for him.

Underlying a lawyer's go-go effort to win every case is the fact that lawyers are themselves victims of the old numbers game. An attorney's professional talent will be measured and his advancement will depend on his scoreboard record of wins and losses. A great many of the cases coming into juvenile court should never have been filed in the first place. As much as one third of the forty thousand cases coming to juvenile court—piggy-bank thefts, truancy, curfew violations—unnecessarily burden the limited resources of the system. One of the most frivolous cases to be filed involved a fifteen-year-old boy and a bus driver. A full trial was scheduled for the boy, requiring the services of a judge, district attorney, public defender, bailiff, clerk, court officer, and stenographer—all at a cost to the public of approximately $1,000. In addition, a policeman was waiting to testify, which meant that he was away from patrol for most of the day. The accused minor was charged with violating Section 415 of the Penal Code: uttering obscenities and otherwise disturbing the peace.

The policeman testified that after the minor had boarded a city bus with another boy, a quarrel arose with the driver over whether the boys had paid the full fare. The defendant had not even been the primary antagonist. A youth who was not in court had unleashed a stream of obscenities at the driver. The only offense for which the accused had been arrested and now stood on trial was this exchange with the driver:

Larry: I put the money in the box.

Driver: No, you're a dime short.

Larry: I'm telling you I put it all in.

Driver: No, you owe it.

Larry: I put the god damn money in.

It was for this last outburst that he was charged with violating the law. I asked the police officer, "Are you telling me the only reason you arrested this boy was because he shouted god damn on the bus?"

"Yes, your honor."

"Well, then I dismiss the god damn case."

Many of these junk matters come to court because of the old numbers game. The police department looks good on paper the more arrests it shows. The district attorney's office enjoys greater political respect the more convictions it racks up. Society is apparently unimpressed by excellence in quality; it has to be fed a quantitative demonstration of performance, a show of numbers.

The juvenile court judge has total jurisdiction over the outcome of a juvenile trial. If a minor is found guilty of the charges, the judge can send him or her home on probation, or to a foster home, a group house, a juvenile hall, a training camp, psychiatric hospital, or one of the prisonlike youth-authority facilities. If the judge decides that the minor is not a fit subject for juvenile court, a transfer can be ordered removing the minor to an adult court, where he or she will face adult prison if found guilty. The salient criteria for removal to adult court are the minor's past record and the nature of the charge against him. In 1974 the Los Angeles juvenile court, for example, quickly transferred to adult court a sixteen-year-old syndicate "hit man." The probation department conducts a study of each juvenile and makes recommendations as to removal, dismissal, and disposition, but these are merely nonbinding guidelines, and ultimately all decisions rest with the judge.

Juvenile judges are a diverse mixture of personalities with a wide range of backgrounds. A decade ago, half of the nation's juvenile judges did not have to be college graduates. Four out of five today still have no psychiatric or psychological experts readily available. The mainstream of court adjudicators are competent, conscientious, able men and women but, as in any field, there are fringe personalities who make everyone else look bad too. Some judges are so conspicuously oriented toward the prosecution that they might be considered extensions of the prosecution staff. A number of incidents have occurred revealing scandalous bias against defendants, particularly minority youths. In one case when a witness was having difficulty recalling the names of the multiple defendants, the judge snapped, "That's all right, just call them Bum 1, Bum 2, and Bum 3." Another judge told a defense lawyer, on the issue of probable cause, "Twelve wetbacks standing in a row is enough probable cause for me." In Brooklyn, a judge once asked two young defendants what they had done with their robbery money, and they answered, "We whacked it up, your honor. You know, divided it up between us." The judge vindictively retorted, "Well, here's sixty years, boys, whack that up." Of course, bias also tilts the other way. In New York City one magistrate is referred to by police as "Cut 'Em Loose Bruce," while in Chicago another judge is known as "Let 'Em Go Joe." What is construed by police as bias in favor of juvenile defendants is sometimes merely an application of "search and seizure" law as handed down by the appellate courts. When a policeman wheedles and coaxes a confession out of a minor, under a fair interpretation of constitutional decisions the juvenile judge is compelled to throw out the confession. "Search and seizure" standards have become so delicately honed—unrealistically so in some instances—that the police either must walk on eggs or subsequently falsify in court to avoid a violation.

A faction of juvenile judges can be intolerably starchy and orthodox in their attitudes. For example, it upset a number of my colleagues that on several occasions I have walked in the courtroom hallway wearing my judicial robe, thus breaching the canons of magisterial decorum. The modern temper has produced some judges who are free spirits, sporting Santa Claus beards and quoting the poetry of Gibran. Mild iconoclasm is even found, as exemplified by one judge who defies convention by bringing his own cans of chicken salad to formal banquets and snubbing the formal fare.

Olympian egotism is a fault of some judges, who make the courtroom their despotic kingdom and feel a godlike power. One such judge has the eccentric habit of referring to himself in all phases of social life as "The Court." For example, talking to his wife at a cocktail reception he has been overheard to ask, "May The Court have this dance?"

A sense of humor is difficult to cultivate in a juvenile court since delinquency cases are basically devoid of any amusing aspects, but occasionally a human drama will tickle the funny side of our imagination. For example, in Long Beach for a long time the most elusive, mysterious, and baffling burglar was a tiny nine-year-old boy who entered houses through the doggie door. In another case, two impish seven-year-olds drove a stolen automobile in tandem, one child down on the floorboard pressing the pedal while the other steered.

Despite the small scattering of colorful judicial personalities, the overwhelming atmosphere of the juvenile bench is necessarily staid, solemn, and detached. The analytical task of judging requires neutral, unobtrusive, and dispassionate equilibrium. The judge cannot inject his personality in the proceedings; he must stand aloof, and impartially, almost invisibly, weigh the facts against experience and law before rendering a judgment.

The most recent study on juvenile court judges in the United States was done in 1973 by Kenneth Smith of the University of Southern California. Replicating a study done ten years earlier, Smith sent questionnaires to juvenile judges across the nation. It was found that only 3.8 per cent of the judges were women. The average age of juvenile court judges was fifty-two. A significant increase in the educational level of juvenile judges was noted, reflecting the increasing number of states that require juvenile court judges to have been admitted to the bar. In 1973, 64 per cent of the juvenile court judges had received bachelor's degrees, as opposed to only 49 per cent in 1963.

One of the most significant findings of the 1973 survey was that the juvenile court judges' view of the problems was exactly the same as it was a decade before, in terms of needed reforms within the system. The judges ranked as their top problem inadequate facilities for detention or shelter care pending disposition. Insufficient foster home placement facilities was listed second, and inadequate correctional institutions was third.

Pretrial detention hearing

There is no right to bail in juvenile court, but an informal hearing is granted to determine whether an accused minor should be detained. During this hearing the judge weighs the evaluations of the probation officer and attorneys. He also considers the nature of the crime and the minor's previous contacts with the law, both arrests and convictions. In a conservative jurisdiction, if the crime has the slightest aura of violence—for example, carrying a switchblade—the minor is invariably recommended for detention. His attorney can then request to have a formal hearing within five days. At this proceeding, called a "Dennis H" hearing—the original precedent involved a boy named Dennis—the prosecution must provide evidence to establish a prima facie case, which means evidence that at first glance supports the supposition that the minor committed the accused offense. The Dennis H hearing is distinguished from a regular trial by the fact that the prosecution need not prove its case beyond a reasonable doubt. Its sole purpose is to challenge the state's right to continue the minor's detention pending trial. At times the Dennis H can be an extravagant waste of the taxpayers' money and needlessly encumber the minor with longer confinement.

For instance, in my court sixteen-year-old Ruddy Jessup was brought in for a Dennis H hearing, charged with burglary. The assistant district attorney had brought all his key witnesses into court for the hearing. Since the prosecution was obviously fully ready to go to trial, I wondered why there should be essentially two trials—one to determine detention and another to determine final guilt or innocence—when all the necessary witnesses were in court and the entire matter could be resolved at once. So, by getting counsel on both sides to agree, we were able to adjudicate the whole case in a single session.

In many cases the defense is not ready for trial and only some of the witnesses are present for the Dennis H, in which case it makes sense to hold this pretrial hearing for a prima facie test of guilt. But often the hearing is an extraneous formality. When a detention hearing is held, the court must decide not only whether the evidence suggests that the minor committed a wrong, but whether the wrong is of such a nature and the minor of a personality that requires his removal from society. California's juvenile courts have been accused of being "detention-happy."

For example, Danny Jones, a sixteen-year-old black youth, was before my court arraigned on a charge of engaging in sexual acts with other male youths. Listed by the police as a transvestite, he appeared in court dressed and fully made up as a woman, wearing white high heels, a bright yellow mini-skirt, and a tight-fitting yellow blouse bulging with a padded bra. His face was rouged and lipsticked, and he was wearing a blond wig.

The matter was scheduled for trial in two weeks, and after the arraignment the district attorney asked that the boy be detained in juvenile hall. The probation officer supported the recommendation. They both argued that the youth's illegal conduct represented a threat to society, and that it was in the minor's best interest to be kept off the street and confined behind bars. Overruling their suggestions, I released the minor to the custody of his parents. It is costly—approximately twelve hundred dollars a month—to maintain a minor in confinement, and it is pointless to spend this money unless there is reasonable certainty that detention will do some good. A youth whose only criminal tendency is homosexuality is not a fit subject for imprisonment. Moreover, there is still a presumption of innocence.

Danny was a timid, nonviolent, nonaggressive person, in no way a danger to life, limb, or property. The only possibility that had to be guarded against was his engaging in sexual acts with other males, but his homosexual appetite would only be fed by placing him in a building crammed with six hundred hard-core male offenders. Being realistic, I also felt that a brief stint behind bars would have absolutely no effect on his psychological penchant for homosexuality. Finally, such an experience could actually be damaging to the minor, instilling an image of himself as a condemned criminal.

The minor as witness

Inevitably a stumbling block to smooth presentation of testimony in juvenile trials is the ages of the witnesses. Trying to extract lucid testimony from an eight-year-old witness can be as tedious as brain surgery. An initial concern is to ascertain whether or not the minor can appreciate the idea of telling the truth and the consequence for lying while on the witness stand. The test for children under twelve used to be belief in God; today it is up to the discretion of the judge. In a 1974 juvenile case in New York, ten-year-old Bobby Retan was questioned by counsel:

"Do you go to Sunday school?"

"No."

"Do you say prayers at night?"

"No."

"Do you believe that if you lie here today God will punish you?"

"No."

"What would your punishment be if you lied?"

"I wouldn't be able to watch Monday-night football."

"I can see the boy is not a liar," the judge said, and swore him in.

In an age of widening agnosticism, child witnesses infrequently express a strong religious faith, and therefore the judge must roam over the flabby moral terrain of modern society to find a solid basis on which to decide whether a minor will tell the truth. No longer can the wrath of God be invoked to assure a truthful answer. Over the years an attorney learns to skillfully interrogate a child witness to ferret out the truth, or to stifle it. A prevailing tactic of defense lawyers is to thunderously shout at the child to produce frightened withdrawal. One prosecutor in Inglewood, California, spends a few hours before trial coaching—along with a great show of affection and attention—a child witness in how to answer all questions, down to the last detail. Above all, the child is instructed to keep his or her eyes on the prosecutor and never to look at the defendant.

Intimidation of juvenile witnesses is a common occurrence. In one month in Los Angeles, four witnesses had their automobiles stolen so they were unable to drive to court. More than one father has enlisted his son in the armed forces rather than have him testify under threats of violence. In Watts, a mother of eight children was prepared to testify that two members of the Crips had snipered at passing motorists. But on the eve of trial, several Molotov cocktails were tossed in her living room window, inflicting hideous third-degree burns on two of her daughters. No one in the entire neighborhood would testify to anything after that.

The terrorization of witnesses by the Crips gang has been well publicized, causing the gang to become known throughout the country. The town of Aliquippa, Pennsylvania, with a population of twenty-six thousand, reportedly has kids in the streets shouting, "Crip here, man! Want some, got some." One police official went so far as to blame the entire rise of gangs on the exhilarating spotlight of media publicity.

Juveniles coming into court to testify as witnesses are more aware of their rights than any other generation in history. They may not know the derivation of the protection from the *Gault* or *Miranda* decisions, but many of them are aware of the right against self-incrimination. A fourteen-year-old Los Angeles girl who was living with an older man as his mistress and was arrested for prostitution was met in court by her distraught, nearly delirious, mother, who asked, "Where have you been? What have you been doing?" The girl replied, "Speak to my attorney. I don't have to answer any questions even from you." Her probation officer in a private interview was also unable to get any explanation for her behavior. She also curtly told him, "Speak to my attorney." In the past, a probation officer might have been able to get at this fourteen-year-old's emotional problem, but no more. Given the sophistication and awareness early teenagers are showing about their legal rights, and their generally accelerated knowledge of the world as seen on television, many policemen and prosecutors are saying, "We don't have children here. These are little people, little adults, and they should be given adult treatment." Perhaps that position goes too far, but common sense should play a larger role in the juvenile system.

Twenty-four-year-old Mrs. Ellen Somer had been visiting her husband at Harbor General Hospital. According to her version, she left the hospital around midnight and entered her car, when she was approached by a young man who asked her if she would give him a ride to his car, parked down the road. She agreed. As they drove down the street he gave instructions as to where to turn, and after they had proceeded about two miles they arrived at a factory parking lot. After telling her to pull over, he asked her for a kiss, and she said she didn't believe in it. He then pulled the keys out of the ignition.

"What happened next?" the district attorney asked.

"He put his arm around my neck and squeezed."

"And what did you do?"

"I struggled. Tried to twist out. He tried to pull up my dress. He told me to take off my clothes."

"Did you?"

"Not at first, but he said if I didn't cooperate he would break my neck."

"So you gave in?"

"Yes, because I was scared."

The accused boy took the stand next. He was a stocky youth, about five feet ten inches tall, with wavy black hair, swarthy skin, and light green eyes. He radiated a rugged masculinity. His version was that at midnight Mrs. Somer had invited him into her car. They drove about five miles, and during the ride—after talking about her husband's convalescence—she seduced him.

"What did she say about her husband?" the defense attorney asked.

"She said he had been in the hospital for six months and she was lonely," he replied.

"Whose idea was it to park the car?"

"Hers. She stopped the car in Winston's Field."

"Whose idea was it to have sex?"

"She just scooted over and started kissing me. Then she took off her top."

The remainder of the youth's testimony raised the prospect of a reasonable doubt. The court had two conflicting, uncorroborated versions of an event, one a morbid story of rape and the other an indiscreet tale of seduction—and obviously one of the two witnesses was lying. Each had a motive to fabricate: the accused boy to escape conviction, and the woman to protect her reputation. The two were caught in the act by a police officer on the factory grounds. A fact that troubled me was Mrs. Somer's testimony that she had volunteered to take a young stranger to his car, a mile away, after midnight. It seemed a strange gesture for a woman alone. Also of some bearing was the fact that her husband had been in the hospital for six months, and that she had supposedly been living an abstinent life; one could imagine sexual pressures building. As a legendary judge once said, "When nature demands its due, youth is prodigal in the payment." Mrs. Somer's testimony was also contradicted by the police officer on certain issues. The boy had spoken unhesitatingly and with logical consistency. He had constructed a plausible prima facie defense. Typically, a defendant's false story is transparently implausible. But this minor's story was supported by reasonable probabilities. I intended to prod counsel to dig deeper into the facts, but the trial was suddenly to end. The district attorney blurted out that the minor had been convicted of rape twice, and once for kidnaping. Under juvenile law a prior petition sustained, unlike a felony conviction in adult court, cannot be used to impeach. Despite the district attorney's request that I judicially wipe his remarks from mind, I granted a mistrial. The matter was transferred to another court for a new adjudication.

Without calling it a felony conviction, perhaps a prior verdict against a minor should be allowed for purposes of impeachment. The empirical relevance and reliability of past offenses are in many instances equal for adult and minor. A six-time forger can be said to have a tendency to forge whether he is sixteen or sixty. The whole area of impeachment needs to be re-examined in juvenile justice. Also in cases of serious offenses such as rape and kidnaping, one wonders what a three-time convicted youth was doing out on the streets.

13 • Sentencing: A Legal Labyrinth

We must reduce laws to basic principles and to numbers of a dimension intelligible to the mind of man.
–Ramsey Clark, Crime in America

The issue of whether a juvenile verdict is a criminal conviction for the narrow purposes of impeachment is less strategically vital than the larger issue of how society will treat the verdict. Lawyers battle adamantly in juvenile court in the belief that if the charge is sustained, the minor will forever have a record. They fear that the juvenile court verdict will be thereafter viewed by society as a criminal conviction.

Juvenile verdict: a criminal record?

This issue was considered by the Supreme Court of Pennsylvania in the case of *In Re Holmes,* when the court ruled that a juvenile proceeding was a civil, rather than a criminal, proceeding. The purpose of a juvenile proceeding, the court stated, is "not penal but protective, aimed to check juvenile delinquency and to turn around a child just starting, perhaps, on an evil course. . . . No suggestion or taint of criminality attaches to any finding of delinquency by a Juvenile Court."

Justice Musmanno, dissenting vigorously, scorned the premise that a youth convicted in juvenile court will not be seen as a criminal by society. The judicial wand wishfully deeming the proceedings civil "is very praiseworthy," Musmanno said, "but this placid bromide commands no authority in the fiercely competitive fields of everyday life. A disturbing fallacy exists in the notion that a juvenile record does its owner no harm. The firm truth is that a juvenile court record will frequently haunt a youngster through childhood, youth, and adulthood."

The numerous cases where an individual's career has been impeded because of a juvenile record bear sorry testimony to the truth of Justice Musmanno's observations. A juvenile record will all too often be used against the person in business and commerce. It will certainly be an obstruction to anyone seeking to enter the legal profession, where attitudes can be remorseless in regard to past transgressions. It may forever bar an individual from high political office.

California wants no part of California Youth Authority children. The community knows who they are and thinks it knows what they are. The principal of a Los Angeles school "knew" about one boy who had been in a Youth Authority camp since the age of seven. Nobody wanted to deal with him, and teachers were warned to expect deviant behavior. Parents ordered their daughters to stay away from him. The boy was in school all of two days before he was expelled. If something went wrong in town, the police immediately picked him up as a suspect.

Though I am now an attorney and sitting on the juvenile court bench, as a teenager I acquired a juvenile court record. During a lecture tour in the South, the following rather cynically slanted headline appeared before my appearance: "Even a Thug Can Improve His Life." While I am happy to know that some people consider that I have improved my life, I am concerned that juvenile offenders may be branded "thugs" or worse for the rest of their lives.

Extensive efforts have been made to establish legal procedures for erasing a delinquent record, and in a number of jurisdictions "sealing" or "expunging" a conviction is theoretically available, but in practice this legal machinery tends to be far from leak-proof. Essentially, "sealing" means that a record or proceeding is "merely" sealed, not destroyed. There is a patent implication that the sealed item may, under certain circumstances, be unsealed. "Expungement" means that the record or proceeding is obliterated as if it had never happened in the first place. The memory of the event is seared out permanently, with no possibility of reinstatement or examination under any circumstances. Often, however, the terms are used interchangeably. To illustrate, the Juvenile Court Act of Utah specifically provides for the "expungement of juvenile court record." The code section, however, makes reference to the fact that the court "shall order sealed all records." An examination of the practices throughout the country in 1970 by criminologists Bernard Kogon and Donald L. Loughery revealed a "singular lack of clarity as to philosophy. . . . It is no exaggeration to declare that confusion is monumental."

An integral part of any discussion on juvenile records is the notion of "setting aside" a conviction. California laws relating to vacation of conviction and restoration of civil rights are erroneously referred to as "expungement laws," when in fact they seek only to remove certain disabilities and not to blot out the record. Legislation in favor of vacating convictions is rather common, but it does not provide for the concealment any more than the declarations of confidentiality regarding juvenile court records keep them immune from scrutiny. Setting aside of a conviction merely clears some disabilities; the record remains.

Beyond the semantic problems—which amount to far more than that in the lives of offenders—the Kogon and Loughery survey found that the vast majority of correctional administrators favor sealing over expungement, and they approved of the proposition that when an offender has paid his debt to society he should not be hounded forever. A number of them indicated that bills pertaining to sealing were currently before their legislatures.

Despite the overwhelming sentiment in favor of concealment laws, however, most states do not actually have such protection. Many laws purport to provide for sealing or expungement, but do not do so. Such misleading laws fall into two categories: (1) those affording the protection provided by privileged juvenile court records, and (2) those specifying the removal of disabilities resulting from a conviction after a "good adjustment."

Unfortunately, these protections exist more in law than in practice, because even if the information is not accessible from juvenile court records it is usually obtainable from police records. The subject of police records is extremely important because virtually all juveniles who come into contact with the police may have police records. In some jurisdictions records are made, complete with mug shots, and maintained on even those juveniles "picked up" by policc and released without further action.

One danger is that police records do not always accurately reflect the minor's conduct. In one article a former probation officer describes the case of an eleven-year-old boy who was charged with burglary by the California police. He had stolen a package of bologna from a grocery store to eat while running away from home because of a conflict with his family. The juvenile court correctly handled the boy as a dependent child but his police record permanently stamped him "arrested for burglary." Another case involved a fourteen-year-old youth whom the police charged with child molesting because he kissed his thirteen-year-old girlfriend in public. The boy was simply reprimanded and sent home, but again the arrest record, labeling him a child molester, was part of his social profile the rest of his life.

The argument that the records must be maintained to help the police protect society is meaningless if the police have not even referred the child to court, or—if they have—if the court has not seen fit to judge the child a delinquent. Yet, in only two states—California and Kansas—are there procedures for the destruction of police records for such youngsters.

This practice, as has already been noted, can be extremely damaging to juveniles. A recent study made by the New York Civil Liberties Union found that 75 per cent of the employment agencies sampled in New York City ask job applicants about arrest records and, as a matter of procedure, do not refer those applicants with arrest records, whether they were convicted or not. Imagine how devastating this must be for the juvenile who was apprehended by the police but was found innocent of any wrongdoing by the court. Even if the court dismissal were reflected on the police record, which it usually is not, the inquirer is likely to conclude the youth "did something" or no police record would exist.

Over half the states have no statutes concerning police records, and presumably in these states such records are public and may be examined by anyone. Twenty states have some provisions concerning juvenile police records, and almost all provide limited access to these records. Thirteen states require a court order to inspect the records, while the other six hold that such records are not open to public inspection for any reason. Seven states have adopted expungement statutes in an effort to balance society's need to be protected from criminals and the juvenile's need to be free of the stigma of being a "criminal," but the offender must meet a number of requirements before his record may be expunged.

Although the public needs protection against crime, it is important to remember that although many adult criminals were juvenile delinquents, only a very small percentage of juveniles who have contact with the police actually become criminals. Juvenile offenders who subsequently achieve satisfactory social adjustments should not have the cloud of police record jeopardizing their future.

The vagaries of juvenile sentencing

One of the most difficult, yet sometimes necessary, decisions a juvenile court judge must make is whether to send a youth to a juvenile institution. One out of seven youthful offenders will be locked up for months or years and sent to a prisonlike security institution where he may learn more about crime than he ever knew before. Incidentally, only one juvenile out of two thousand in Los Angeles appeals his decision. The majority of arrested youths come from undereducated poor families who know little of the appellate process, and public defenders are generally too overworked to concern themselves with giving their clients much advice about appeal. The net result is that the appellate route is effectively closed to youths enmeshed in the juvenile justice system.

One of the great injustices in juvenile dispositions is that a probation report lists every contact a minor has had with the police. A list of a dozen or so such contacts on a youth's record creates a strong bias against him. Yet a contact may not even mean an arrest, and even an arrest is nothing more than an informal accusation. If the matter never proceeded to trial, theoretically the minor has been cleared. But the inference made by most judges is that "where there's smoke there's fire"—if the youth has been hauled in so many times by the police, he must be a "bad" kid. Yet in the ghetto areas of our cities, the police frequently round up certain youths every time a particular offense is committed. Nothing more than fishing expeditions by the police, these contacts often unfairly damage the youth at his disposition hearing. On this particular question, the appellate court has ruled in *People v. Calloway* that a juvenile court may not consider a youth's police record in passing sentence. The probation department and judges, however, continue to ignore this ruling. Most lawyers consider plea bargaining a futile exercise in the juvenile courts because even if the district attorney agrees to drop a charge against a minor in exchange for an admission to other counts, the dropped charges will appear on the probation report. Anything a youth is even remotely suspected of by the police appears on his or her record on judgment day in court.

In my own court I ignore mere contacts with the police; I do, however, give significant weight to prior petitions sustained against a minor. If he has been found guilty of an offense half a dozen times, I must assume that he has strong criminal habits. A minor in this category must be removed from the community and given close supervision.

By defining crimes in terms of penalties prescribed, the criminal law implies concern for, and attempts to take into account, the extent of harm done to the victim. For example, extent of bodily injury to the victim is a basic distinction between murder, which usually carries the penalty of life imprisonment or death, and aggravated battery, which may carry a fine of $2,500 and imprisonment for five years. In the juvenile justice system, however, although minors are charged with violating statutory laws whose penalties are set by adult standards, the judge is not bound to follow the prescription. This is so because the minor's age exempts him from going to prison unless his case is transferred to an adult court.

My basic judicial philosophy is to keep a youth out of a detention camp unless the protection of the community demands it. Sending a young person into confinement is nothing more than shoving him down the road to becoming a hardened criminal. Seventy per cent of those in California prisons were at one time inmates of a California Youth Authority camp. Despite the best efforts of the staff at a detention camp, the dominance of the hard-core minors within the institution strongly influences a newcomer's attitude.

The first thing I do in contemplating sentence is to look at the nature of the offense charged. If the minor was convicted of a violent crime such as rape, armed robbery, or attempted murder, I must give appropriate weight to the seriousness of the crime in deciding whether to send him back to the community or to a security institution.

But even a serious offense does not automatically mean that a youth must be sent to a camp. If it is his first offense, and if he shows the proper attitude, he might still be a fit subject for community-based treatment. A youth's genuine remorse has a good deal of bearing on my decision. If he pleads guilty, he is showing an appreciation of his obligations as a member of society and his consideration for the public, in contrast to the anti-social attitude necessarily manifested by the commission of a crime. Since a first step toward reformation and rehabilitation has already been demonstrated in the guilty plea, it is reasonable to believe that a correspondingly smaller amount of correctional discipline is necessary to complete the process of reformation and rehabilitation.

Naturally the family environment of the child is a prime

consideration in whether I send a child to camp or home on probation. Where a minor has two interested parents pulling for him, he has a much better chance on the outside for rehabilitation. To help the family as a unit, and to aid them in guiding the child in the right way, I will prescribe family counseling.

If the child has no parents, or only one apathetic parent, however, I must lean more toward an institutional approach to his case. For if he is not learning anything right at home, he is being raised wrong in the streets. Sending such a youth home may mean nothing more than sending him back to the streets to continue his criminal education. Lack of family does not automatically require institutionalization; a minor can be placed in a foster or group home. A good school record is also a strong plus in keeping a juvenile offender out of camp, as is the prospect of a good job opportunity. If the youth has something positive to go back to—a successful school career or honest work opportunities—there is much less need to send him to camp for rehabilitation. Such a child is well on the way to rehabilitating himself.

Given the overcrowded conditions of juvenile halls and the camps, the court must give priority to those youth most dangerous to society. The juvenile halls are overcrowded not only in Los Angeles but all over urban America. There are waiting lists for security camps. Los Angeles has only five such camps to serve the county population of over seven million people. Each camp can accommodate about 175 inmates, while more than forty thousand cases came through Los Angeles Juvenile Court in 1974. Complaints are heaped on juvenile judges for not sending more of these gang toughs to camp. Obviously, lack of space is a limitation.

If we are putting most of the hard-core kids away, it will do more harm than good to put lesser offenders in with them. At the Nellis School for Boys, to which the Los Angeles juvenile courts refer hard-core cases, there are forty murderers in residence. It is an axiom that penal institutions are academies of crime. What kids boast about inside, what they value, is a form of indoctrination into crime. I know, because I was an inmate in three such places as a teenager. My main concern in considering whether to confine a youth is whether he is potentially dangerous or a hard-core repeater. How much of a threat is he to people and property if he is allowed to remain in the community? The greater the threat, the more likely will be confinement.

Whenever possible, to instill a sense of personal responsibility I will order a minor to make restitution to his victim. For acts of vandalism, I will try to teach the minor the seriousness of his wrong through some chore which will demonstrate the effort that it takes to build something. For example, in the case of a Santa Monica boy who poured a gallon of glue on a printing press, I ordered him to scrub the equipment until it was restored to its original condition. For a ghetto youth who could not return the money he had stolen from a woman, I ordered him to perform compensatory labor—that is, to clean her windows, wash her dishes, and mow her lawn for a three-week period.

When a youth has committed an offense for which confinement has been recommended by the probation officer, I will sometimes give the minor one last chance for rehabilitation in the community by staying his sentence pending the result of a twelve-month job experiment. If the minor applies himself to the job, demonstrates a rehabilitated attitude, and has worked diligently, I will allow him to remain on the job and out of the reformatory. But if during the twelve-month period the minor fails at the job and exhibits a negative attitude, he will be sent to detention. The alternative of going away to a reformatory becomes an incentive for the minor to apply himself on the job. I have been criticized for supposedly placing cruel pressure on the minor by threatening him with confinement. My view is that in reality I am being anything but cruel; the minor is being given the key to keeping himself out of jail by showing the right attitude. Special consideration must be given to the nature of the crimes committed by a minor given this opportunity, and the court's decision should be predicated on a reasonable prospect of success.

Sentencing should also be a time when the judge attempts to educate the minor for his improvement. Truants coming into court remind me of my own boyhood attitudes toward school. The ghetto youth is usually eager to drop out. His visions of life out of school are euphoric: he pictures himself sharply dressed and driving a long, smooth car. He doesn't care what his job is as long as he is getting a paycheck so that he can afford to "live in style." He wants to have pocket money to date girls on the weekends. School is only in his way.

A youngster finds it nearly impossible to project himself into the future. He can only see clearly what is important now. The film *Easy Rider* showed a young man rising early to sprinkle corn for the commune's chickens. This image seemed to appeal to many young people, but had the producer shown that scene 365 times, multiplied by ten years, it probably would not have seemed so idyllic.

To make a teen offender feel the future now, I will order an activity that may jolt him into an awareness of what life can hold in store. I will tell the boy to go down and watch the chicken pluckers at the local chicken market for a week, or spend a day with the orderlies in a hospital. "That's the kind of job you can expect," I tell them, "if you drop out of school." I once asked a teenage boy to dig ditches in his backyard to get acclimated to such a job. I advised him to stay in school so that he could become a prosperous man like his attorney, at which point the public defender representing the boy interrupted: "Your honor, ditchdiggers make more than we do now."

The most important rehabilitative function a juvenile court judge can perform is to inspire a young person to develop his or her best potential. So many children come through the legal system being discouraged, mocked, denounced, and put down at every turn that they suffer from tremendous insecurity and feelings of inferiority. Even the most gifted have strong doubts about themselves. They view themselves as permanent losers, and everyone around them reinforces that image. If a youth experiences a stretch of success, he still has a constant fear it will all disintegrate, that he will again start being a loser. The odds are stacked against ghetto youth, and they desperately need transfusions of encouragement.

Too many judges cynically hold and project the belief that the kids in front of them are the garbage of society, incorrigible deviants, hopeless losers. My own experience gives me a different perspective. I know that many of the kids don't want to be at the bottom, that a good number of them have the ability to compete in society. Eleanor Roosevelt once said, "No one can make us feel inferior unless we give our consent." I speak to "second-chance" youths as individuals in my court, and in groups at high schools, junior high schools, and juvenile camps, and I write to them. I tell them to have pride in themselves: they are as good as any rich kids anywhere in this country. I tell them that they can climb up to their dreams. The human spirit is the individual's last refuge, where he can achieve his dreams despite grim disadvantages and stark limitations. I tell them to reach up to the stars, for they can ultimately be the arbiters of their own destiny.

Frontiers of juvenile jurisprudence

Until the eighteenth century, American justice had been a bedlam with everyone held accountable for his actions—adults, children, and even animals. American courts in some jurisdictions ordered the execution of dogs for biting people. In the landmark canine case of Provetie, a dog who bit a child, the court scroll noted for posterity: "The prisoner is to be hanged to the gallows until death ensues as an example to other evilly disposed dogs."

Traditional jurisprudence in America rests on the Judeo-Christian model of human nature, which says that an individual has free will and is morally responsible for his acts. Thus an offender is an evildoer and deserves to be punished. In modern times the law has adapted to an alternative vision of human nature, the so-called deterministic model, in which crime is a form of social sickness, a symptom of emotional maladjustment, and the proper response is not condemnation but therapy.

One of the proponents of this view, Dr. Karl Menninger, says in *The Crime of Punishment:* "We must renounce the philosophy of punishment, the obsolete vengeful penal attitude, if we are to have a society safe from crime." He calls for a greater role for the social sciences in dealing with crime and offenders. Dr. Robert Sadoff of Temple University states, "Some psychiatrists consider all criminals to be mentally disturbed." They see the therapeutic approach as a humane and effective method of dealing with deviant behavior.

Not everyone agrees, of course. "Psychology is watered-down religion," says California Governor Edmund G. Brown, "and I'll take mine in the pure form. I don't believe in the overliberal view that human beings are so malleable that by a little social engineering you can create a new person." A totally therapeutic approach may actually do the offender more harm than good in that it removes from the law the concept of showing that an individual is responsible for his or her actions and should receive a punishment equal to the offense committed, the only logical connection between punishment and justice. The therapeutic system removes sentencing from judges and places it instead in the hands of social technicians who do not even acknowledge rights or justice. Under the traditional system the offender was let out of prison after a definite term. Under the new theory, the offender presumably is detained until he is "cured." It is small consolation to the individual that his compulsory confinement is in a hospital, perhaps in a straitjacket or padded room, rather than in a prison cell.

Interest is growing in the "mentally disordered juvenile," although opinions vary as to who, exactly, is to be termed "disordered." The social sciences definitely have a role in the criminal process, as do medical theories, but juvenile offenders should not be turned over to their exclusive jurisdiction. Empirically the social sciences are too unproven to be entrusted with the control of crime. We must not embrace either extreme—moral or medical—in correcting youthful offenders. Our approach should be comprehensive and constructive, therapeutic in some instances, restraining in others, and disciplining as well, but preventive in its social impact. The young individual is morally responsible, but society should recognize problems of adjustment and environmental pressures. It is inhumane to place all the blame on the youngster, and at the same time it is dehumanizing to place no blame on him. The answer is a balanced compromise, a fusion of medicine and morality, science and freedom.

14 • Juvenile Hall U.S.A.

The juvenile reform system is more destructive than constructive.
–Milton G. Rector, President,
National Council on Crime and Delinquency

The prevailing philosophy of correctional work with minors is summarized by social scientist Pauline Young:

> Every child has numerous possibilities for adjustment to society if properly trained and guided. A child grows, develops, and gains social consciousness through whole-group participation. A child's misconduct is in response to his conditioning environment, and therefore punishment is futile. . . . A child is not a fit subject for correction in a penal institution where the atmosphere tends to stunt his growth and moral development. He needs love, security, encouragement, self-expression, and a chance to belong.

These conceptions are a clear departure from those of the criminal court system for adults, which recognizes retributive justice and the doctrine of "an eye for an eye."

The goal of rehabilitation

The Institute for Juvenile Court Judges states the credo that juvenile courts, more than any other courts with criminal jurisdiction, are imbued with the goal of rehabilitation. Less accent is placed on punishing an offender to deter others, or on frightening an offender to inhibit him from future offenses, while more emphasis is placed on using scientific methods to change an offender's motivation. Herbert Jacobs, in *Justice in America,* reminds us that the punitive sanctions taken against adults should not be used in the same degree with minors because children are not generally considered responsible for their actions to the same degree as adults and because they offer greater promise for rehabilitation. Special stress is given to providing the proper institutional environment to youthful offenders.

Customarily institutions for juveniles publish statements setting forth their program objectives. They express elaborate psychological methods of reclaiming the wayward youth for constructive citizenship. At the O. H. Close School for Boys, transactional analysis, as developed by Dr. Eric Berne, has been adopted as the major treatment method. The Karl Horton School proudly boasts a "specific treatment approach for each ward using behavior modification principles." The Ventura School for Girls says it applies "reality therapy to change delinquent behavior." The Nellis School for Boys uses "principles of operant conditioning through contingency management." Whatever the method chosen, the uniformly stated aim of juvenile institutions is to reform, not punish, delinquents.

In practice, however, the institutional goal of rehabilitating young offenders has not been as effective as it was hoped. As early as 1967, the President's Commission on Law Enforcement reported that recidivism rates for juveniles were higher than for any other age group. The odds that a juvenile graduating from a reformatory or training school is rehabilitated are less than fifty-fifty, notes the National Council on Crime and Delinquency. When the FBI studied several thousand repeaters of all ages it found three out of four who were under twenty became repeaters within four years following their incarceration.

Authorities are certainly aware of the problems that exist in our juvenile institutions, and everyone has an explanation for their failure. Alan F. Breed, California Youth Authority Director, blames apathetic politicians and a generally apathetic public. John Shea, a hall supervisor for fourteen years, says, "They can call it juvenile hall, but the way things are now it's really a hell hole—and just about anybody's kid can end up there." He suggests that society is responsible for not supporting better facilities. Administrator Jean Sides, a dedicated public servant, blames the problem mainly on substandard facilities, severe overcrowding, and a rapid turnover of personnel—sometimes as high as 40 per cent each year. My own view is that no generalization can cover the problems afflicting juvenile camps and detention halls around the nation. The only uncomplicated fact is the clear record of failure.

Juvenile hall in the fifties

In the 1950s the New York Youth House was a filthy brick building with caged windows crowded between warehouses and commercial buildings, and lacking any outside space for fresh air or recreation. At fourteen, charged with assault in a gang rumble, I was taken there by paddy wagon to begin an indefinite term of confinement. Getting out of the wagon, I looked up at the building's prisonlike facade and I felt a stirring of pride, sensing that I was about to take a step into manhood. I had felt left out before when the older boys talked about Warwick, Coxsackie, Elmira, and the other prisons they had been in. In the mentality of the street, it was a badge of status to serve time in jail. We were locked in twenty-four hours a day and we trudged through a daily routine that was so empty it made us numb yet tense. At six-thirty in the morning a burly counselor in a grouchy mood pounded on the door to wake us up. Then, draped in towels, we stepped out into an icy hallway to receive dungarees and polo shirts, our uniform for the day. After dressing we were marched military style to the cafeteria where we were served a breakfast of powdered eggs and powdered milk.

During the meal the counselors passed out cigarettes, strictly warning us to only have one smoke, but attempts to get around this restriction never ceased. My roommate had his sister smuggle in a pack of cigarettes on visiting day, then hid each cigarette in a separate cranny or vent and Scotch-taped the matches individually to the underside of fixtures and furniture. Overnight, everything was confiscated, even the match fastened inside the toilet ballast. Staff members were microscopically keen searchers.

Mandatory classes were held in the morning from nine to noon. When the science teacher entered the room, he was usually welcomed with raucous jeers to which he inevitably responded with a yawn. He could be counted on to sink half the class into drowsiness by reading the day's lesson from a book. In math, the teacher often diverged from the multiplication tables to probe into our sexual escapades.

Youth House was primarily a waiting station, so at lunch the "flap" (talk) was often about the prison sentence someone had received that morning. One boy returned from court beaming because he got a "zip-five" (zero to five year) sentence at Otisville. He was happy because at Otisville he would be reunited with his big brother. For a number of wards like myself, Youth House was the final place of detention, since we had not committed felonies.

An implacable brand of bigotry from the streets was carried over into Youth House. Friction between whites and blacks was never-ending. Naturally, I had my share of brushes with blacks. Once I almost got into a fight with another boy who tried to pull a comic book out of my hand. He was less interested in the comic book than in testing to see if he could dump on me. I got up to fight him and was quickly encircled by a dozen blacks. If a counselor had not intervened, they would have mangled me. Whites who didn't know each other did not stick together as instinctively as blacks did. Eventually I became friends with a black through boxing, and we spent a lot of time together.

Youth House residents ranged in age from ten to sixteen. The youngest were usually there for minor wrongs such as truancy or running away from home, but whatever bad habits they had been developing were accentuated while they were there. In the evening all age groups and all types of offenders mingled in the recreation gym. Like predators, the older boys ferreted out the weakest or most sickly of the younger boys and forced them into the gym shower for sodomy. One night a counselor discovered ten older boys taking turns sodomizing a helpless twelve-year-old. The only girls allowed were those on pin-up pictures. When India's Madame Gandhi toured Youth House, she was shocked by the pornographic pictures on the walls. Onc sixteen-year-old, desperate for sexual release, was caught having intercourse with an artificial vagina made from a slice of raw liver stolen from the kitchen and stuffed into the head of a bottle.

The greatest diversion at Youth House, though, was decorating one's body with homemade tattoos. First we drew a figure in pen or pencil on our arms, chest, or leg. Then ashes or ink were spread over the area outlined, and the ashes or ink were driven under the skin with a thousand pricks of a safety pin. It stung, but the results were worthwhile—to our eyes, at least.

The New York youth house was demolished during the sixties and replaced by a new juvenile detention center made up of several high-rise buildings in the Bronx. From a distance the new building looks like an attractive apartment house, but up close it reeks with a sterile emptiness. Any attempt at creating a homelike atmosphere is stifled by electronic locks, security guards, and sealed windows. Young inmates walking about the grounds have somber faces, and—most telling—their arms are tracked with homemade tattoos.

Juvenile hall today

According to the National Council on Crime and Delinquency, a half million juveniles were placed in detention centers in 1974. In addition, more than a hundred thousand children of juvenile-court age were held in adult jails or prisons. Traveling across the nation in 1973, I had an opportunity to inspect many of these facilities personally and to interview both inmates and officials. Based on my observations and the data I collected, I must conclude that conditions have not improved much since my own boyhood experience.

Located in a smoggy basin adjacent to old railroad tracks, the Los Angeles Central Juvenile Hall is the nation's largest, accommodating up to six hundred boys and girls from eight to eighteen. The high-walled stone dormitories, with their heavily screened windows and iron doors, make it seem like a concentration camp. Periodically, due to overcrowding, mattresses have been scattered in the hallways so that as many as two hundred kids could sleep on the floor.

Despite newspaper and television reports on the deplorable conditions, and despite promises of reform by politicians, no substantive efforts have been made to change things at Los Angeles Central Juvenile Hall. In 1947 the superintendent of the hall said, "Proper segregation is our biggest problem. . . . Sleeping in the same dormitories at juvenile hall are delinquents who have been associated with criminals of the lowest type." In 1974 the *Los Angeles Times* wrote: "Behind its cagelike entrance and heavily screened windows, curfew violators, runaways, and hubcap thieves are thrown in with muggers, attempted-murder suspects, sexual psychopaths, dope addicts, and psychotics deemed too dangerous even for mental institutions." The first thing I noticed in my visit to the institution was the number of boys and girls who were decorated with homemade tattoos.

One of the great but by no means unusual tragedies of juvenile halls today is the number of children confined for minor mistakes. During my visit to Los Angeles Juvenile Hall I talked to several very young boys who were confined for no more than running away from home. Children as young as seven have been thrown into surroundings that often serve as a school for felonious crime.

In the female wing of the hall I asked a pretty eighteen-year-old girl why she was being held.

"Because my mother doesn't want me to marry my boyfriend," she told me.

"Well, is that a crime?"

"My mother signed me in," she answered simply.

"You mean your mother put you in here because you wanted to get married?" I asked incredulously.

"She filled out a complaint that said I was incorrigible."

"How long have you been here?"

"Three months," she sobbed.

"Why is your mother so angry about your marrying this boy? Is he a drug addict or something?"

"No, she just doesn't want me to get married now, period."

"How long is she planning on keeping you here?"

"She says as long as it takes—until I promise not to marry him. She won't take me home until then." She buried her face in her hands, sobbing.

It seems a bizarre legal system that permits a mother to jail a daughter merely to prevent her from getting married.

Not only does overcrowding of Juvenile Hall mingle novices with hardened criminals, it also brings out racial tension and friction, creating an explosive mixture. One group of blacks bragged about how they tormented white boys to vent their frustrations against the white society they blamed for all their troubles. They called the hall "Disneyland" and said it was a "place to have fun playing with the white dudes' heads. White boy is used to having his way on the outs, but in here the brothers run things."

"The white boys and their pig protectors and their rich fathers think they're superior outside," one boy told me. "There ain't no pigs or rich daddy in the halls, jails, and camps. We make those boys remember what they done to us!"

"We're as good as the whites," said a seventeen-year-old armed robber, "but they keep ripping us off and keeping us down. If I had my way, I'd blow away all the white dudes."

Counselors who work with these particular black youths said most of them come from direly poor, fatherless families. They view life in the ghetto with hopeless desperation. When they get into Juvenile Hall, they form a power nucleus. Told by militants that they're in because they are black and oppressed and that their crimes were not actually crimes but rather acts in support of the whole class struggle, they lash out in resentment at the white inmates.

Seven doctors who work on a rotating basis at the Juvenile Hall infirmary complained of its poor medical facilities. Night and weekend doctors must often wait many hours, even several days, to get a child to a hospital for nonemergency care. Psychiatric treatment barely exists for emotionally disturbed youngsters. Dr. John Stalfberg said that he has had two cases of self-destructive youngsters brought to the infirmary because they had slashed their wrists and were banging their heads against the wall. Another boy, dissatisfied with his male sexuality, nearly bled to death when he attempted to cut off his penis with a sharp piece of glass. He was rushed to the hospital, where surgeons were able to save him.

The doctors said that much of the problem is due to lack of proper training for counselors in handling violent or disturbed youngsters. Dr. Stalfberg noted that counselors are sometimes quick to call for tranquilizers for the youngsters because they cannot control them. Another doctor recalled, "I had one girl in here recently who used to stick pins in herself to get response from the staff."

A number of maximum-security facilities in Texas are overcrowded, located far from the homes of the children, and, according to the National Council on Crime and Delinquency, control their inmates by physical repression. For example, at the Gatesville State School for Boys in Texas, Senate investigators were told, "Security is maintained by a twenty-four-hour horse patrol, a twenty-four-hour jeep patrol, and an eager kennel of dogs who are trained to chase younger children. In April of 1968, two hundred of the school's inmates were under twelve. A day without a beating is the exception, and torment is the order of the day."

Young troublemakers are dealt with in a more sophisticated but equally brutal way in a North Carolina reform school.

Instead of being physically subdued, rebellious youths are injected with heavy doses of tranquilizing drugs, which keep them in a tame stupor.

The Wayne County Juvenile Hall serving the greater Detroit area has been plagued by overcrowding. Recently the hall made headlines because of an inside murder. Two fifteen-year-old boys had an argument in the mess hall over a piece of fudge. The wrangle erupted into a fistfight, but the boys were quickly separated. It appeared that the matter was settled, and everyone went to the recreation room to watch television. As one of the boys involved in the fight sat absorbed in a program, however, the other came up behind him with a fire extinguisher and split his skull open, killing him.

The Oakland Juvenile Detention Center in Pittsburgh is an ancient structure with a small recreation yard secured by a wire-mesh fence, patched in many places where inmates have cut holes to escape. Counselors recall a game of basketball during which all of the boys suddenly stopped playing, headed for the fence, and ran right through it. Friends on the outside had snipped away a big chunk of fence at night, but had left it precariously intact so that it fell away with a slight nudge.

Given a tour of the hall, I was introduced to a sixteen-year-old boy who was back at the detention center for his twenty-first time. The center's library consisted of a few shelves of paperbacks, with such titles as *Soul on Ice, Manchild in the Promised Land, Knock on Any Door,* and other books of interest to ghetto kids. Tiny Brown, the 250-pound director of the center, who impressed me with his affectionate concern for his wards, was apprehensive about the new detention facility under construction. He said the mammoth center would have a capacity for five hundred inmates and he wondered how something so massive, impersonal, and crowded could help emotionally starved youngsters. I wondered, too.

The Wilkes-Barre, Pennsylvania, Juvenile Hall looms like a gothic fortress on a cliff. This enigmatic structure is sculpted out of rock. Among its tragic inmates was a fourteen-year-old girl called "The Entertainer" because she allegedly had intercourse with almost an entire battalion of soldiers. As far as I could tell from talking to her, she appeared to be suffering from a severe emotional disorder and probably should have been in a mental hospital rather than a juvenile hall. She was a threat only to herself; I could see no justification for keeping her in a fortress.

Another youth in the hall, a fifteen-year-old arsonist, had to be kept in an extra-security cell with steel bars to prevent him from escaping, which was relatively easy for him because he had a unique ability to pitch his voice to an intense high-frequency tone, comparable to that of a dog whistle. Until this endowment was discovered he had driven local police crazy when, while confined in a police car, he correctly pitched his voice so that he could shatter all the vehicle's windows. Naturally, he also applied this almost magical ability to break windows in jails and juvenile halls. The staff at Wilkes-Barre did the best they could with the limited facilities available to them.

At the Corona Rehabilitation Center in California, an institution whose sole purpose is to treat drug addicts, inmates confided to me that more drugs were floating around inside than on the streets. Girlfriends baked cookies spiced with marijuana and mailed them in, and even parents smuggled narcotics to their children.

The Dade County Juvenile Hall is the main intake and detention center for Miami and the surrounding Florida communities. Just a short ride away from the luxurious hotels and yachts along the beach, it is a dingy stone building with a window-box-sized playground. A post-Civil War shanty serves as a classroom for arts and crafts. The capacity of this facility, serving Florida's most populated area, is fifty-four beds—but they have long been stuffing in nearly four times that number of young people. In the past ten years, eleven grand jury probes have exposed the scandalous conditions at Dade Hall, but there has been little external evidence of change. David Boris, its young assistant supervisor, was candid in his description of the place as a "cesspool."

A caring, compassionate person, who typically worked eleven- and twelve-hour days with no overtime pay, the twenty-four-year-old Boris ushered me through the institution. "Things are bad now," he said, "but when I first came here this place was a raging zoo. I lost a tooth from a punch within a couple of hours. The tension was hyper-explosive."

He told proudly of how he had labored to try and improve

conditions for the kids. He had the place scrubbed down, repainted all the walls in a cheery yellow, issued fresh bedding, revised the menu to include nutritious and tasty food, recruited a night staff, and—most important in his own mind—created a multipurpose school to reduce tension. The school offered unstructured lessons in pottery, ceramics, painting, macrame, and other creative activities that helped to siphon off accumulated energy. Violent outbreaks still occurred, but with far less frequency than before.

Dade Hall's worst problem in the past had been an inept and brutish staff with a high turnover rate. David Boris brought people like himself—able, concerned, and committed—to Dade. But by the time I met him he was bitter, and in fact he resigned the day after we talked. He complained that the new policies he had fought to establish were being erased by bureaucrats and politicians who had never even visited Dade Hall. They were cutting the budget for youth services in Miami, including salaries for teachers at Juvenile Hall. Thus the school, which Boris had correctly felt was so uplifting and beneficial to the kids, had to be closed. That was too much of a heartbreak for him.

In his resignation letter, David Boris wrote: "I see no reason to put up with this anymore. I have found what people say and what they do are poles apart. The problem gets a lot of play in the press, but little is done. Ninety per cent of the money gets diverted from its proper focus. Officials ride in Cadillacs, they have plush offices. I have never been in a high official's office that did not look better than his own home. He's not paying for it. The public's money never reaches the kids."

Statistical backup

My own observations in 1974 only confirmed what had already been reported by the President's Commission on Law Enforcement in 1967. The commission examined 220 state-operated juvenile facilities, in all states, constituting 86 per cent of the juvenile holding capacity in the United States. At a time when juvenile crime was substantially less than it is today, the survey found severe overcrowding in the detention facilities of many big cities. In eleven states, in institutions housing nearly ten thousand children, the average daily population was 10 per cent more than any given system's capacity. The survey also found important differences between what services were available "on paper" and what was available in reality. Improvements of all types of services were badly needed. Support for this view was based on the existing ratios of treatment personnel to inmates. Forty-two jurisdictions were operating training-facility systems without a separate reception and diagnostic center, which would have helped to individualize institutional placements. Facilities in thirty-seven states did not even have one full-time psychiatrist on staff. The survey found that at least a hundred more psychologists were needed to bring the psychologist-delinquent ratio up to minimum standards. The survey also found that only 66 per cent of the needed caseworkers were available. The impact of a program of rehabilitation upon children is largely determined by the adequacy of staff, both quantitatively and qualitatively. Children failing in reformatories appear to have been failed *by* the reformatories.

In *Youthful Offender*, Elmer Reeves reports how one probationer expressed the positive effects of a relationship with an officer who shows a genuine concern for the offender as a human being:

> I know talk is cheap. I never did much talking. I guess I done more right here in this office in the last two years than I ever did before. I was a pretty tough kid. I been through a lot of this racket. Homes, social workers, parole officers, cops, bug-doctors—they don't mean a thing to me. And I always took my own rap, see? No one ever took no raps for me. You're the first guy ever had the idea I might be a man, not a monkey that's got to be shut up in a cage. That's all I got tn say, Mister. Except this, you went to bat for me for a lot of things—the judge,

> my relatives, my boss, and many other things. If I go sour, they're on your neck. So long, and I am telling you, you ain't never gonna have to take no raps for me.

One probation officer with a spark of loving quality can overcome the ocean of negative forces besieging a youngster.

15 • Overloading the Probation System

How can my probation officer rehabilitate me when I was never habilitated to begin with?
—Ex-Inmate, Corona Rehabilitation Center, Los Angeles, California

Probation operates on the theory that offenders have a better chance of adapting to society's rules if they are rehabilitated within the community. Juvenile probation allows the offender to live and work as part of the community under the "guardianship" of a probation officer instead of serving a penal term. It usually involves a court finding that the minor has been guilty of a wrong, the imposition of conditions upon his continued freedom, and the provision of means for helping him to meet these conditions. Probation implies more than giving the child "another chance." Its main intent is to give him positive assistance in adjusting while in the community. Henry Chandler, former director of the United States Courts, says of probation, "The theory is that in the offender there is a core of sound impulse which by an understanding person can be brought out and made effective. Probation is really the application of wise and compassionate friendship."

The probation system

In the United States juvenile probation developed as part of the wave of social reform in the latter half of the nineteenth century, when the new and enlarged definition of the state's responsibilities to its children yielded laws of a protective nature. Probation emerged as one of the means of blunting the harshness of criminal law and of utilizing the behavioral sciences in behalf of the child. In 1869 Massachusetts became the first state to inaugurate a probation program; such programs are now in operation in all fifty states.

As of the mid-1970s, juvenile probation is one of the major and most complex social institutions affecting the lives of an enormous number of children and young people. In 1974 well over a million delinquents, dependent and neglected children, and juvenile traffic violators were referred to the juvenile courts, with juvenile probation having the main responsibility for processing and servicing these cases. The correctional system relies on the interrelated effects of both deterrence and rehabilitation. Within this general scheme, juvenile probation's specific assignment is to prevent a repetition of the child's delinquent conduct as well as to avert a long-time deviant career and assist the child in developing his potential as a productive citizen.

Juvenile probation is vested with the loftiest of goals, but like any other major social institution, its worth in the long run must be judged by its performance. The premise that probation contributes to the attainment of its goals depends on the merit of two prior assumptions: first, that probation actually does have the tools of knowledge that would enable it to influence conduct and, second, that the manpower, money, and other resources necessary to effective performance actually are available.

The tools with which probation operates are still in the process of formation, and are nowhere clearly stated. Traditionally, the theory embodied in the law has been that you can change a person by punishment—that is, coerce him to reform by penal deterrence. Probation cannot function in a way that would subvert the deterrent power of the law. However, most people are aware of the peril in relying too complacently on the assumption that deterrents do in fact work. Our prisons are brimming over with unintimidated repeaters. We can instill fear in the offender, but in doing so we also foment venom and vengeance. Further, most young people do not seem capable of weighing the pleasure of immediate gratification against future uncertain "if I'm caught" punishment, and they are of course always subject to the subtle tyranny of peer pressure. Confinement remains a realistic necessity to take dangerous offenders out of circulation, but we cannot rely on it as an effective means for removing criminal traits.

Modern probation is generally dedicated to the pioneering horizons of behavioral change. Among the cherished precepts of probation work are to help the youngster find normal satisfactions in socially acceptable ways, to guide him or her in getting along with parents, developing proper study habits, doing well in a job, and choosing the right friends. Toward these ends, some probation officers are not concerned with theory, operating mainly on the basis of common sense. Others are committed to any of a dozen theoretical frameworks, some of which stress the pre-eminence of one variable or another—the family, the subculture, the self-image—as the cause of criminal behavior. Perennially, these theories seem to accentuate only the grand origins of crime and do not offer pragmatic guidelines for dealing with the individual offender. Grandiloquent treatises on the qualitative impact of defective child-rearing provide no clues to the probation officer on how to do his job. One of the prime challenges in the probation field today is to formulate a set of flexible, professional tools. At present, the approach is an unscientific patchwork of intuition, ideas, and gut instincts.

Fundamental to effective probation practice also is the availability of full-time paid probation services to all courts and children needing them. A federal survey reveals that in only thirty-one states do all counties have probation staff service, and in some of these it is only token. In the big cities where juvenile crime is an emergency crisis, the caseload for one practitioner ranges from forty to more than a hundred offenders. To get the job done—whether it is in commercial business or criminal probation—there has to be adequate staff. The probation circuit of America's juvenile court is generally too overloaded for best results.

Probation subsidy program

A study commissioned by the California legislature in 1964 laid the groundwork for the California Probation Subsidy program. The plan is based on the assumption that treating an offender in the community is less expensive and more effective than institutional rehabilitation, and that an increase in probation does not cause more crime and is intended to promote cooperation between the county and state government in handling both adult and juvenile offenders. Traditionally, most of the responsibility rested with the counties, with the state lending only minimal support in the form of consultation and limited subsidies for juvenile camps. The state now directly participates in probation by partially subsidizing the counties as a "reward" for reducing commitments to state institutions.

State funds are based on the percentage by which the county reduces each year's commitments to penal facilities. If, for example, based on past experience the state expected a particular county to commit a hundred offenders to state institutions but the county actually sends only ninety, the county has registered a 10 per cent decrease in the commitment rate, thus saving the state over $40,000. A portion of those savings will go to the county for probation programs, up to $4,000 for each offender.

In addition, the probation system enlists help from the community. Medical and psychiatric services are available, including counseling and therapy, and there are recreational programs and the possibility of job training through career agencies. These funds make possible a more direct officer-to-probationer relationship, along with experimental programs involving foster homes, day-care centers, and drug-education sessions.

Supporters claim the California Probation Subsidy program

has led to a reduction in the number of prison sentences, an increase in the probation population, and a marked saving in state-tax dollars. They hail it as an enlightened approach to corrections, allowing the offender to work within the community. Evidence of its achievement can be seen in the fact that a number of prison wings have closed down because of fewer inmates. The number of convicted defendants sent to state prisons dropped from 23.3 per cent in 1965 to 9.8 per cent in 1971, while those receiving probation during this period increased statewide approximately 25 per cent.

Critics, however, have assailed the policy of reducing prison commitments and increasing probations. Los Angeles Police Chief Edward Davis pegs the subsidies "blood money" because he feels the program permits the release of violent and dangerous individuals. He claims such a lenient philosophy endangers the lives and safety of citizens in return for a small amount of money to bolster a basically inept probation system. Sheriff Duane Crowe of Sacramento County maintains that the probation subsidy allows criminals to have little or no fear of the judicial system. Captain Stephen Downing of the Los Angeles Police Department's juvenile division decries the subsidy for leaving hard-core offenders to propagate in the community like "germs."

The probation system has not stopped crime, and money has become the focus in some cases. Probation departments have not made as effective use of training as was hoped, and drug programs and special-care centers have not materialized as expected. Even its effectiveness in reducing crime has been viewed with pessimism. The imperfections, faults, and potential risks of the system are obvious, but one must remember that the program has been in operation only since 1966. Further, it seems clear that prison itself does not help greatly in reducing or stopping crime, and in fact often aggravates the crime problem by converting petty offenders into felons. The U.S. Attorney General's office finds that while prisons are successful in restraining dangerous offenders, minor offenders come out "worse social misfits than when they entered." Probation represents a more promising approach for the lesser offender and the young, malleable delinquent who is not yet a danger to the community, and it can be effective if the offenders are chosen with care, supervisory work is done with professionalism, and there is ample staff.

The probation officer and the minor

Once placed on two years' probation as a teenager, I envisioned a long period of restrictive living. I expected to see a probation officer every week in his office and that he would be slyly dropping by at my home, my job, and pool-hall hangout and would question my parents, employer, and friends. I assumed that he would become a steadying influence in my life, a moral centurion, keeping a close vigil on all my activities. Every one of these preconceptions proved to be a misconception.

Once a month I pushed out of a crowded elevator to enter the Brooklyn Youth Division where several benches were always filled with young people waiting for their probation officers, each of whom was responsible for about a hundred cases. I fidgeted and felt the way I felt waiting to see a priest for confession—except that I never once made any confessions to Mr. Mirgon, my probation officer. If I had been involved in anything illegal, he was the last person I would have confided in. In my eyes, far from being a friend, he was a branch of the court, a lawman, the enemy. If I revealed my wrongs to him, I was afraid I'd be taken off probation and put in jail.

During our half-hour interview each month, I sensed that he was trying to take my moral pulse—asking me how everything was going at work, at home, and in the neighborhood. Whatever the reality might have been, I always covered it with a patina of conformity. I answered calculatingly, shaping my image to meet his approval, making him hear what he hoped to hear.

It was not that I didn't have good rapport with Mr. Mirgon, who was a friendly, jovial man and easy to get along with, but I still felt an alien distance between us. He represented a fleeting communication once a month, and he was a bona fide member of the establishment. Counteracting his once-a-month influence were the hundreds of hours on the streets with my friends. The streets dominated my feelings, urges, and motivations, not this man I knew remotely and called "mister."

My probation experience was in the fifties, and despite some improvements in modifying the ratio of probation officers to probationers, the number of individuals that one officer must still handle today makes the quality and efficiency of the service highly questionable. To these obstacles must be added the crunch of competing with the minor's environment in influencing him. The care and attention of one individual *can* do a lot in inspiring an offender to change, but a poor community or home environment raises formidable obstacles in reaching a soul or forging a new direction. With the responsibility of guiding the minor to socially acceptable behavior, the officer must serve as both a supervisor and a counselor, blending discipline with caring concern for the youth. He acts for both the community and the delinquent and must be sensitive to the desires and needs of both. The offender needs to be regarded foremost as a human being, not just another case to be reprogramed to function in society.

Hans Weiss, a former supervisor of probation with the juvenile court in Washington, D.C., characterized several levels on which the officer can relate to a youth. At the lowest level he listed the "card-index" or "clerk" type of officer who limits an understanding of his "cases" to the information he puts on cards and who avoids real conversation. The officer on the second level, the "parson" type, lectures with the same veiled threats to all his probationers without understanding their individual situations and backgrounds. On the next level is the officer with a "touch of technique" who knows something about social investigation, but whose lack of organization and sporadic contacts lead to poor interaction with his charges and to ineffective treatment. The "supervisor" type simply acts as the watchful eye of the court and does little to involve himself in helping the probationer in rehabilitation. The "social technician" knows the process of social casework and investigation well, diagnoses his cases, and is efficient, but he fails to build a relationship with his ward. He discusses rather than guides, and then fails to make meaningful contact with the probationer. At a higher level, the "leader" type of officer makes use of probationers in their reconditioning. By attempting to understand the offender's total situation and its psychological elements, he communicates true and direct concern for the probationer rather than for his symptomatic delinquent acts.

PART FOUR

Preventive Measures and Antidotes

16 • One-to-One Caring

I escaped from the ghetto only for one reason:
Nana, my maternal grandmother.
—Ralph Bunche, 1965

Probably nothing can help a young person with problems more than a supportive, inspiring relationship. The Michie Study of disadvantaged youths with successful employment records demonstrated that these young men and women had been greatly influenced by teachers who showed warm, personal interest in their students. The control group—the boys and girls who did not do well on their jobs—did not report such relationships.

Escape from the ghetto

Of course, all relationships are two-way streets, and teenagers who are determined to succeed may seek out and bring more to a relationship than their less able or motivated peers. Nevertheless, it is important that an older person be there with support, love, faith, guidance, and the standards upon which to model new behavior and attitudes at a time when a young person is still open to help. Ralph Bunche put it this way: "You couldn't develop ambition in that [the ghetto] atmosphere, because where the hell were you going—where could you go? You could see nothing ahead for you in life. Nothing open to you. I escaped for only one reason: Nana, my maternal grandmother. She was the greatest woman I have ever known. She made me go to college—I know where I would have been and what I would have become if it hadn't been for her."

For Claude Brown, author of *Manchild in the Promised Land,* meeting Counselor Papanek at Wiltwyck, a detention home in New York State, was a turning point in his life. Papanek was the first person Brown had ever known "who could handle life without lying, hitting, or getting angry." Brown felt Papanek's deep understanding of people, and his caring for them. "He was the first person I ever wanted to do anything for," he remembers. "I wanted to stay out of there so Papanek would be right." Malcolm X had a similar experience while in prison. He began to study after meeting Bimbi, a man who could command respect merely by the strength of his words. Bimbi cared for the young Malcolm, and this one-to-one caring was an important part of the impetus that Malcolm needed to reshape his life.

In my own past, there were my religious parents, a caring teacher, a concerned priest, and a bowling-alley owner with tremendous insight. When I was twenty, a close friend was killed, a traumatic experience that caused the inner balance within me to shift irrevocably toward the creative. But it might not have worked out that way. Even before that grisly event I was fortunate that there were people in my life who cared on a one-to-one basis.

For a long time I had been a hopeless student—until I met Miss Lawsen, my seventh-grade teacher. As a result of her concern and confidence, I applied myself to learning and eventually achieved the highest grade average in junior high school. Regrettably, peer pressure in high school tipped my inner balance back to destructiveness and street violence—fighting every week, failing all my subjects until I was finally expelled at the end of my freshman year. But when I returned to night high school at twenty, I had the memory of Miss Lawsen and the academic aptitude she had nurtured in me.

One-to-one caring is not a Hollywood answer. It is not a script of love merging into trauma and tragedy, of a kid rising from the depths of despair into the sunlight. It is a quieter drama, of real people going through real problems, listening to each other when they need it most. It is one person caring enough about another just to help at a crucial point.

My friend Chuck Platy

I have a friend named Chuck. We don't see each other very often, but we're still good friends. Chuck's work day as a milkman begins at three in the morning and he goes to college at night, so it's not easy for us to get together. But we do get a chance to talk on the phone from time to time, and we once carried on a brisk correspondence. At that time Chuck was in a juvenile correctional camp. Our correspondence began with the following letter:

> Dear Mr. Sorrentino,
>
> . . . there are hundreds of ways (it seems) that the problems you've had are the ones I've had, exception of two, I've had dope problems, you have had gang problems. But what I wanted to ask you was this! I want to start myself off *right* from where I am right now, which is in a work camp in Calif. I had recently got busted for being on downers at a drive-in show. Before my court date came up I was arrested for robbery and it really broke my family to pieces. But how can I start a new type of life for myself?
>
> I figured you would wonder why I don't go to someone a little closer to me, but you've been through most of what I might be headed for, or already have past. I thought maybe if you would write me back with a little advice or something. I do have some ideas on what kind of career I want. Being in juvenile hall, camp, etc., I've sort of wondered what I would be like on the other side, like being a Group Supervisor. . . . Is that the answer. Maybe to go to school you think? But to tell you the truth I never really had any dislike toward school, after the 10 grade, before then there was a few problems, but then I found a school I liked. Well, I'm hoping for a little help really I'm asking and hoping! . . . I'll leave an address if you decide to write and I really do hope you will.

In my answer I encouraged him to continue his good attitude and make an effort to do well at the camp school, as boring as it might be. Gratified that I might be able to influence him, I invited him to write as often as he felt like it, to tell me more about himself, his street past, his family situation, his dreams . . .

His reply, in part, was this:

> I've had a lot of time to think where I'm going to be in the future. The school here is starting a brake-muffler program, so I'll be going into that as a starter, so I can earn a few bucks to go to college. . . . I am trying to figure out what exactly I'm going to try to reach for in the days to come. I think the letter from Mr. Laraby will explain the way the teachers are, which is fantastic. They seem to take more of an interest in us than some counselors.
>
> I hope if you decide to come up to visit, that you won't be too disappointed with some of the dudes here, cause I know some of them will be acting their part to their friends, and themselves. Thank you for writing.

The man Chuck mentioned in his letter, Mr. Laraby, was an English teacher in the camp's school, who wrote to me at about the same time, telling me a little about Chuck. It seems Chuck had read my autobiography, *Up From Never*, and had written a book report about it—and then, having found that I lived in the Los Angeles area, had decided to write me. Mr. Laraby felt that Chuck lacked a sense of self-worth at a very deep level but that my letter had helped him start to develop one. What had impressed Chuck, he said, was that a man as busy as I must obviously be had taken the time to write a personal reply to his letter. Mr. Laraby invited me to come up to the camp as a guest speaker. He said that not only Chuck but many of the other young men would like to meet someone who had been like them as a kid but had overcome it. As he said in closing, "I believe the interest level would be very high."

The interest level was general pandemonium punctuated with flak from some totally alienated inmates. Even so, I shook hands with about two hundred boys after my talk. I was full of emotional anticipation, like an expectant father, waiting for Chuck to come up and introduce himself. When he did, I met a husky young man with broad shoulders and the posture of a Marine. His features were handsome but slightly blemished by a skin rash on his cheeks. Most important, he was as sincere and intelligent in person as he had been in his letters. He was clearly someone with potential who, with guidance and affection, could make something useful and worthwhile of his life.

That was late in February. I next heard from Chuck in April 1973:

> I have been doing alright, except for the minor agitation that always seems to go on up here. I want to apologize for not writing sooner, except I have been kept real busy. I hope you'll understand. They have set a definite date for me to leave, May 10. There is one problem. If I leave then, I will lose up to 25 points of credit for all of the fall semester. Mr. Anderson, the principal, says that the school board set the cut off date for the 17. I'll most likely be staying. I really think that I might have some problems though, when and if I do stay. I mean problems with the other dudes here. I know a week doesn't seem that long, but I just hope I can handle it.
>
> There really isn't too much more going on. . . . I seem, also, to be getting a little paranoid about going home, having to face certain people. I am losing confidence in myself. I really shouldn't be, 'cause there isn't anything to worry about.

In my reply, I wrote:

> There is a saying, to everything there is a season. You will find in life that experience, like the weather, ranges from sunshine to storms. You have to face the storms, knowing that they will be over soon, and that there will be sunny days ahead. You must not allow the prospect of bad times or struggle or crisis to get the best of you or to beat you.
>
> I have great confidence in you. I know you have a good head on your shoulders, a strong healthy body, a nice personality. There is no reason you can't make a good

> life for yourself. The only one defeating you is yourself. You dwell on the negative, you remember past failures, you worry about yesterdays too much.
>
> Don't let the dudes down there get to you. Remember that only a few months more and it all will be behind you. In a short time that place and the bad people will be a forgotten, evaporating haze in your past. Ignore troublemakers, go your own way, endure what has to be endured.
>
> Remember when you get out of there, you have a friend.

The next time I heard from Chuck, he had been released from the camp.

> I'm a milkman! I work four days a week out at Foothill Dairy delivering door to door. I work from 3:00 until 11:00. I'm up before the roosters. I usually put in some hours overtime everyday. It works out to a rough $30.00 a day and commission, if I go out and try to sell milk.
>
> I'm off on Wednesday so I'm planning on going down to P.C.C. [Pasadena City College] on my night off. I believe I'll be able to draw an A, without a doubt, 'cause for right now I'm only going to take one class. Now I'm not sure exactly what I should take to start out with, I guess psychology would be about the best. Do you have any suggestions? I would really appreciate it. Well, it's a worknight, so I'm going to hit the sack. Take care.

Chuck and I have seen each other and we talk on the phone every once in a while. The culmination for me in this effort to help a youngster was a letter from Chuck's parents, which began: "Why are there not more words in the English language to express Thank You?" The letter, written by Chuck's mother, went on to say that Chuck had let her and his father read our correspondence, and that they wanted to thank me for taking the time to care for their son. She closed the letter as follows: "Our thanks again for taking the time to read this. How reassuring it is to know that there are still so many that truly care. A reply to this letter is not necessary. It was the only way we could let you know that we care too."

One-to-one caring is the influence that helped to bring Chuck

Platy back to society. I'm glad to have been a part of it, and I am also glad to know that Chuck has parents who love him, understand him, and care deeply about his future. We can't legislate one-to-one caring. It is a quality that can only come from within ourselves. All of us have this capacity; it merely needs to be summoned to help those who need it so desperately. More people expressing concern for troubled youngsters can be of supreme importance in curing juvenile crime in America.

17 • Schools That Ignite the Inner Spark

Schools, in terms of the sheer length and intensity of the child's exposure in educational institutions, must be reckoned with as a major force shaping the lives of American youth.
—Edwin M. Schur, Our Criminal Society

Education—vocational, academic, and moral—is vitally important as a barrier to crime. I know from my own experience that even one dedicated, inspiring teacher can change a young person's life. Caught up in the exciting heroics of the street cult, rumbles, building a rep, and proving my machismo, I entered the seventh grade at P.S. 259 in Brooklyn with a school history that included mediocre grades, atrocious conduct, and a flip attitude that was summed up in "School is fa creeps." But one teacher—a twenty-five-year-old Norwegian-American woman—turned me away from the streets to books.

The teacher as catalyst

An inspiring teacher can not only channel a child's energy and curiosity into constructive areas but can also serve as an effective example of good social behavior. Delinquency-prone youngsters consistently have fragile, distorted images of themselves. A sensitive teacher can help these youngsters develop healthy self-images.

Herbert Kohl, in his book *36 Children,* gives us abundant examples of how a good teacher can go into a ghetto elementary school and, using imaginative and affectionate methods, free and expand the brilliant potentials of disadvantaged children.

Kohl found the reading skills of his sixth-grade students at P.S. 103 in Harlem to be dismal. For the first six weeks he tried to use the standard books assigned to the class and teach the official curriculum, but it was hopeless. The class went through the readers perfunctorily and droned through their other subjects, absorbing nothing. He felt as burdened as the children did by the inappropriateness of the materials and methods he was supposed to use. The students came to life, it seemed, only during the ten-minute breaks he gave them when they could do anything they wanted.

Unwilling to lose this will and energy, Kohl brought in chess and checker games and other objects he thought the class might find interesting, and spent some time each morning describing them. For example, he gave them a brief history of chess, and he told them about the wise man who asked a king, as a reward for a favor, for the number of grains of wheat that resulted from placing one on the first square of a checker board and then progressively doubling the amount until all the squares were covered. Several children realized that the king must have been out of money by the end of the exercise, showing how far they had gotten in trying to figure out how much wheat the king owed the wise man.

The children learned how to play checkers, and some also learned chess. During their games they came to understand that winning does not always depend on using physical force, a big insight for them. The rights of both winners and losers were established and respected. Kohl was an observer of his class as well as a leader and participant, and studied the children to discover how they related to each other and to their school environment. A year of teacher training at Columbia had never given him any hint of the importance of really paying attention to the children.

When students asked questions, Kohl listened carefully, trying to find a way to convert their curiosity into creative expression. One of the boys showed him a copy of the *New York Enquirer* and asked him what he thought about it. Kohl remarked that he thought the student could do a better job of telling the truth, and asked the boy to report on what was happening in his neighborhood. The boy sat down and composed his own "magazine" on Harlem. Another student asked, "Mr. Kohl, can't we study the language we're talking about instead of spelling and grammar?" Kohl decided they could, and began with an exciting expedition into the study of language and myths, the origins and history of words and of their changing uses and functions in different eras. He found that by showing students the origins of words they became really interested and found it easier to master and acquire a vocabulary than they did by tedious rote memorization.

Kohl brought his own books to class to supplement the boring standard texts. The children were curious about those Greeks and Latins who had contributed so many words and concepts to the English language, so they were interested in books on Greek and Roman architecture and art, and even in the Larousse Encyclopedia of Mythology and the Iliad. After studying a book on Greek architecture, one of the students constructed a reasonably accurate scale model of the Parthenon. Two others created a clay volcano, using a chemistry text to learn how to simulate the volcano's eruption. A number of girls in the class were reading romantic novels, and in some cases went on to such writers as Thurber and O. Henry. Kohl learned that practically nothing was beyond their capacity if they were really motivated.

Most importantly, Kohl was expressive with his feelings; he said deeply affecting things, moved children to tears with unexpected kindness, and praised them lavishly. At the end of a year there were no signs of pre-delinquency among his students, and they were reading enthusiastically, writing intelligent stories that had real content, and creating art that expressed their innermost feelings.

Herbert Kohl's experiences are not unique. In every school

system there are teachers who are improvising, using their imagination and their creative talents in an effort to reach children who are bored and frustrated by the generally bland, middle-of-the-road public-school concept of education. There are not enough of these teachers, of course. It isn't easy to find ways to get around standard procedures and to fight the red tape and obstructionism that seem to be inherent in school systems. Many quit in despair after a few years.

But those who persevere can literally mean the difference between life and death for some children, no matter how few, by igniting a spark, by giving a child the tools to think with, feel with, explore with—and the motivation to want to use these tools. The time has long since passed when the school marm equipped to teach the three R's by rote and impose irrelevant moral standards can be considered a sound approach to public education.

Broadening the dimensions of learning

A child's natural perception of the world is open-ended. He or she will gaze at everything, not discriminate, roam boundlessly in fantasy, juxtapose objects and ideas that are rigidly separated in "educated" minds. A child has no qualms about seeing the sun sitting on a blade of grass, or putting a star in his pocket, or wondering why Almighty God inflicts such terrible natural disasters as hurricanes or floods or droughts.

During the educational process, however, the child's mind is placed in a vise and molded to fit preconceived ideas of what is beneficial, what he or she "should" learn. The protests of college students in the sixties about the lack of relevance of their education to the world around them were valid—but the separation of education from life experiences begins long before college, or even high school. Our educational standards, of course, reflect a general narrowness of thinking in our society: the Great Ideas Syntopticon of the Encyclopedia Britannica, for one prime example, has managed to compress the "ideational concepts" evolved throughout the entire history of humankind into one hundred and two neat categories. Ultimately, this kind of constricted thinking seeps down into our educational system, becoming ever narrower the farther down it trickles. The educational process is a building with endless doors, almost all of which are sealed shut. These doors should be opened and the students encouraged to roam at will, with some guidance, wherever their needs and their curiosity—and those of their teachers—lead them.

The Prime of Miss Jean Brodie is an indictment of the "stuff-in, stamp-on, zip-up" practices found in too many of our schools. During one of her classes at a provincial girls' school in Scotland, Miss Brodie asks, "Who was the greatest Italian painter?"

"DaVinci," one girl answers.

"Wrong. Giotto. He's my favorite." This remark is typical of Miss Brodie's teaching. Her tastes become the only touchstone, her politics the only truth. "I am in the business," she announces loftily, "of putting old heads on young bodies." To get a good grade in Miss Brodie's class, students must regurgitate her preferences and her perceptions of the correct ordering of the universe.

A nobler goal of education, and one more enriching and contributory to democracy, would be to teach students how to think, how to reason, how to analyze, how to explore, how to break down the barriers of stereotyped thinking and the need to conform to others' standards without questioning the value of those standards.

Few educators would disagree that there is a need to make the curriculum more relevant and teaching methods less rigid; dispute arises only over how these goals should be accomplished. The Parkway Program in Philadelphia is one example of how this can be done—an integration of "compulsory education into the realities of world situations." In an effort to deal with overcrowded high schools, the city's board of education suggested setting up a school that would use the city's cultural facilities and libraries for its classrooms. What has developed from this is an "on location" program in which students attend classes taught by professionals in various fields and held at various locations around the city—shops, offices, museums, concert halls. The course offerings range from gem-cutting to art history, and both the students' academic wants and needs are considered.

The freedom and variety of the Parkway curriculum create a unique learning environment. Although the school is structured informally, student responsibility is an important part of the plan. On the administrative side, students and faculty work together in three self-governing units that meet together weekly. No marks are given, but teachers write frequent evaluations of each student's work. Attendance is not compulsory for the most part, and students maintain an informal relationship with their teachers.

The Parkway's style of freedom has had significant effects on students. Most of them not only mature faster, but they also learn more. Disciplinary problems are minimal, although many of the students had delinquency problems in the schools they attended before going to Parkway. There are no hard-drug problems, nor have there been any racial incidents.

Mario Fantini, an official of the Ford Foundation, says the Parkway program "breaks down the dichotomy between living and learning." The school's very positive results demonstrate the importance of making the curriculum relevant to living and of bridging the distance between a sterile school existence and the "real" world.

Another successful educational experiment is the Street Academy of South Bend, Indiana. Henry James, a participant in the program, who prefers the name "Chango," now knows what freedom means to him. He's never talked about it much before, because nobody seemed interested. Now that he's a Street Academy student, where someone does want to know, he can express his concept of freedom in writing, in the Academy's student newspaper, the *Frederick Douglass Observer:*

"Freedom is Pride, Unity, and a feeling of calmness inside you. Freedom is talking about anything you wish, without any restrictions. Freedom is when you decide for yourself what is wrong and what is right. Freedom is a black man speaking what he wants, without being afraid. Freedom is living your life the way you want to, without anyone telling you what to do or say. Freedom is what blacks want, but must achieve because most of us can't even define it."

Chango and fifty-one other students—black, white, and brown—are in their first year of academic studies at the Academy, which is housed in an old manufacturing building in downtown South Bend. The money from the subscriptions and single-copy sales of the *Frederick Douglass Observer* goes into a scholarship fund for students who want to go on to college. Another flourishing activity, which students rarely took part in at "regular" school, is student government. By their choice, it is patterned after the South Bend city government, which has a cabinet form of administration.

The street academy, an innovative approach to school reform, was pioneered by the New York Urban League. The South Bend Academy opened in January 1972, with the financial backing of the National Urban League and Youth Advocacy. Each invested $50,000 for youths aged sixteen to twenty-three who had been "short-changed in their search for education." Four months of intensive planning by the Academy staff—five teachers, a social worker, a director, and secretary—preceded the opening.

High school students who had dropped out, or been "pushed out," of school were actively recruited. The school system provided the academy with transcripts of the students' records to assist in the design of the Academy's programs. The emphasis at the Academy is on quality education. Graduation is based on the standard accumulation of academic credits but student learning is enriched through programs involving local police, museums, universities, and industry, and students also participate in encounter-group sessions conducted by teachers and professional consultants. Above all, there is genuine student participation in the decision-making process at the Academy on all levels.

Roosevelt Thomas, the director of the Academy, knows that they have only taken one small step. "But," Thomas reasons, "someone had to prove the need, and the kids who are sticking with it are showing others it can be done. They're making history." And the students do seem to be proving themselves.

Indiana University has agreed to accept Academy graduates, as have other institutions of higher learning.

Nobody would argue that the street academy has a long way to go before it becomes a viable alternative to the traditional high school, but it *is* a beginning. As Bob Gemengnini, former president of National Youth Development, says, it is one way to "make ghetto kids feel comfortable with education, doing it on their terms, and using values they are used to."

Educational first aid and rescue missions

The hollows of West Virginia are another kind of ghetto strangled by poverty. The children of the hollows come from homes in which neither parent usually has more than a third-grade education and where the atmosphere does not inspire hope, much less encourage education.

In 1966, Mrs. Jane Galyean, wife of one of West Virginia's prominent business leaders, became alarmed over the dropout rate in the hollows. She was even more distressed that students quit school in the early grades because they lacked proper clothes and schoolbooks (at that time pupils in West Virginia public schools were required to buy their own schoolbooks).

Together with concerned citizens, Mrs. Galyean founded the Keep a Child in School program. The idea was to work closely with the board of education and find out which children were potential dropouts. These children, with the permission of their parents, would be referred to a sponsor, an individual or couple who had volunteered for the program. Using their own money, the sponsors provided the books and clothes necessary for the children to attend school. Many youngsters could not attend gym classes simply because they did not own gym suits, so gym suits were also donated.

The group found, however, that most children had dropped out of school because they had had an unhappy experience in school. The lack of confidence and fears typical of most grade-schoolers can usually be overcome by attentive parents, but if the parents are neither interested nor educated themselves, their children don't have much of a chance. The child who is sponsored by Keep a Child in School receives, in a sense, emergency assistance. Child and sponsor spend several hours a week together, discussing lessons, exploring crafts, and dealing with any problems that may be troubling the youngster. In five years the group has helped more than a thousand children stay in school.

"In the beginning," says Mrs. Galyean, "prospective sponsors would ask, 'How involved do you expect us to get with these children?' And we answered, 'We don't expect you to get involved—we expect you to fall in love.' "

The most remarkable aspect of Keep a Child in School is the evidence that hundreds of lives *can* be rescued from emptiness and failure with a very small investment in time and money. Scores of young people helped by the program are now attending college. As journalist Edwin Roberts observes, "It does require a measure of humanity, a humanity we possess but often neglect because it seems so frail. At the soul of a civilized society there must be a consensus about individual responsibility—our responsibility to each other." The Keep a Child in School program is proof that concerned citizens can have a real effect on the lives of young people whom they care enough about to feel responsible for.

Life education values

Many people deplore what they consider to be a "breakdown in moral values within our younger generation," a cry that has been heard since the dawn of civilization. Moral values are changing, but to what degree, and what the long-range effects will be, cannot yet be judged. Certainly no new agreed-upon moral standards have emerged, and at times adults are sanctimoniously self-righteous in their criticism of members of the younger generation who will not abide by the old rules. Nevertheless, in the age of "future shock," many adolescents and young adults feel overwhelmed by forces and events, unable to accept traditional social and moral norms and yet adrift without any guidelines. They often express their helpless feelings in a "sickness of the soul," rootlessness, nihilism, and moral anarchy.

This highlights a need for moral education of the young and the establishment of real moral foundations early in life. In a society committed to the separation of church and state, specific religious morality cannot be imposed within the school system, which, in any case, many people would see as dogmatic indoctrination of the worst sort. And, sad to say, the teaching of moral values within the family, in the home, seems to have become a lost art.

But moral excellence does need to be nurtured in our society, and it can be done without religious indoctrination. Basic to moral education is the objective examination of all values, and Lawrence Kohlberg, in *Research in Moral Development,* suggests that the key to giving children such an education is the stimulation of their moral judgment. This approach, says Kohlberg, utilizes an adaptation of the Socratic method, of having a teacher conduct discussions about values in the areas of social studies, humanities, religion, sex education, and even the sciences. Part of the process is to ask the student to put himself in another's shoes, to see a problem from another point of view. Through this method, the children learn to empathize with other people and to see all sides of an issue. The teacher, in helping the child consider genuine moral conflicts and think about the reasoning he uses in solving such conflicts, helps him to see inconsistencies and inadequacies in his way of thinking and find ways of dealing with them.

A new discipline, called "Life Values Education," is being taught in some schools, with the aim of helping youngsters examine more critically the logic of their own thinking about the moral and ethical values of their society. Within this discipline, a number of school districts are also offering courses in law as a part of the regular curriculum to help youth respect the law and understand how the legal system works.

In Los Angeles this aspect of the program was the brainchild of Los Angeles District Attorney Joseph Busch. "Curbing juvenile crime is my primary concern," Busch says. "After nearly a quarter of a century as a prosecutor, I'm more convinced than ever that proper education and communication with our young people are essential in our continuing efforts to reduce crime." Students at Beverly Hills High School attend seminars conducted by lawyers on such topics as consumer protection, criminal felonies, and legal defense of the poor in the hope that they will become more aware of the law's impact on everyday life.

Something new is also being tried at Monroe High School in the San Fernando Valley section of Los Angeles: a "rap room" where students can get together with other students and counselors in an informal atmosphere to exchange ideas on matters ranging from the most innocuous problems to the most raspingly controversial moral issues. An extension of the program is a crisis-intervention center where youngsters facing serious moral dilemmas, often centered around involvement with drugs, get immediate and strictly confidential guidance.

There are myriad other experimental programs being tried across the country, with varying degrees of success—and usually enmeshed in controversy as to their merits. There is no one "final" or complete answer to the question of how to actively involve our youngsters in a meaningful educational experience, to keep what one teacher has called the "pre-prisoner" ghetto teenager from actually winding up behind bars. Much more needs to be done, but until the educational system is completely overhauled, it is basically up to each teacher to see students as individual human beings and to try every means possible to make the time they spend in the classroom challenging and relevant to the "real world" they will have to deal with when they leave.

18 • Preventing Youthful Drug Abuse

In one year alone, the sale of tranquilizers in America soared to $150,000,000.
–Robert S. DeRopp, Drugs and the Mind

We cannot help but be aware of the severity of the drug abuse problem, since it affects all ages and all social classes. Insofar as it affects youth, it is poignantly tragic, as it not only leads to wasted lives in terms of personal fulfillment but is a major cause of crime and a serious threat to social welfare. The need to support a drug habit is undoubtedly responsible for more violence toward people and property than all the gang wars ever fought. Drug abuse is a complex problem, and reacting to it wisely requires a concerted effort of understanding.

Drug education

Initially we must recognize that drugs have been used in almost every culture since prehistoric times. The desire to experiment with mind-altering substances is one of the features that distinguishes human beings from animals. Throughout history drugs have been used to change perception, for relaxation, in medicine, and as part of religious rituals. As far back as 2700 B.C. the Chinese recommended marijuana for gout, constipation, and "absent-mindedness." The Greeks had a word for the pursuit of drugs—"ataraxia," a virginal state of perfection in which mental serenity is harmoniously blended with physical rapture. The history of drugs represents humankind's attempt to wiggle, worm, and slither its way out of its natural self. As the French philosopher Pascal once observed, "The greatest ailment of man is his inability to sit quietly in his own chamber."

Efforts to stop the spread of drugs in the general public date back to the sixteenth century in America. Fantastic stories were concocted and disseminated to keep the common man from harvesting certain medicinal plants and thus destroying a profitable market. Today the young are particularly vulnerable to the psychological stresses and insecurities of society, and are therefore quite vulnerable to the alluring inducements of transcendent flight from one's consciousness and the promise of soothing release. In a climate of increasing social pressure and discord, we can expect the young to become even more attracted to the siren call of drug use. It has been estimated that Americans consume twenty-one tons of aspirin a day. Dr. Allen Cohen, a Los Angeles psychologist, believes that we must be practical and admit that the question is no longer whether people will use drugs, but rather which drugs they will use, and how often.

Society as a whole and youngsters in particular must be informed about the nature of drugs. Since there are so many kinds of drugs—barbiturates, euphorics, psychedelics, narcotics—we must be aware of their differences and their particular effects and of the dangers and risks in using them. Some drugs are habit-forming, some have overdose levels, and some wreak mental and physiological devastation. For an educational program to be effective, it must be honest. If young people are told, for example (as they often are), that marijuana is addictive and causes severe brain damage, they will not be influenced by anything else they are told about narcotics. Scare tactics and brainwashing have proved counterproductive. Today's youth live in an age of space satellites beaming the facts to them from the four corners of the earth; they can no longer be spoon-fed false information to make them docile. They are too sophisticated, and sooner or later they will realize they are being deceived—and lose all trust for adults in the process. Nor will moralizing be effective, for it may tend to produce a reverse reaction; the forbidden can seem fascinating. Above all, then, drug education for youth must be factual, accurate, and nonmoralistic.

Drug education should be offered in the schools but not as a crash lecture by an unprepared English or physical-education teacher. We need, from the sixth grade on, factual, objective programs of drug education that survey the full spectrum of mind-altering drugs, including alcohol, presented by specially trained, knowledgeable teachers. The program should be comprehensive and should be presented over a period of time, taking up at least two hours each week. It should use a combination of instruction, class discussions, and audiovisual materials and be continued each year through high school, with the material upgraded to the age level, knowledge, and sophistication of freshmen through seniors. An important objective of the drug program should be to desensationalize and demythologize drugs—in other words, to counteract the propaganda of drug advertisers, politicians, and drug cultists. College campuses should sponsor drug-education seminars for students, faculty, and administrators similar to those that have been carried out in recent years by the U.S. National Student Association. Special national conferences should be held to bring together the country's top experts to evaluate the present state of knowledge and make recommendations to the public and legislative bodies.

For purposes of drug education, the remainder of this section will outline the major categories of drugs being used by young people, their distinguishing characteristics, and their harmful or innocuous effects.

Benzedrine, or "uppers," commonly known as pep pills, are stimulants that speed up the mental processes, depress the appetite, cause a swirling dizziness, and make sleep impossible. To ward off sleepiness on long hauls, truck drivers sometimes use Benzedrine, a dangerous practice since it often results in mental confusion, which may lead to accidents. One driver became so confused under the influence of Benzedrine that he was convinced that "Benny" was driving the truck, and he crawled into his sleeping berth, leaving the truck to steer itself. The driver survived, but the truck did not. Half of the total annual production of these pills is estimated to go into illicit channels.

Barbiturates are depressants, or "downers," known on the street as "red devils," "rainbows," and "blue heavens," and are among the most dangerous drugs. Legitimately available as sleeping pills and tranquilizers, they affect the nervous system, slow down the heart, and lower the blood pressure, transforming an abusive user into a mental sloth. Overdosage will drag the victim from intoxicating lethargy into deep coma. Downers can be dangerous because they may dull one's consciousness to such an extent that normal inhibitions are loosened. An extreme example of this is a sixteen-year-old whom Los Angeles police call "Mad Dog" and believe has killed six people since age eleven. He is said to glut himself on "red devils" and sink into a zombielike trance before knocking on the door of a potential victim and unloading the clip of a .45 into the person. No one has dared to testify against Mad Dog.

Amphetamine and methamphetamine, or "speed," come in a crystallized powder and are often taken intravenously in "runs" of every four hours for six consecutive days. During this period, the user's blood pumps furiously and his adrenalin races at top speed. Thus overstimulated, he can represent a danger to himself and the community. A youth in a "speed run" can suffer toxic psychosis, which may induce a state of paranoia, leading him to believe that people are plotting against him. In rare cases, he may feel he must kill or be killed. Chronic use of speed can cause disintegration of the brain; this was graphically illustrated in a Los Angeles autopsy on a speed freak whose brain virtually crumbled into cerebral sawdust.

Euphorics pose the greatest menace to early teens for they are cheaply available at any local supermarket as an ingredient of plastic cement, aerosol sprays, lighter fluid, airplane glue, and paint thinner. The giddiness they cause may sometimes be a prelude to hallucinations, and persistent use can cause degeneration of the brain cells.

The opiate heroin, a deadly addictive white powder, is injected intravenously and produces a serene and dreamy surrealistic escape. A gang friend of mine under the influence of heroin fell on a steaming radiator, scorching his nude body into oozing blisters. Heroin abuse affects metabolic change in the nervous system and generates a narcotic hunger or craving that can last a lifetime. A heroin addict's body often will be splotched with abscesses at the site of injections from dirty needles, and every inch of vein on his limbs and neck may be tracked with needle marks. To satisfy his habit, a heroin addict may need as much as a hundred dollars a day. Thus while little crime is committed by the person under the influence of heroin, a great deal is committed by the impoverished addict who must somehow raise the money for his next fix.

Cocaine, known as "the aristocratic drug" because it is so expensive, is a sugarlike powder derived from coca plants, and is ingested by chewing or "snorting" through the nose. Cocaine induces a cozy sense of contentment while at the same time overstimulating the mind; it is simultaneously a narcotic and a stimulant. The ecstatic sensations it causes may dissolve quickly into the darkness of depression. Psychologically addictive, cocaine can be destructive to one's health and, as with heroin, can lead to criminal acts in order to get the money necessary to buy the drug.

Hallucinogens and psychedelics, or acid, are found in such mind-altering chemicals as LSD and STP and in a natural form in peyote. On an "acid trip" feelings and images tumble through the mind in profusion, colors and shapes are intensified, and one's sense of time is distorted. Praised for their alleged lift to creativity, hallucinogens are allegedly capable of burning the cerebral cortex of the brain, damaging chromosomes, and producing birth defects.

Marijuana and hashish are derivatives of the Indian hemp plant cannabis sativa, marijuana being the dried plant and hashish, the stronger substance, the resin of the plant. A mild psychedelic, marijuana accentuates sense perception, causes time to unfold in slow motion, and subdues the ego. In *The Man God,* Baudelaire describes this experience: "Your personality disappears to such an abnormal degree that contemplation of outward objects makes you forget your own existence, and soon melt into them. A bird soaring beneath a blue sky at first merely represents the immortal yearning to soar above life, but already you are the bird itself." In 1944 the New York Academy of Medicine published a report concluding that marijuana neither produced any harmful effects nor led to addiction. Since then countless investigations have been conducted, private and governmental, and all basically support the Academy findings. When used sparingly it does not appear to have any harmful side effects, but according to a 1974 NBC News series, heavy and continual use of marijuana can possibly become psychologically habit forming, cause psychotic derangement, and produce genetic damage.

Treatment and rehabilitation

Treatment and rehabilitation programs in our country have been a finger in the dike, a Band-Aid of resources and token institutions to turn back a tidal wave. The scene is a loose scattering of specialized parole, methadone, and self-help or extramural programs for narcotics addicts, and several ineffectual federal prison hospital programs at Lexington, Kentucky, and Forth Worth, Texas. The only comprehensive rehabilitation program for drug abusers is San Francisco's Center for Special Problems, which deals with the full gamut of drug abusers, including alcoholism, chronic cigarette smoking, amphetamine abuse, narcotics addiction, and so forth. "Treatment of drug abuse," says Dr. Joel Fort, "must include case-finding or early detection of illness through public-information programs; the availability of specialized programs; and detoxification and withdrawal treatment for those addicted to alcohol, sedatives, or narcotics, which ordinarily requires a period of in-patient hospital care." Still more important is long-term outpatient help, including group and individual psychotherapy, social-work services, vocational counseling and placement, and self-help approaches.

Lately, with the growing evidence that drug abuse is spreading throughout all segments of society, there is less talk about "getting the addicts off the streets" and more about what can be done to salvage them. One result is that the treatment of addicts is becoming a growth industry, with proponents of vying theories fiercely competing for public funds to support their enterprises. Treating addicts is a task for missionaries because, in the words of writer Marion Sanders, "it is heart-and-back-breaking and generally unprofitable work."

Synanon is a "therapeutic community" that operates on the theory that the addict can change his faulty behavior only by voluntarily joining a sternly disciplined but loving pseudo-family. His pseudo-parents are ex-addicts who have unique insight into his weaknesses and evasions and provide living proof that his habit can be overcome. The program emphasizes a "self-help" regime that includes hard physical work along with the now-familiar technique of group encounter, where members sit around a circle and blisteringly tear down each other's defenses to reach the core of personality. Eventually the new member phases into pensive re-evaluation and develops a sense of belonging and the strength to overcome drug dependence. Synanon has been criticized for wooing the addict away from drugs in exchange for permanent allegiance and duty to Synanon itself.

The Roosevelt Hospital Mental Health Center in New York City concentrates on rehabilitating the teenage drug offender by using the young addict's parents as the therapeutic group. Associate Director Saul Pavlin explains: "You cannot deal with addicts just as individuals. An addict usually comes from a family that is malfunctioning. If you send an addict back home without making changes in the family situation which produced his sickness, he'll go back in his old role." In Roosevelt's program a group of young addicts and their parents meet weekly at the center in an encounter type of setting. Interacting with each other provides them with a medium of communication otherwise not available. "One of the program's accomplishments," says Pavlin, "is that the families go past the point of saying that nothing is wrong, that it is only the addict who is sick."

New York City now operates a chain of therapeutic communities known as Phoenix House, as well as a growing network of storefront outposts aimed at reaching young people and staffed with a new civil service category, "addiction specialist." Part of the cost of operating Phoenix House is met by having residents who are on welfare contribute their welfare checks. The residents, approximately a thousand addicts, range in age from young adolescence to middle age. They do all the work, making a dilapidated building livable through a strenuous roach and rat extermination campaign, plastering, rewiring, and replumbing. Residents start out with the lowliest tasks such as KP and scrubbing toilets, but by demonstrating progress in personality change they can be promoted to clerical and administrative positions. There are three inviolable rules: no chemicals, no violence, no threats of violence. Infractions are dealt with by demotion to scrubbing toilets or by what are known as "learning experiences." The minor offender may incur a "haircut"—that is, temporary ostracism by the group—or have to wear a sign reading "I am a baby," or "I must stop testing this program."

A candidate for admission to Phoenix House must submit to an "induction encounter," which is designed to test his or her readiness for the program. The air is thick with cigarette smoke as a verbal fusillade is directed at a plump, swarthy girl named Dolores who has been in and out of several treatment centers.

"Talk about your hangups?" someone asks her.

"I don't have no hangups."

"You're a lying bitch. There's a lifetime ban on somebody like you. You're like cancer. You sound fucking poisonous."

"I think she's dealing."

"She's a spoiled brat with a cute little body."

"You know what a whore is?"

"I know. But I'm not a whore. Sure, I turned tricks when

my boyfriend didn't have money for dope. He got me tricks. But I'm no whore."

"Then why you go around balling everybody?"

Though her prospects of success seem dim, Dolores will probably be admitted whenever space is available. Most applicants are no more promising. Few addicts spontaneously seek salvation in a place where they know they will be under scrutiny. Many come because of pressure from parents, a court order, or the threat of losing their welfare checks.

Daytop Village in New York State is a full-service drug-rehabilitation center providing therapy, counseling, vocational training, and job placement—all designed not only to help the addict kick his habit but to become an integral and useful member of society. Daytop has a follow-up program to assist the addict who may be floundering and to nudge those who may be faltering in facing up to life. A play performed by Daytop residents became an off-Broadway hit in 1968 and offered persuasive evidence to hundreds of theatergoers that "The Concept" (its title) actually worked.

Prevention and early treatment

Clearly the soundest approach is not only to rehabilitate addicts, but to take intelligent preventive measures. In this respect community action can be more vital and effective than state agencies and hospitals, because it can deal with the root causes of addiction—the alienation and desocialization of the potential drug user.

A promising and exciting example of community concern is the Brotherhood Establishment in the Bronx, New York, started at James Monroe High School by a few students who were helping one another kick their habit. Their program is founded on the premise that "since kids turn each other on, they are the best ones to turn each other off." One part of their program deals with drug crisis at the school itself. If a student "ODs" in class, a "crisis unit" tries to find out what the student was using so that the medical staff can treat him quickly and correctly. If a student is suspected of being a drug abuser, he is referred to the BE for counseling and help. When the BE team, run entirely by students, comes to speak in class the teacher leaves the room, allowing students to talk without being afraid of betrayal. With the cooperation of school administrators, BE also conducts after-school counseling seminars for parents.

Another example of community involvement, in this case on the part of mothers, is MAD–Mothers Against Drugs–also in New York. One of the mothers explained: "We had so many pushers in the community and so many deaths were occurring as a result of the drug traffic, that we got upset and decided to do something about it." Among the things they did was to march to places which they knew were drug drops carrying signs that read "Drugs Are Sold Here" and "A Pusher Lives Here." MAD's program has five main points: visits to homes of teenagers in the neighborhood; advising parents who have addicted children; drug information workshops; school symposiums; and retreats.

Project DARE (Drug Abuse Research and Education) is unique in that it crusades to prevent drug use with the aid of junior and senior high school students who have never touched drugs. These teenagers are a living demonstration that young people don't have to use drugs to enjoy psychedelic art and hard rock or to have long hair. Their life style cannot be distinguished from that of other hip teenagers. The Stayns, DARE's rock group, performs wherever the kids congregate, radiating "togetherness" and true rock sounds–all without help from artificial stimulants.

Free clinics were the fruit of the "hip" culture in the sixties. Models of community action when run intelligently, they involve professionals and paraprofessionals, young and old, all on a volunteer basis, aimed at early treatment and prevention of drug abuse. Free clinics seek to help the young offender in his own environment by not preaching or pontificating, minimizing bureaucratic confusion and official snags, and creating a comfortable atmosphere of secure trust.

Legislation and law enforcement

In 1963 President Kennedy established the Advisory Commission on Narcotics and Drug Abuse, the first coherent drug-legislation arm in the United States. At that time criminal activity involving amphetamines, barbiturates, and hallucinogens was not covered at all by federal laws, and drug-law-enforcement officers were splintered among the various departments of the federal government and there were only a handful of narcotic agents stationed overseas. Since 1963 the situation has changed markedly, with one comprehensive federal statute encompassing all forms of drug abuse, and more than two thousand special agents have been assigned to enforce the law, all responsible to the Department of Justice.

Yet despite these advances, the legal forces against drugs are meager. Illegal drug traffic has become a multi-billion-dollar international industry with big-time overlords presiding over an army of sophisticated and ruthless troops and controlling a criminal empire around the globe. The factual story told in the book and movie *Serpico* illustrates the enormous financial power of drug chiefs to freeze drug enforcement by corruption.

The inadequacy of existing laws and penalties for narcotics traffickers is revealed in recent statistics which show that more than a quarter of those convicted at the federal level are receiving mere probation. Obviously the laws must be changed to remedy this situation. Legislation has been proposed that would provide for mandatory sentences permitting judges to deny bail under certain circumstances—for example, if the defendant has been previously convicted of a trafficking offense. Trafficking must be retaliated against with swift and sure penalties.

One of the most frustrating aspects of the drug problem is diversion. The General Accounting Office reported in 1972 that 90 per cent of the dangerous drugs sold illicitly are diverted from licensed sources—manufacturers, distributors, doctors, and pharmacists. Diversion includes leaks in the production phase, distribution, thefts, employee pilferage, unauthorized sales, and excessive prescribing and dispensing. In response to this problem, John R. Bartels, chief of the Drug Enforcement Administration, ordered new and stricter federal controls over the manufacture, distribution, and prescription of barbiturates.

Again, this is only a first step, and there remains a score of other legitimate drugs that are subject to abuse that should be placed under similar regulation. The existing practice of producing millions of pills far beyond the limits needed for legitimate uses, which are then shipped to Mexico and other neighboring countries only to be smuggled back into the United States for illicit sale, must be checked by imposing the strictest controls on purchaser qualifications and maintaining surveillance in these foreign nations to trace the cycle of the pills.

The passage of new laws and regulations is only half the effort. The other half, the task of law enforcement, is more formidable. In the United States there are over four hundred thousand doctors, veterinarians, pharmacists, and other professionals registered to handle controlled narcotics and drugs. Any one of them is a possible point of diversion into illicit channels. Compounding the difficulty is an absence of adequate coordination among the various agencies having jurisdiction over drug handlers at the state and federal level.

Realizing the need to coordinate the efforts of state and local agencies into a strong and cohesive campaign against drug diversion at the retail level, the Drug Enforcement Administration (DEA) has recently launched a pilot program—the Diversion Investigative Unit (DIU). Specially trained DEA agents, state policemen, and officers of the state boards of pharmacy have been relieved of other duties and assigned to DIU to concentrate solely on retail diversion. To insure the necessary legal support, county and district prosecutors have been asked to attend DEA-sponsored seminars to acquaint them with the fine points of convicting those accused of misappropriating controlled substances. Pilot programs in Alabama, Texas, and Michigan have proven successful and point the way to a new direction in law enforcement. Based on DIU success so far, a Senate committee on government operations has recommended that high priority should be given to establishing more

DIU types of projects, to bring to the war against pills the sophistication and coordination that law enforcement brings to the war on heroin.

A critical issue in the area of law enforcement is how to most effectively deploy our limited police resources. Should the police be reconnoitering teenage locations to make arrests for drug possession or should they be mobilized in a massive assault on the manufacture, cultivation, and distribution of drugs? I believe that society must concentrate on cutting up the roots of the drug forest instead of sending police to rake up the falling leaves. In 1962 the U.S. Supreme Court in *People v. Robinson* rendered the milestone decision that narcotics addiction, as such, must be medically treated, not penalized. Thus the court exempted from police business the pursuit of individuals who are under the influence of narcotics unless they are actually in the process of using drugs or have them in their possession. Future decisions may conceivably extend the *Robinson* rule to decriminalize even use and possession, limiting prosecution for drugs to illegal manufacture, cultivation, and distribution. Insofar as the juvenile courts are concerned, minors apprehended for dangerous drug use or possession should be referred for treatment, not punishment.

Understanding young people's attitude toward drugs

While both young and old take drugs, there are salient differences in their attitudes about the use of drugs. These differences are part of a larger antagonism which must be understood if we are to communicate with and educate our youth. By and large, adults take drugs as isolated individuals trying to cope with personal problems, or, as Shakespeare said of the sedative-aphrodisiac Mandragora in *Antony and Cleopatra*, "Give me to drink Mandragora–that I might sleep out this great gap of time." A Guatemalan Indian says, "Man must sometimes take a rest from his memory."

But for many young people drug use is an integral part of an emotional rejection of society, an attitude that is not individual but bound to a social consciousness. If adult society is to honestly accept responsibility and effectively cope with the problem of drug abuse, it must sensitively face this issue. Youth must be furnished with constructive ways to express their disavowal of adult values. Moreover, society must take the issue to heart, do some soul searching, and seriously question those values that alienate so many young people.

The generation gap is also obstructed by radically different philosophies on the use of mild mind-altering psychedelics such as marijuana. When Margaret Mead suggested that such substances should be legalized, Governor Claude Kirk of Florida furiously denounced her as a "dirty old lady." Older people tend to find the idea of altering one's consciousness as repugnant and unwholesome. Yet millions of young people do so without any qualms. One recent study, for example, indicated that 33 per cent of Californians between the ages of sixteen and twenty-nine use marijuana. Mild psychedelics are, for the young, mental journeys to voluptuous sensuousity and higher self-discovery.

The issue to be resolved is not who is right but whether those who think they are right have either the right or the widom to impose their convictions on others through legislation. We must recognize that an element of puritanism exists in drug legislation and public policy, which denies not only pleasure and any unusual state of mind, but also any nonpragmatic endeavor. An element of fear pervades present drug legislation—fear of the unknown and the unpredictable. A society that stresses a mechanical, perfunctory, well-ordered, and controlled life fears a chemically altered state of mind. What society must do is rationally, scientifically, and definitively proceed to divide drugs into harmful and nonharmful status. By placing moderate marijuana use outside the law, while hypocritically indulging in tobacco and alcohol, which cause cancer, heart disease, cirrhosis, and drunk driving, the older generation undermines its legal and moral authority over the young, creating conflicts between youth and law-enforcement officers that, in the case of middle-class youngsters, would not ordinarily exist. Young people see the illegality of marijuana as a tool which the police use against them.

Dabbling in drugs is a permanent part of our society, and we must unite to handle this phenomenon. Criminal penalties for drug use will not intimidate young people. Deeper research is needed in exploring the link between mind and chemicals. The real frontier of research lies in the human brain.

19 • Juvenile Courts and Laws

Juvenile cases are given even lower priority than traffic and misdemeanor cases.
—Anthony M. Platt,
The Child Savers: The Invention of Delinquency

Tens of thousands of dollars are spent each year to study the causes of crime; millions are spent on bricks and mortar and steel to confine adults in jails and prisons. The lawmakers of this land should realize that they might better spend more of this on preventive measures, and the practical place to begin is with the children who appear in juvenile courts.

The philosophy of juvenile justice

Every juvenile code in the land should be emblazoned with these words: "The juvenile court cannot substitute for the family in helping a child develop into a stable adult." Neither the Spartan gymnasium, the Russian creches, the Israeli kibbutz, nor scientifically run childrens' homes have been able to successfully duplicate the special ambiance of the family, which nurtures a bundle of instincts into a civilized human being. The juvenile court judge is not a father, a runaway house is not a home, a camp matron is not a mother, and a juvenile court counselor is not an older brother. No matter how capable they may be, all these people are functionaries of the state, enforcers of standardized rules, constrained by institutional controls, and bureaucratically bound to an impersonal organization. Pious legislative claims that the juvenile court simulates or approximates "the care and custody of the family" should be deleted from our statutes because it is incapable of replacing family care and affection.

In its objectives and aspirations, the juvenile court must reaffirm its primary responsibility: protecting the welfare of the community by any means legitimately at its disposal. Frequently, as for example in California's Welfare and Institutions Code, the law will stipulate that the court has the joint purpose of advancing the welfare of the minor and protecting the best interest of the community, with the implication that these aims are always consistent. They often are not. In the case of the totally alienated young sociopath, society's best interest may have to come before that of the minor. The jurisdictional principle which must be emphasized is that the court is concerned first and foremost with protecting the community from dangerous behavior.

On the surface the juvenile court seems to have a firm purpose, but behind the facade it hovers in an ambivalent limbo, not sure whether it is a benign paternal agency seeking to rehabilitate wayward youngsters or a vindictive tribunal ready to inflict harsh punishment. A tug-of-war rages, sometimes subtle and subterranean but more often caustically open, between prosecutors and police on one side and social workers and probation officers on the other. If juvenile crime rates continue to soar and public confidence in rehabilitation continues to be eroded away by skepticism and fear, the scales may tilt decisively toward making juvenile court a carbon copy of the adult court, with teenagers being treated no differently than adults, subjected to the same standards, and banished to similar prisons.

Underlying this tug-of-war is a fundamental conflict over a minor's accountability to society. The punitive-minded faction, strictly applying the traditional Judeo-Christian concept of free will, holds that the minor who has committed a felony should be responsible to the same degree as an adult. They are skeptical about the benefits of rehabilitation. "Get the young robbers and rapists off the streets and behind bars for a long time," says one police sergeant. "Never mind this coddling nonsense of 'home on probation' so he can rob and rape again the next day." Rehabilitation is seen as a farce, a prohibitively expensive luxury, and an indulgence at the expense of the community, costing untold injury to lives and property.

Proponents of sociological and medical concepts of human behavior hold that the juvenile offender should be afforded special dispensation because his criminal behavior stems from socioeconomic disadvantages or emotional maladjustment. If they discuss free will at all, they say it is impaired in a minor—as it is in an insane person—because of an immature mind, and therefore the minor should not be held fully accountable. They feel that minors, properly treated, will eventually become contributing members of society, and that any community which does not provide its wayward children with proper therapy will inevitably suffer the effects of self-inflicted wounds. In the long run, they insist, by sending children to grim prisonlike institutions society is only aggravating the problem, for when the children come out they will surely be permanently entrenched in crime.

In my own view, it is unrealistic to pin *all* one's hopes on rehabilitation. A human being is a bundle of habits and needs that have been forged over many years, and attempts to change them by a few hours of talk with a psychologist each week is not going to work in every case. In 1967 sociologist Robert Martinson began to analyze every known rehabilitation experiment; after compiling his results in two encyclopedic volumes, he concluded that nothing is guaranteed to work. In January 1973, the National Advisory Commission on Criminal Justice Standards and Goals pessimistically reported that all juvenile institutions should be closed because they are such miserable failures; the Commission feels community programs are a better answer. But the experiments analyzed by Martinson don't give us much hope for success through parole, probation, work furlough, and halfway houses, which are usually the programs that constitute "community corrections."

The American Friends Service Committee, in its report *Struggle for Justice,* concluded that greater use of probation, indeterminate sentences, small cottages, and halfway houses has failed to retard the growth of crime, and prescribed a massive onslaught on the social environment that produces juvenile delinquency. My own view is that rehabilitation can and does work in many cases, and should remain our main response to the youthful offender. But I also believe that it will not work in all cases, and that dangerous offenders must be imprisoned to protect society. Since the social sciences and the psychiatric disciplines are still so new and unproved, we cannot trust them to deal exclusively with young sociopaths, at least not outside the walls of a secure institution.

Treating hard-core youthful offenders harshly may also have a deterrent effect on their cronies and followers. If gang members know they can no longer get probation for armed robbery or serve only eighteen months for murder, they might not be quite so cavalier in their attitudes toward the law. If the leaders of today's marauding street gangs are given stiff sentences and taken out of the community, perhaps some lives will be saved and perhaps some gangs will collapse. In the fifties in New York City, for example, when the Cape Man, the Twinny Brothers, and Tony Bavimo were removed from the community, their respective gangs fluttered for a while like headless chickens and then folded.

But recognizing the need to remove certain young malefactors from society does not relieve the juvenile justice system of the responsibility of trying to rehabilitate them or treating them compassionately. Restraint and discipline are not necessarily incompatible with rehabilitation—a good parent uses discipline along with love to help children mature. Totally alienated young offenders usually respect toughness in other people, and tend to look down on law-enforcement representatives who try to appease them or act obsequious. Thus a juvenile court judge who appears to be as tough as a good Marine Corps drill instructor and yet obviously and sincerely is willing to help the minor, treats him or her with respect and dignity, shows care and concern, gives compassion and love—this judge will win the minor's respect. This respect, bolstered by confinement in a secure but not oppressive institution and some solid attempts at rehabilitation, may finally help the minor cope with his problems and re-enter society with a changed attitude. Preventive programs in the community remain our best bet to reduce or redirect gang activity, but judicial toughness combined with fairness can play an important role.

Most juvenile offenders, however, are not confirmed sociopaths and do not represent an immediate or continuing threat to society—*if* they are helped. For them, community-based rehabilitation may be effective. It cannot be repeated too often that we can expect more success in rehabilitation programs based in the offender's immediate community than in a prison community, even if his area is a slum; but before the slum community can really rehabilitate its delinquent youths effectively, society must first rehabilitate the slums, because in the ghetto, delinquency may not be deviant behavior, but rather completely in accord with subcultural patterns of crime, militancy, and revolution.

On the premise that the protection of society is the primary responsibility of juvenile justice, in each case the juvenile court judge should first ascertain whether the minor truly represents —in legally technical terms—a "clear and present danger to the community" or an "imminently probable source of seriously disruptive behavior" by assessing such criteria as the minor's past record, the nature of his current offense, and the strength of his ties with family, school, church, and employment. If the minor is considered to be dangerous according to these standards, he must be removed from the community for rehabilitation in a secure institution. All other juvenile offenders should, if possible, be referred for treatment in community-based programs.

State legislators must provide more funds for rehabilitation of the juvenile offender, both in the community and in institutions. At present, state governments invariably allocate the largest proportion of their judicial and correctional budgets to the adult system, which means that a larger amount will be spent on the juvenile offender when—almost inevitably—he comes through the court later as an adult. Clearly, this represents a serious inversion of priorities; it is with the more malleable young that we should make the larger investment.

Finally, lawmakers have a duty to realistically assess the nature and extent of the contribution the juvenile court can make to the solution of the larger problem of crime and delinquency. Whatever goals early supporters of the juvenile court movement may have had, with the rising tide of youthful crime there is an urgent need for more effective techniques and resources than the court alone can provide. Morally, society has an obligation to deal with the root causes of juvenile crime instead of burying its head in the sand by resorting to more walls and cages to lock alienated children out of sight. Ultimately, as a nation, we are culpable for the moral malaise of our young.

Too many juvenile trials

Unraveling the mass of cases coming into juvenile court for trial, they can generally be classified in two categories: juveniles who have committed acts recognized as crimes in the adult court, and those who have committed what are considered exclusively juvenile offenses. The latter category is further divided into violations of specific ordinances—such as curfew, truancy, and alcohol or tobacco possession—and cases in which no specific law has been broken but in which the minor is designated as "beyond control," "incorrigible," "ungovernable," "runaway" or "in need of supervision."

The number of children coming to trial on noncriminal charges is substantial. Criminologist William Sheridan, in his article "Juveniles Who Commit Noncriminal Acts," says a conservative estimate is that this group comprises 26 per cent of the total number of cases coming into the juvenile courts of the nation. At least a third of the approximately forty thousand cases that came to trial in Los Angeles Juvenile Court in 1974, for example, did not involve criminal acts.

This situation is detrimental both to the children and to the courts. The truant or "minor in need of supervision" suffers the stigma of being labeled delinquent, although no criminal law has been violated. Moreover, such offenders are usually detained at juvenile hall, where they are subject to the corrupting influence of truly hard-core delinquents. And if they are institutionalized and given long-term therapy or rehabilitation, these minors will probably end up permanently associating with the professional criminals who are their fellow inmates. For its part, the juvenile court, already frantically trying to deal with a chronic overload of serious criminal cases, finds itself overwhelmed by these relatively petty matters that are brought to trial. Every additional case the juvenile court must handle diminishes the quality of litigation, detracts from the concentration needed for serious offenders, and strains treatment facilities. Finally, the taxpayers are also victimized. If more people were aware of the thousands of tax dollars used to pay for trials dealing with curfew violations, beer drinking, bubble-gum swiping, frivolous pranks, truancy, unruliness, and school shenanigans, they would be marching on the courthouse in protest.

Obviously, a way must be found to rationally limit the juvenile caseload to a manageable number. Most noncriminal matters and borderline criminal acts should be screened out of the trial process. At present, probation departments are responsible for filing petitions for trial in juvenile court, and why they file thousands of petty matters can only be guessed. Is it because bureaucracies by their very nature tend to enlarge their jurisdiction over whatever matters they are responsible for? Is it that the more children a probation department sends to juvenile court, the larger and more powerful is its role in the juvenile justice system, and in society? Surely this is part of the explanation. Another reason is that the probation department may be oversolicitous, or apprehensive, about the children in its jurisdiction and doesn't quite know how to handle them. Deputy District Attorney James Blatt of Los Angeles charges that "probation sometimes files matters for trial because of lack of legal expertise." For example, in one recent case the Los Angeles probation department sought murder convictions against eleven youngsters who were part of a group aboard a bus during a shooting, although there was no evidence at all against ten of them. The trial of these eleven minors dragged on for weeks before the foregone verdict of not guilty was returned for everyone except the actual gunman.

Noncriminal juvenile offenders should be diverted from the courts to other social agencies and given rehabilitative assistance without the ritual of a trial. The juvenile justice system should not be so inflexibly bound to the Supreme Court's *Gault* ruling–requiring due process for minors–that it loses its common sense. Probation departments, or even schools if it is a school matter, can conduct informal hearings in cases of minors charged with lesser offenses and, if necessary, prescribe suitable disciplinary action. The procedures mandated by the *Gault* ruling would not be required in such hearings because the minor would not be facing incarceration or unduly restrictive controls. The only time a court trial is needed is when the offense is a criminal violation or there are indications that the minor should be removed from the home or placed in detention.

As long as we insist on full due process in handling every juvenile act of misconduct, there can be no workable solution for reducing the onerous workload of the juvenile justice system. In Northern Europe lesser categories of delinquency are generally handled administratively, and in England 95 per cent of all criminal cases are disposed of by justices of the peace. As Supreme Court Chief Justice Warren Burger has observed: "To take these problems out of our conventional judicial process calls for some basic rethinking. But the trend . . . is the other way. Supreme Court holdings are gradually converting juvenile courts, for example, into full-blown criminal courts. What the juvenile courts need is not more but fewer trappings of legal procedure and judicial formalism. The system requires breathing room and flexibility to survive. On the present course, the juvenile system is doomed."

Alternatives to trial for noncriminal offenders

Primarily in response to the need to divert substantial numbers of juvenile cases away from the juvenile court, Los

Angeles County is planning a Juvenile Justice Center, which will bring together representatives from the juvenile court, probation department, police department, city schools, district attorney's and public defender's offices, and the Department of Community Services. All juvenile offenders from an experimental target area will go through a screening process by a joint committee of school, police, and probation officials.

Each agency, instead of reviewing the minor's case in isolation, will work with the others to arrive at the most effective procedure to protect the community and rehabilitate the youth. Their recommendations will be sent to the committee chairman, representing the probation department, to be used as the basis for deciding whether to send the minor to juvenile court or to public or private agencies for treatment.

The community will participate in the center through a Community Advisory Board composed of a cross-section of residents of the target area. Thus parents and students will be able to contribute to the philosophy and operation of the center and through it receive attention to community needs.

The Juvenile Justice Center, which will cost an estimated $737,000, hopes to pay for itself. By designating test and control areas, the center's effectiveness will be measured by comparing reductions in repeated offenses by both first and hard-core offenders, and also by the total number of juvenile arrests in both areas. An independent contractor will collect and analyze data from the two areas over a one-year period to evaluate how well the center fulfills its objectives. If the evaluation shows positive results, the test area will serve as a model for similar centers around the state.

Other types of community-based programs are already in operation, for example FIND (Friends in Deed), which is located in Auburn, California. Originally designed to help young drug addicts, it was so successful that the probation department is now referring all types of young offenders to it, from joy riders to girls who mug truck drivers. The central concept of the program is creative dynamics, a technique that channels young energy into creative crafts such as ceramics, sculpturing, leatherwork, and macramé. The craftsmen are provided with a sales outlet to earn money from their creations. Another popular feature of FIND is its "natural high" game, in which youngsters are helped to achieve the effect of using mind-altering substances without ingesting anything, by utilizing theories and techniques presented in Andrew Weil's book, *Natural Mind.* The youngsters do yoga exercises, breathing in smooth cadence, and then, through the catalyst of a narrative medium, they embark on a glittering fantasy trip in their imagination. Of the hundreds of young offenders diverted to FIND, in three years only one participant has been in trouble with the police, and even this case was dropped.

The Seventh Step Organization, run almost exclusively by ex-felons, has established a number of diversionary programs throughout the United States. In Santa Barbara, California, for example, the county probation office sends young offenders to a Seventh Step board composed of five ex-felons, who question the minor and then decide on the best program of rehabilitation for him. At the first session the board members challenge the minor's ideas—debunking the glamour of crime as presented on television, relating the nitty gritty of prison life, recounting the degrading truth about being an ex-con—in order to destroy any stereotypes he may have about a life of crime. The youngster is then assigned to a Helper-Helpee Program, a one-to-one approach, to be guided through the organization's seven steps of improvement; the first step is facing the truth about the need to change, and the last is pledging to help others. In its three years of operation, the Seventh Step claims a recidivism rate of only 23 per cent, making it enormously successful when compared to prison performance.

The city of Compton, California, has established a Community Service Center to which a minor who admits guilt to a petty offense can be referred to be assigned some kind of community work as punishment for his misconduct. His assignment might be cleaning city streets, trimming park lawns, or assisting elderly people. The program is operated on a voluntary basis—that is, the youth must agree to enrollment in the program instead of a court trial. Along the same lines, the Los Angeles Fire Department has agreed to help fight juvenile crime by making a thousand firemen available as counselors for minors diverted away from court. Each fireman will spend several hours a week with a young offender, trying to guide him in the right direction. Usually the kids are excited about the prospect of hanging around a fire station, and have a certain amount of respect for firemen, so they tend to be receptive to such guidance.

These are only some of the constructive programs that exist to help ease the juvenile court caseload and help young offenders in the community. They should become an integral part of the juvenile justice system throughout the country.

Juvenile court judges and court procedures

While most presiding officers in the juvenile court are able, the system would benefit from higher requirements for appointment and higher compensation in order to attract persons with outstanding credentials. In light of the legal ramifications of the *Gault* ruling, a law degree is now a necessity for hearing officers. The current smorgasbord arrangement of having referees, commissioners, and judges performing identical functions under different titles should be phased out and replaced by one designation for all adjudicators: juvenile court judge. More members of the lower and working classes are needed on the bench to replace some of the predominantly upper-middle-class judges, who tend to see lower-class life in terms of abstractions and generalities. More trial judges should come from the ranks of the working people so that they will have greater empathy and compassion for disadvantaged citizens.

Instead of being appointed by a higher court, the presiding judge of the juvenile court should be elected and should serve a minimum of five years. Judge William Hogoboom, a talented and compassionate jurist, spent two years learning about juvenile justice systems throughout the world after his appointment as presiding judge of the Juvenile Court in Los Angeles, only to be appointed as presiding judge of the Superior Court at that point. Obviously, in two years one can only begin to get a feeling for the special needs of the juvenile offender, and the system should not permit a man as capable as Judge Hogoboom to be whisked away so soon. This is especially true when the appointee comes from the ranks of judges in the adult courts. It may take years to adapt to the different approach necessary in juvenile court.

To reduce the long waiting periods for witnesses who come to testify in juvenile court, the judge should have those present take the stand even though all the necessary witnesses are not present and even though it may mean the case will last more than one day. Since the testimony is transcribed, the lawyers and the judge can refer to previous testimony, so it should present no hardship. Also, present requirements that the trial be held in the jurisdiction where the accused minor lives should be changed so that the trial may be held in the community where the crime occurred, eliminating the need for witnesses to travel long distances to testify. According to the Witness Project pioneered by Judge Joan Dempsey Klein, the rate of conviction in adult criminal cases is falling off due to the fact that many witnesses refuse to appear because they are inadequately compensated and often lose days of pay on their jobs as well. Further, some crimes are not even reported because people know that if they report a crime it will obligate them to be a witness. The situation is much worse in juvenile court because there is absolutely no compensation for witnesses, and they can expect a much longer waiting period before actually taking the stand. To remedy this problem, the state legislatures should guarantee witness fees for juvenile court appearances and require employers to compensate witnesses who must take off from work for juvenile court duty.

As for the required appearance of parents in court for the trial of their child, much more vigorous enforcement of this responsibility is necessary. The existing policy of allowing parents to sign a waiver form excusing their appearance contributes to delinquent conduct by parents. No trial should proceed unless at least one parent, and preferably both, is present in the court. The most extreme proposal for parental responsibility was made in Camden, New Jersey, where some legislators want parents placed in jail for the offenses committed by their children. This proposal, however, is of questionable constitutionality and might actually do more harm than good. If the father of seven children, for example, were jailed he could be prevented from earning a living and his family would be forced to go on welfare. Certainly that would not help the cause of juvenile justice.

A significant segment of legal opinion holds that the juvenile court should be exempt from the evidentiary rules and practices of the adversary system that are essential in adult trials. They say formal rigmarole and elaborate machinery of procedure interfere with the primary task of the juvenile court, which is rehabilitation, and that allowing an attorney to make technical objections disrupts the desired informality of the proceedings. Appellate courts have generally upheld the constitutionality of the informal approach on the ground that juvenile courts are not criminal courts.

If it were true—as in theory it is—that a juvenile court conviction did not lead to punishment or affect a young person's future, then relaxation of the rules of evidence in juvenile trials might be acceptable. However, too often the punishment given to a delinquent is in reality no different from that imposed on adults found guilty in criminal trials, and the consequence to his career no less devastating. On the premise that a juvenile conviction is in fact a serious consequence, the juvenile hearing should be governed by the same evidentiary safeguards that apply in adult criminal court. Rules of evidence are not merely technical or historical invocations, but have a sound basis in human experience, and are meant to maximize the reliability of information admitted into proof.

A number of juvenile court judges throughout the country report that they are satisfied with the operation of their courts even though they must abide by the formal rules of evidence. The proper places for flexibility are in the approaches of the attorneys toward their clients, the role of the law, and the filing of petitions—not in the rules of evidence, which are merely guideposts to the truth.

The role of attorneys

In the landmark *Gault* decision, the Supreme Court declared: "A proceeding where the issue is whether a child will be found to be delinquent and subjected to the loss of his liberty for years is comparable to a felony prosecution. The juvenile needs the assistance of counsel to cope with the problems of law, to make skilled inquiry into the facts, to insist upon regularity of the proceedings, and to ascertain whether he has a defense and to prepare and submit it. The child requires the guiding hand of counsel at every step in the proceedings against him."

But even though the Supreme Court conferred upon minors the right to counsel in juvenile proceedings, it failed to give lawyers additional guidance on their proper role in juvenile court. Therefore, decisions about the proper role of counsel must be made by each individual attorney or the state legislature in each case. Many authorities believe the lawyer's obligations toward his juvenile clients do not differ from his responsibilities to his adult criminal defendants, and that he ought to play the role of unyielding advocate at all stages of the proceeding. Others believe that an adversary posture should be followed only during the fact-finding phase of the case but that the attorney should join the bench at the time of disposition. Still others believe that the concept of guardianship requires consideration of the child's general welfare as well as his legal rights, and hence the lawyer should modify his advocate's role.

In Los Angeles and New York City, attorneys for juvenile clients have adopted the unbending role of advocate, strictly urging all the rights and privileges of their clients at every stage of the proceeding. In Indiana the public defender combines two functions in the attorney, adding to advocate the role of "guardian" or "social worker" in some cases. In Texas, seemingly in breach of the privilege of confidentiality, a survey revealed that 76 per cent of the attorneys associated with juvenile court would report any admission of guilt by a juvenile client to the judge, believing it is their duty to present all facts that come to their attention, including any incriminating statements. (It should be noted, however, that many of the respondents to the survey were associated with the district attorney's office.) This view would seem to be counter to the intent of the *Gault* ruling, which recognizes the minor's need for counsel to help prepare a defense and to assist the minor in the proceeding every step of the way. But it is consistent with the "parens patriae" function of the juvenile court—that is, to help a young offender change his ways and to protect society, not merely to obtain an acquittal even if the client has admitted guilt.

It is my belief that until claims for rehabilitation of juvenile offenders become a reality rather than a fiction, an attorney is obligated to play the role of staunch advocate for his juvenile clients. If the consequences of a juvenile conviction are as severe as they are for an adult, the minor should not be denied the rights of due process merely because of his age. In certain kinds of cases, however—such as glue sniffing or other activities that are harmful primarily to the juvenile—the attorney must be flexible enough to adjust his advocate's role so that he makes sure his client gets the best therapy possible. For the present, at least, there should be no universal policy in regard to juvenile court lawyers. In each case the attorney must make a determination as to how far to depart from traditional advocacy, taking into consideration the nature of the offense, the quality of the rehabilitative programs, the future handicap to the minor, the welfare of society, and the attitudes of the minor and his family.

In dealing with juvenile matters, the lawyer may find himself in the position of a personal ombudsman to his client's family, often in the middle of family disputes. He will encounter problems that his legal education never even mentioned, because little or no concern has been expressed in traditional law-school courses for such important extra-legal considerations as family dynamics. Even more reprehensible, scant attention is given to juvenile law in most of America's law schools. In the face of escalating juvenile crime rates, it is time for our law schools to lend their resources in solving this serious social problem. At the very least, juvenile law courses should be required for all freshman law students, and all applicants to the bar should be examined in juvenile law. Inexplicably, juvenile justice has always been shunted aside as the ugly duckling of the legal profession. We can no longer afford this attitude.

The formation of a juvenile bar association would be a worthwhile innovation, affording attorneys who practice in juvenile court an opportunity to discuss their problems with juvenile court judges, probation officers, and other experts so that they could share ideas and learn from one another.

Also helpful would be the establishment of juvenile court clinics modeled upon the facility recently opened in Boston. Meant to provide a therapeutic milieu associated with the juvenile court and to serve as a liaison between attorneys, minors, and the juvenile justice system, a juvenile court clinic operates in behalf of the child so that his particular offense can be better understood in relation to his psychosocial development and his home environment.

At the Boston juvenile court clinic a team of professional psychologists, psychiatrists, and social workers skilled in dealing with delinquent children formulate a diagnosis and report to court with recommendations for treatment. The clinic works closely with probation officers, helping to clarify the psychiatric and social status of the youth and his family.

The clinic is extremely useful to overburdened juvenile court lawyers in that its reports highlight the psychosocial aspects of each case and help the lawyer to prepare his cases by providing well-developed treatment plans for his clients. For example, an offender charged with breaking and entering may be a drug addict, which the clinic can verify. Then, citing the clinic's report, the lawyer can show that his client has been accepted in a drug-treatment program, which may prompt the court to place him in the program rather than merely put him in a detention facility. If a lawyer feels that his client is in need of therapy, he can request a clinic referral either before or after trial and can, in fact, suggest that the client's entire family be referred for help. In short, the clinic helps the attorney as both a social and legal advocate.

Pruning our juvenile laws

Laws proliferate in the United States with the maddening abandon of crabgrass. All the substantive laws of France are contained in just one volume, while California—with less than half the French population—has a tangled web of ninety-nine volumes of statutes, in addition to a legal tower of babel from federal, county, and municipal lawmakers. For the sake of efficiency, if nothing else, we must simplify some of our categories of criminal law as they relate to minors. For example, if an adult is chronically absent from work he will normally be dismissed, and that is the end of the matter. But if a child misses school repeatedly, he is a truant and could face a court trial and possible confinement.

Truancy in England is handled much more simply. Authorities visit the school to see if the problem can be solved at that level. If it cannot be, the youngster is placed in a state-operated hostel where he lives with six to eleven other children under the supervision of a professional social worker. He must either resume school or go to work, but in either case he lives a normal life, totally accepted by society, and is spared the embroilment of a trial. This procedure is a result of the Children and Young Persons Act, passed by Parliament in 1970, a comprehensive but simple set of statutes dealing with young persons. It is a legal concept that should be copied by state legislatures in this country.

Statutes that make criminal such essentially self-destructive acts as glue sniffing and paint inhalation should be removed from the juvenile codes, as should the offense of being drunk. More than thirty-six thousand cases of juvenile inebriation cluttered up the Los Angeles court calendar in 1974. Acts which represent a health hazard to the individual or a nuisance to society should be handled under joint civil-medical auspices. A kid who is sniffing glue is doing enough harm to himself without being saddled with a criminal record because of it. Any acts that represent a personal problem more than a social threat should be decriminalized. To safeguard individual rights, the minor's case could be subject to judicial review if a program of therapy exceeded a certain period of time, possibly thirty days. The details need far more refinement, of course, but this is the direction our juvenile laws should take.

There is also the problem of interpreting and applying the laws fairly and uniformly throughout the country. A Rand Corporation study in the early seventies found that in California one offender who stole millions of dollars worth of equipment received a forty-day sentence—as did another who stole only a can of spinach in a jurisdiction only a few miles away. The case of Frank La Vorr, the almost definitive "all-American boy"—track star, top student—attracted headlines. He was convicted in Virginia for possessing twenty-five grains of marijuana and received a twenty-five-year prison sentence. On the same day in New York and Los Angeles, several teenagers were sent home on probation for the same offense. The law should not vary so flagrantly from place to place. The state legislature has the authority to impose rational limits to judicial discretion, and a Uniform Sentencing Code could compile a series of guidelines for judges to use at the sentencing stage or disposition hearing in juvenile court.

20 • Detention and Rehabilitation

A hundred and twenty-five bucks buys a shotgun.
—Saying in Missouri prisons, where inmates are given $125 on their release

In the late sixties the Ford Foundation made a sizable grant to the Institute for the Study of Crime and Delinquency to develop a model treatment program for young offenders. In its report, *Design for Change,* the Institute concluded that the model youth correctional center would be located where the problems are, "right in the middle of high-delinquency areas." Ideally it would accommodate forty-eight offenders in three separate living areas and look, from the outside, more like a motel or apartment house than a detention center. Qualified wards would be permitted to go out in the community while under treatment.

The President's Commission on Law Enforcement recommended a similar community-based program based upon the same logic, with educational and vocational activities carried on in the community or in concert with community agencies. In both proposals the focus shifts from placing offenders in distant high-security institutions to working with them in a carefully planned combination of control and treatment. Institutional restraint is preserved but in a flexible and community-oriented context.

Under both plans the modern barbarism of lumping all juvenile offenders together without considering age differences would be ended. Anyone with a minimal sense of social responsibility recognizes that a seven-year-old runaway does not belong with teenaged robbers, rapists, and murderers. Runaways and other noncriminal minors should be housed in separate institutions.

Variations on a theme

Boise, Idaho, has a model correctional facility divided into four sections, ranging from maximum security, through moderate and minimum, to a section in which the inmates have free movement. The Los Angeles Central Juvenile Hall has introduced a similar multi-unit system based on age and type of behavioral problem. A minor with a serious emotional disturbance, for instance, is sent to the intensive-care unit. Ideally, young offenders should be housed in smaller, separate facilities categorized by age and the nature of problem to be treated, rather than in different wings of a large institution, but in the meantime existing institutions can be reorganized into specialized departments.

Undoubtedly the most encouraging experiment in juvenile rehabilitation is being carried out in Massachusetts. In 1970 the Massachusetts Department of Youth Services closed its juvenile jails, where about eight hundred had been kept in maximum-security facilities. Then the counties closed their juvenile halls, and both state and county facilities were replaced by an innovative program of rehabilitation.

Under the old system, Massachusetts had been spending $15,000 to $25,000 each year to institutionalize a minor. Instead of perpetuating this system, the state decided to use its funds to extend to all families the option that had been open only to middle-class and upper-class families. Now virtually all problem youngsters are placed—at state expense—in boarding schools, free private schools, and specialized foster and group homes. Some teenagers have been placed in university dormitories where they receive tutorial attention and individual supervision from qualified college students. Amherst, for example, has a number of such residents.

Massachusetts still maintains state residential facilities for juveniles, but it has fewer than six hundred in custody, about half the number in Los Angeles Juvenile Hall. An additional hundred and twenty-five youngsters deemed by the Massachusetts courts to be truly violent are held in maximum-security lockups, where they receive intensive psychiatric treatment at an annual cost of $20,000 to $40,000.

According to a 1974 study by Harvard University, the Massachusetts system has cut in half the number of repeaters. Some increase in the rate of recidivism is expected over an extended period, but there is every sign that it will never reach the old rate of 48 per cent.

A halfway house is any relatively small facility, either residential or nonresidential, usually located in or near a city. Persons participating in the program take part in the daily life of the open community, either working or going to school "outside." Halfway houses may be publicly or privately supported, oriented along psychotherapeutic or reality-based lines, and administered under secular or religious auspices. The residents are expected to undergo a group experience of limited duration. The halfway house stands literally halfway between the community and the institution, and may serve persons who are released from an institution as well as those received directly from court.

A variation of the halfway house is the halfway-out program, designed to assist the person who is ready to leave an institution but needs special help in readjusting to society. An apt parallel is drawn by criminologists Oliver Keller and Benedict Alper between this process in the life of a convicted offender and the decompression chamber through which the deep-sea diver passes in order to gradually adjust to sea level pressure before being permitted to surface completely.

Small population is an essential ingredient of the halfway house. Some houses accommodate as few as ten boys or girls, yet others may have facilities for thirty, while the pioneer Dismas House, one of the best-known halfway houses in the

United States, has as many as sixty residents. Opinions differ as to what kind of persons should be referred to halfway houses. While the primary concern is with the youthful offender, precise age limitations are by no means universal, and many places house teenagers along with octogenarians. Almost any kind of physical setting is suitable. While some facilities are conventional in appearance, others are housed in private houses, converted motels, YMCA's, remodeled schools, an Odd Fellows Hall, a former parish house, a beach club, and a nursing home. The effectiveness of halfway houses is currently a subject of lively disputation.

A study of the Elizabeth Fry Center, a California halfway house for young women who have been paroled, released from institutions, or just out of luck shows a recidivism rate of only 28 per cent in contrast to the 50 per cent rate for the female inmate population as a whole. There are six halfway houses for women in California. Some are state-run and restrictive; others, like Elizabeth Fry, are liberal, with few rules. In the words of one resident: "Nobody is on your back here." There are no curfews, no room searches, no signs outside the building. The residents are asked to pay twenty-eight dollars a week for room, board, and counseling, and each woman is asked to attend one group-therapy session a week. During the day some residents work—as nurses' aides, waitresses, or in factories. The majority of the young women are in their late teens or early twenties.

A young Mexican-American, Amanda Sanchez, illustrates the success of the halfway house. She came from a broken home where she was mistreated by her parents and had to take care of her six younger brothers and sisters. Eventually she became a heroin addict and then a burglar to support her drug use. She spent her adolescence in and out of correctional institutions, never receiving an academic education. At eighteen she heard about the center while incarcerated at the Correctional Institution for Women. Eager to be paroled, she wrote a letter to the Elizabeth Fry Center and was accepted.

One of the unusual features of this halfway house is that there are no criteria whatsoever for screening applicants.

Young women are taken in on a first-come, first-serve basis. Unlike programs that accept only women showing potential for success, EFC accepts almost anyone. Amanda lived at EFC different times in seasonal cycles, summers from EFC to the streets, in winter to jail, then back to EFC. For years she was a scrupulous recluse, refusing to talk with director Tom Nelson, but in 1968 she overdosed and it was Nelson and his wife who stood by her. "For the first time I noticed that I was hurting them," she said. "They were trying hard to help me. So I started fixing at the gas station rather than at the house, but I overdosed again and again. I died for four hours once." Eventually Amanda was able to break away from the bondage of heroin, and has stayed off drugs for over seven years. She now leads a self-sufficient life.

Numerous other young women have been helped to achieve a normal life in society because of their experience in a halfway house. In Pittsburgh the Nova House has utilized the concept of peer-group counseling to enhance its effectiveness. Former offenders who have gone straight counsel younger offenders, hoping to help them follow their own examples. The halfway house provides a family atmosphere that many young people have never experienced and which is not available in large correctional institutions. Piloted by the American Friends Service Committee as a progressive idea in penology, halfway houses should be supported by federal or state funds so that they may continue to perform their unique role.

Barry Harbison, disc jockey on station KSUE in Susanville, California, was on the air in January 1974, strumming his guitar and lazily singing the "Conservation-Center-Is-Closing Blues." "Ten million dollars to build her from the ground," he warbled, "Now the taxes we paid to get her made will be spent to tear her down." A minimum-security correctional facility, the Susanville Conservation Center was built to train its young inmates to fight fires and do other conservation work. "The closure doesn't make sense," says Susanville's mayor, Ivor Lanigar. "The state comes in here, spends ten and a half million dollars building the most modern correctional facility in the nation at the time, only nine years ago. Another six million is spent on furnishing the facility and on landscaping. And now the place is being shut down when crime is at an all-time high."

Penologists throughout America have cited the Susanville facility as the type of institution that can truly humanize corrections. Pleasantly landscaped, the grounds contain a baseball diamond, football field, basketball court, and, in winter, an ice-skating rink. The prison basketball team was a member of the Lassen County League, and Little League baseball teams played inside the prison walls for the entertainment of inmates. Streamlined indoor workshops and classrooms are the setting for courses in various trades, degree programs for high school and college, and intramural debating competition. But this ideal minimum-security institution was going to be torn down because of lack of inmates.

Fortunately, aroused legislators have learned about the proposed closure, and they have criticized the Department of Corrections for creating a shortage of prisoners to send to the institution through what they charge is a "promiscuous practice of paroling." Recently the Susanville center, though still slated for oblivion, received a stay of execution. It will tentatively remain open until future notice. In light of the fact that Susanville combines security with a radiantly versatile number of educational, ecological, and recreational programs, it might well be the model for the type of institution to be used to house hard-core delinquents and young sociopaths.

Job training

The delinquency rate in California is five times greater than it is in France, and one of the major reasons, aside from cultural differences, is the French emphasis on apprenticeship programs. Young people in correctional institutions in Paris are trained by master craftsmen, and many youths volunteer to extend their confinement so that they can complete their apprenticeships under the same master. Similar practices prevail in Israel, where vocational training is regarded as a primary weapon in closing the educational and social schism between African Israelis and their countrymen of European extraction.

Paul Bohem, principal of the boys' school at Los Angeles Central Juvenile Hall, has been urging the inauguration of apprenticeship programs in U.S. detention centers and camps. "But it shouldn't just be in the correctional system," he says. "A child should not have to be punished to learn a trade." In many European nations, the average age of students in apprenticeship programs is fifteen. Swiss law states succinctly that "every child at sixteen is either in school or in apprenticeship training."

There are apprenticeship programs in the United States, but few are for young people under eighteen, and they last only about six months. Unions, industry, government, and schools should insist that our child-labor laws be changed to provide apprenticeships for anyone who wants them. "We are an industrial society, yet people under eighteen are not allowed to work with heavy machinery," says Paul Bohem. "How can they learn it?" More must be changed than laws, however. In Europe there is a consistent and respected system of professional training as a way of life for all future citizens, not only as the cornerstone of the rehabilitation process. The word professional is applied to vocational pursuits as a means of imbuing trade students with a pride in their future careers.

Workman's Compensation Insurance laws are also an obstacle to hiring young people. An example is that of a sixteen-year-old who wanted to be a sign painter; after much pleading he was finally allowed to join the union and a small shop gave him a job, but because he was only sixteen the boy's Workmen's Compensation premiums were so high that his employer could not afford to keep him on, so he was let go. A year later he was caught committing a felony.

Beyond being trained for an occupation, a young offender must have help in obtaining employment when he is released if he does not return to school. Young or old, the ex-offender has tremendous obstacles in finding a secure place in society.

Correctional institutions must do more than put a youth back on the street—disoriented, discriminated against, and unable, because of the conditioning of confinement, to "discern between two donuts." The youth must be given skills and confidence in his ability to function, and assistance in finding suitable work. In England the national government finances job-training agencies that place young people in work during confinement to provide them with a decent start on the outside.

An encouraging community rehabilitation program is being carried out on an experimental basis at Long Island University in New York. Young parolees are given tuition, room and board, and an allowance for a full semester's work at the university in order to give them a sound basis on which to re-enter society after imprisonment. After a semester the parolees may continue at LIU, with the aid of counselors in obtaining part-time work, loans, or scholarship money. The most important aspect of the program is that the parolee is given all the privileges of full citizenship as well as responsibilities that go with those rights. This program, so far with less than a hundred participants, has had an 80 per cent success rate, in stark contrast with the normal 30 per cent for penitentiary parolees returning to society.

Full-service institutions

To be most effective, juvenile correctional facilities should be amply staffed with qualified psychiatrists, psychologists, and counselors specially trained at newly formed "rehabilitation academies." Full-time schools must function within the juvenile hall, with high-quality teachers and adequate funding for materials, and, beyond vocational and academic training, they should offer "self-image" courses aimed at widening young offenders' vistas, improving their confidence, and dispelling images of worthlessness.

Selective programs would allow inmates to visit and work in the community on a furlough basis. Boys in Camp Mendenhall in California, for example, may leave when there is a need for their services in fighting forest fires. The youngsters who volunteer for this work are trained by professional fire-fighters and go out in twenty-man crews when necessary.

Caviling critics maintain that all these programs are tremendously expensive and that society cannot afford to provide them—all it can afford is incarceration as a response to the juvenile crime problem. Yet from a cost-benefit angle, spending money on improving juvenile facilities is a comparative bargain. The Department of Commerce reports that in 1967—the latest figures accessible—Americans spent $36.6 billion on automobiles. Another $14.5 billion went for alcoholic beverages, and a whopping $9.2 billion was spent on tobacco products. In 1974 Americans pampered their pets to the sum of $2.5 billion. In contrast, according to the Department of Health, Education, and Welfare, "Total expenditures for 110,000 children locked up in reform schools was a meager $209 million dollars, less than the cost of one B-1 bomber." Far more research has been done (and more money spent) on raising hogs, chickens, or cucumbers than on solving the problem of our troubled youth. One reform official said, "Farmers have an effective lobby. Children in trouble have no one they can count on. If they had someone, they wouldn't be in trouble."

Simply spending money, however, is not the answer, nor is building new model structures. Coordination has to be tightened between diverse programs, both legal and social. The Los Angeles Department of Community Services lists more than six hundred programs, but many law-enforcement agencies ignore them. Instead, they set up their own, stretching resources to the vanishing point and functioning as a secondary probation department. This, says one county official, "aces out the community" from its proper role in helping combat juvenile crime.

No matter how much is done to the system, anyone with eyes knows the problem really lies on the outside. Dr. Hiawatha Harris, a nationally respected psychiatrist, says, "The older children in the juvenile justice system are manifesting the despair and apathy of their parents. There needs to be prevention—we need to find ways to prevent people from getting into the system, and that's going to mean a massive pragmatic thing, not only in financial outlay but in philosophical and spiritual commitment to the preservation and saving of all children."

Chemical and surgical "rehabilitation"

Because of the high recidivism rate of both juvenile and adult offenders and the apparent unreliability of present psychological-therapeutic methods, some corrections and law-enforcement authorities are looking to the sciences for more sophisticated techniques of rehabilitation. To a limited extent, chemistry could be a useful tool in corrections. For example, hair tests, glucose tolerance tests, and blood tests can be conducted to ascertain if a violent young offender is lacking in particular vitamins and minerals, which might be a contributory factor in his criminal behavior. Research into the causes of violence would also be helpful. Unfortunately, the advocates of scientific rehabilitation are often proposing far more ambitious schemes.

In his "State-of-the-State" message in January 1973, Governor Ronald Reagan suggested the formation of a Center for the Reduction of Life-Threatening Behavior. At the time, this proposal was generally overlooked, but now, given the escalating juvenile violence in Los Angeles, the idea has been resurrected as the Center for the Study of Violent Behavior, to be based at UCLA. The California Department of Corrections is extremely enthusiastic about the center and is seeking federal funding through the Law Enforcement Assistance Administration. Dr. J. M. Stubblebine, state director of Health Care Services, has also been an active supporter. The aim of the program will be to explore advanced scientific techniques for the prevention and cure of violent behavior in both juveniles and adults.

A great many people fear that any such undertaking will become a Clockwork Orange type of mental butcher shop, and some of the suggestions for "scientific rehabilitation" are indeed chilling. For example, Dr. Louis West of UCLA states, "In some patients, outbursts of uncontrolled rage have been definitely linked to abnormal electrical activity in deeply buried areas in the brain. Techniques have been devised which may permit surgical treatment of this condition." Elaborating further, he contends that by implanting tiny electrodes deep within the brain, electrical activity can be followed in areas that cannot be measured from the surface of the scalp. "New drugs being tested in Europe and in America hold promise for diminishing violent outbursts without dulling other brain processes," says Dr. West. "These drugs should be tested in the laboratory and in prisons, mental hospitals, and special community facilities. Proper experiments must be done as soon as possible."

At the Vacaville Correctional Facility in California, research has been carried on in hormonal-imbalance rehabilitation, a form of chemical castration in which female hormones are injected into a male offender to quell his aggressiveness. Also in California three prisoners were subjected to psychosurgery in an attempt to change their behavior. The experiment failed and the program was dropped when the public learned about it. One of the prisoners—who was reported by officials to be the "most improved"—now suffers from memory loss and disequilibrium. In Springfield, Missouri, the federal government has funded a program of chemical therapy whose aim is to pacify "incorrigibles." At the Los Angeles Central Juvenile Hall, tranquilizing drugs are used to mollify "hard-to-control" youngsters, and in North Carolina heavy dosages are applied to subdue young troublemakers.

Dr. Frank R. Ervin, co-author of the book *Violence and the Brain,* discusses the destruction of tiny areas of the brain, which will often eliminate dangerous behavior in assaultive people. His co-author, Dr. Vernon Marks, speaks of mass screening methods to predict violence through a battery of tests that would be administered to both juveniles and adults. Presumably the focus would be on the young, since the spearhead of the program would be to uproot violent inclinations before they matured into adult characteristics. At the present time Los Angeles law-enforcement agencies maintain "alpha files" on thousands of youngsters regarded as potentially dangerous.

Many behavioral scientists, legal experts, and advocates of

prison reform are deeply distressed by the ethical, legal, and social implications of these new developments in "prevention and rehabilitation." Among the groups which have criticized the UCLA Center for the Study of Violent Behavior are the Children's Defense Fund of the Washington Research Project, the American Civil Liberties Union, and the American Psychiatric Association of California. Former Senator Sam Ervin, then chairman of the U.S. Senate subcommittee on constitutional rights, was adamantly opposed to the center.

Scientific studies on the causes and cures of violent behavior do have a social utility, and they should be pursued, but only with the most stringent procedural safeguards as to their application to human subjects. Violence per se is not necessarily abnormal behavior. Our founding fathers established independence by the violent overthrow of British colonial rule. Police must often use violence in their daily job. America is—now and in the past—not averse to the violence of war. When, then, do we label violence sick?

There is the danger of transforming a basically social and political issue into a medical one, and a temptation to quiet the malcontent have-nots and minority rebels on the cheap by cutting out their rage. We must not permit science to be used as a shield to preserve the status quo or to "rehabilitate" the angry ghetto kid by converting him into a vegetable.

21 • Improving Police Performance

Cops act without a face. People feel they're talking to a robot.
—Patrolman John Miller,
New York City Police Department

Out of the tens of thousands of municipal law-enforcement agencies, only one—that in Portland, Oregon—requires a college degree for the position of police officer. Generally, police educational requirements are minimal, and occasionally they are nonexistent. Moreover, the screening procedures for character are typically shallow and inadequate.

A policeman is subjected to tremendous strain in situations ranging from a confrontation with a cornered gunman to a hysterical wife throwing dishes, and one would expect that a rigorous examination of an applicant's character would be standard procedure. Yet in current practice, according to James H. Scheurer, in *To Walk the Streets Safely,* "Those characteristics that are so vital today to good police work—maturity, discretion, sympathy, coolness under conflict and stress—are often ignored."

Upgrading recruitment and training

Police work occasionally attracts men with neurotic needs to have authority. Such recruits must be weeded out before their personal problems erupt in incidents of racial bigotry, sadism, and brutality against young people. Surveys by the Los Angeles Police Department in the seventies disclosed that 86 out of 760 persons tested—about 11 per cent—had personality disorders serious enough to disqualify them for service, yet only one in six police departments conducts any tests aimed at finding such imbalanced individuals. We might therefore speculate that in the five out of six departments that do not perform extensive psychological testing, as many as 10 per cent of the men on the force are potentially unfit. Recurringly, these are the men who bring discredit upon the police by prematurely firing their weapons and bullying youngsters in the inner cities and on college campuses.

Higher standards of recruitment should be implemented for modern policemen, stressing a broad educational background and the fittest possible moral and mental character, tested by in-depth screening methods. Minimum age limits should be lowered to eighteen, or even sixteen. Cadet programs have been established in several cities, including New York, Cincinatti, and Washington, to utilize late teens in police investigation. Unquestionably, in the area of undercover drug surveillance, using teenagers has enormous advantages. The focus of "mod squads," however, should be the older corruptors of children, not their peers on campus, and should be governed by sensitive, democratic policies. Even more important, a significant increase must be made in the hiring of minority representatives to be assigned to ghetto areas. Blacks policing blacks eliminates the sense of white troops occupying the ghettos, and might increase the police understanding of ghetto problems and life styles.

Training programs for policemen should be longer and more comprehensive. According to the President's Commission on Law Enforcement, the average police officer in America receives two hundred hours of preparation for his job, compared to two thousand training hours for barbers and sixteen thousand for doctors. Also according to this report, in 1934 the primary courses offered to recruits during training were traffic signals with hand and arm; military calisthenics; military drill; jujitsu holds and breaks; first aid to the sick and injured; use of gas masks and gas bombs; use of bulletproof vests and riot shotguns; use and care of the revolver; criminal law of the state; common law; and ordinances and bylaws of the city. Thirty-three years later, the Commission found that "few of our smaller police departments provided even this amount of training." What little training is received instills little sense of the policeman's position in relation to the community and little understanding of contemporary life.

Modernization and urban density in Western Europe have created massive problems, often involving young people, for European police, who have responded with a revolutionary overhauling of their training programs. Trail blazers in experimentation, German police academies require recruits to complete a program which lasts four years and offers intensive study in psychology, government, and history, with an emphasis on the inhumanities and injustices of the Nazi regime. Mimeographed copies of complaints that have been made against policemen are studied by recruits so that they can avoid repeating past mistakes. In psychology, the need for human understanding and a sense of humor are stressed, and at the same time recruits are alerted to the dangers of prejudice and stereotyping. The recruit is prepared for the frustrations that traffic jams and octopus bureaucratization can create, and tries to see the average person in a total context. In contrast, American policemen tend to be trained to a simplistic narrowness.

In Sweden, police trainees undergo a ten-month program devoted to a broad spectrum of nonpolice subjects. Law and social studies make up 40 per cent of the curriculum. Their civics text opens with Lincoln's famous quotation that democracy is government of, by, and for the people, and then goes on to underscore such concepts as civil liberties and minority rights. The French recruit goes through six months of training that structures his allegiances so that he is first a citizen, second a civil servant, and finally a policeman. New French officers are encouraged to play a role in the twenty-two summer recreational camps for youth operated and staffed exclusively by policemen. Before a French candidate can become an officer he must go before a jury consisting of several police superiors, a judge, and a university professor. The French department is also reaching out for more women on the job, following the example of Germany, where policewomen handle all children under the age of fourteen. Italy's police-training program runs for two years and includes the study of humanities and the arts.

Virtually only one institution exists in the United States—the California Regional Criminal Justice Training Center—which offers American policemen comparable breadth and scope in training. The school, which is open to policemen, parole officers, and probation officers, provides the most advanced techniques in police science along with the most sophisticated study of psychodynamics. Policemen watch instant replays of their investigative conduct on video tapes. They accompany experienced officers in the field who tutor them by "show and tell." In the area of youth rehabilitation, they delve into transactional analysis and behavioral-modification theories, and mind games and role playing are emphasized to teach empathy. A recruit going through the program will play the role of a teenager being picked up for marijuana possession and attempt to feel his feelings. (I was invited to participate in their "mind games," where I was first introduced as a gang leader from Brooklyn, which provoked a room full of scowling faces; midway through the talks I was reintroduced as a current juvenile court judge, and the scowling changed to deference.)

The courses dealing with the juvenile stress the minor's value as a social resource. The trainees are taught to look for and nurture the minor's good side. Ethnic and race history are offered for "development of an adequate social perspective, an awareness, and understanding of the multiple factors which cause individual and group differences." Fully abreast of the modern age, the institute incorporates sociology, psychology, constitutional law, and a touch of philosophy into forging a well-rounded police officer ably equipped to deal with the urban frontier.

Police and community interaction

"Okay, break it up," ordered an abrasive voice from the squad car pulling up to a Brooklyn street corner.

The youths picked up their props and hurried across the street to resume their street-corner production of the movie *Shane*. One teenager lagged behind the rest, trying to light a cigarette in the wind.

"I told ya to move," snarled a wiry cop, getting out of the car and brandishing his nightstick.

The youth looked over his shoulder with a sarcastic simper, but he started to walk to the other side.

"Why you little bastard!" The officer rushed at the young man with a kick and a swing of his nightstick.

On another beat—in Milwaukee, Wisconsin—Patrolman Mike Sullivan moved unhurriedly toward a group of boys hanging around a street corner, but his approach caused no panicked scurrying. Patrolman Sullivan said firmly but without antagonism, "Listen, fellers, you'll have to break it up and find a better place to get together. You're blocking traffic here and I can't allow it. It's against the law. I know it's hard to find a decent place to hold a huddle, but you'll have to find one."

Two approaches to the same problem—which is more functional for police objectives? The Brooklyn example represents the old nightstick discipline, the growling, hard-boiled insistence on a pound of flesh for juvenile misconduct. Many voices are clamoring for the unmuzzling of old-fashioned police ferocity; they say what we need to stop juvenile crime is a revival of swift, uncomplicated truncheon justice. The Milwaukee policeman's approach to juveniles exemplifies vanguard thinking in police science. The premise is that a kindly officer's approach to the juvenile in his work can make the difference between a future good citizen and a confirmed cop hater.

There are incurably malignant and hostile youngsters, but the damning approach is not going to change them one iota. On the other hand, a firm, no-nonsense but friendly attitude may make young people see the policeman as an interested human being who is only doing his job as a referee in the game of life. Defensively, too many young people and too many policemen often automatically relate to each other with unmitigated hostility. The average policeman's attitude is cemented in rigid stereotypes. At the California Regional Criminal Justice

Training Center, recruits are instructed that without abandoning caution and shrewd instincts, without endangering themselves, good police officers go beyond reflexively enforcing the laws. They try to find the borderline youth who is not fully committed to the criminal way of life, who is in a state of internalized warfare, pulled by conflicting moral forces, and they try to help nurture the minor in the right direction.

I remember in the days when I was running with a gang how responsive I was to the efforts of one particular concerned and sincere police officer. As part of a cumulative process, he ultimately helped me to become another person. I believe that life is always in the process of becoming, that we all have the potential of becoming another person. Perhaps thousands of other selves are locked within our subconscious. Joseph Conrad's *Lord Jim* depicts the metamorphosis of a coward into a hero of steely courage. The life of St. Augustine shows a debauched spirit rejuvenated into an immortal saint. I have traveled 180 degrees from juvenile defendant to juvenile judge. Aspiring to excellence, a good police officer helps to nourish the seeds of promise in a youth, hoping that they will eventually outgrow the weeds of delinquency.

To promote the positive aspects of troubled youngsters, the Pasadena Police Department has moved forward with several innovative programs, establishing the position of Youth Services Coordinator and an Intensive Care Unit, in which specially trained police officers work on a one-to-one basis with juveniles who have gotten into trouble with the law, acting simultaneously as informal probation officers, counselors, and big brothers. Members of the Intensive Care Unit are assigned to the school system to counsel students who show signs of incipient criminal behavior—the pre-prisoners. Several of these officers have received provisional teaching credentials and actually teach classes. It should be emphasized that the young people know they are dealing with members of the police department, and the program has received popular acceptance among both students and the police.

Encounter-group sessions between police and residents of the Houston ghettos are being used to promote better mutual understanding. The sessions begin with an intensive examination of the attitudes the police and the community groups have about themselves and each other. "Why don't you niggers like being called niggers?" one policeman asked. "You call yourselves that, don't you?" The response was, "Shut up, you blue honky!" The policeman flushed with fury, but instead of lashing out with a fist or nightstick, he sat and nodded when asked, "Now do you understand?"

Required by the city government to attend, at first Houston police mumbled and grumbled; some played checkers during the initial session, and Chief of Police Herman Short snidely remarked, "Bunch of slobbering sociologists." Eventually, as the meetings progressed, the ridicule retreated, interest grew, and the chief apologized for his earlier comment. At one meeting a veteran police sergeant blurted out, "I've hated niggers all my life." The group gave him a rousing ovation for his frankness. A militant expressed his feelings about the police: "Racism is part of the air we breathe, and you white cops represent the worst of it. You're all fascists." Attending for six weeks in groups of twelve, more than fourteen hundred Houston police officers have completed the program and have benefited from it by gaining a deeper understanding of the people on the "other side of the tracks."

"Operation Empathy" was the brainchild of the police department in Covina, California. The policemen of Covina, frankly examining the deficiencies in their training, realized that they knew very little about the arrestee's emotional reactions to police contact. What are a youth's feelings as he is seized by uniformed, armed strangers, booked, showered, deloused, and finally shuttled in a grilled bus to the walled compound of juvenile hall? Why do first offenders often panic and lash out at the officers? Searching for answers, a number of Covina's police personnel posed as members of a captured forgery ring and experienced the anxieties and discomforts of being treated as prisoners at Riverside County Jail.

In another exercise, Tom Courtney, a young juvenile officer, posed as a skid-row loiterer, complete with thrift-shop clothing, shopping bags filled with junk, and a muscatel bottle camouflaged in a brown paper bag. He and his co-derelict partner roamed the skid-row streets and alleys of Los Angeles, and at dusk they paused in a deserted parking lot and took turns tipping a bottle of wine. Suddenly, out of nowhere, two uniformed policemen materialized. Tom and his partner were spread-eagled against a building and searched. Forgetting the instruction not to reveal identities, Tom panicked and exclaimed, "We're police officers. We're police officers." Later, Tom explained to senior officers why he had been so quick in his revelation: "I thought I might get shot." Today, Tom is still telling department personnel, "For God's sake, smile when you can. And above all, tell the man you're shaking down what you are going to do."

For years the security police on campuses around the nation have been taunted with choruses from the "Mickey Mouse" song. In attempt to promote greater tolerance toward policemen on campus, a number of university police agencies have switched from the starchy outfits complete with boots, cartridge belt, handcuffs, and helmet to more casual blazer-and-slacks attire. As Patrolman John Miller of New York City observes, "A cop's uniform accentuates his impersonality. People feel they're talking to a robot." Police departments in Orange County, California, have also switched from military dress to more informal uniforms, and several other municipal departments are considering a similar change in the hope that they will appear more human to young people.

Alvin Nierenberg, a former New York policeman now practicing law in California, believes that the press badly hurts the image of the police officer by highlighting only the incidents of abuse or brutality: "How many times do you hear of the cop breathing air into a baby's mouth or helping firemen go into a burning building?" He thinks the police should distribute press releases about their good deeds, and he would also like to see policemen have a more general education. "Cops are not broad enough to look at the over-all picture. It's hard enough for the average citizen, let alone the cop, who is always on the defensive. You're damned if you do and damned if you don't."

The question of arrest quotas

Considerable uproar has been churned over the alleged practice of arrest quotas, with some groups contending that officers who have not made sufficient arrests will resort to making frivolous or marginally justifiable arrests and hounding teenagers to ferret out any minor breach of the law. The police generally deny that such quotas exist. The U.S. Commission on Law Enforcement found in both a midwestern and a western city that one criterion for evaluating police officers was the number of "field interrogations" each had made. In one of these cities a ranking officer stated, "Our first-line supervisors have a responsibility to keep statistics on each officer to find out whether a particular officer's [arrest] performance is consistent with what his squad's average might be. As a result, if a particular man is low, we expect an explanation."

My brother, Detective Anthony Sorrentino of the New York City Police Department, recalls that when he was on the vice squad his commander frequently issued the injunction: "I don't want anybody back tonight until he gets on the sheet [makes an arrest]." Under this pressure, one ineffectual and unscrupulous policeman attempted to arrest a woman who was merely standing in front of a restaurant on charges of soliciting for prostitution, but before the officer could drag her off to the patrol car her husband came out of the restaurant to stop him. While I was employed by the U.S. Justice Department in 1967, former U.S. Attorney Mathew Byrne, in charge of criminal prosecutions, called several meetings to tell us that Washington was interested in statistics. Presumably for political ammunition, President Johnson wanted more convictions to report in the war against crime.

Police work is a far too complicated and delicate job to judge an officer's work or qualifications for promotion on the number of arrests he has made. Furthermore, quotas, if they do exist as either explicit requirements or implied expectations, can lead to improper activity by policemen. Patrolling officers have the complex and difficult responsibility of exercising discretion, and that responsibility should not be weighted by any kind of quotas.

With limited resources, the police should concentrate on the main dangers to society. It seems like a super waste of precious time for a policeman to station himself all day on a restroom roof, as has been reported, waiting to arrest homosexuals, or to spend a half day in court waiting to testify that a minor was drinking a can of beer on the street. In Scotland, where juvenile courts have been replaced with Children's Panels, when an offense has been committed by a juvenile and there is sufficient evidence to establish a prima facie case, the police have to first consider whether to seek prosecution or issue a formal or informal warning. Instead of alienating a teenager by prosecuting him for a petty wrong, an informal warning impresses upon the minor that there is fairness in the system and that a subsequent lapse may bring him to court. If a formal warning is issued, the Scottish minor is brought before a senior officer at the police station with the consent and presence of the parents. This action is not an attempt to decide the appropriate course of treatment or to invoke punishment, but to warn the minor firmly as to its consequences. This warning is given only when there is adequate evidence and an admission of guilt. A formal warning is noted on the minor's record but does not have the same stigma as a court conviction. A system of formal and informal warnings might well be instituted in many of our cities.

Upholding juvenile court

One respected police executive expressed the view that most of the police problems in the juvenile field can be laid directly at the door of juvenile courts that attempt to treat with kindness and decency antisocial youths who deliberately seek to take advantage of the system. From the bench I have to confirm the partial validity of this observation. There have been several occasions when, after offering a more-than-fair disposition to a minor and asking him to express his contrition and future intent to obey society's laws, the youth has looked up at me and drawled, "Yeah, sure, I'll be straight. Sure, man, I mean your honor. Anything you say, man. I mean, your honor." The contempt in such a response is only faintly veiled. Do you reverse your decision in this case? A juvenile court judge should be flexible enough to reverse himself if the facts truly warrant it.

A chronic complaint expressed by policemen is that the juvenile court fails to take strong, positive action. Some police officers feel that probation is not effective as a corrective measure and that referring juvenile offenders to various community programs or welfare and social agencies is practically useless. They are usually eager to see the erring juvenile placed in detention or committed to a security institution.

There is a widespread feeling on the part of the police, unquestionably justified in some cases, that the action taken by the court does not impress upon the minor the seriousness of his action. The police chief of Sierra Madre, California, relates that during a talk to a class of third-graders on the dangers of drug violations, one seven-year-old said, "But they can't do nothin' to you the first time ya caught. The court always lets you go the first time, no matter what." Police are disturbed that the youth who has been repeatedly in trouble with the law is still released on probation or his case dismissed on constitutional grounds. In one case, after I was forced to dismiss a matter because of a clear infringement of search-and-seizure law, the angered police officer arbitrarily arrested the youth outside the courthouse for "disturbing the peace." Police object to the fact that juvenile offenders may not be fingerprinted, photographed, or have their identities disclosed to the public. In some jurisdictions, the police may not even question a juvenile suspect, being required by law to immediately deliver minors to the probation department. The police often see probation officers as primarily oriented toward the best interest of the offender rather than of society, and feel that a probation officer is inclined to take unwarranted chances on behalf of his probationers.

Many policemen believe that the juvenile court judge is supposed to side with them rather than give serious attention to the abstract concepts of constitutional rights. Of course the judge is not supposed to "side" with anyone—he should remain scrupulously neutral; but, candidly speaking, at a gut level it is sometimes painful for me to obey the constitutional law if it means I must release a clearly guilty person who will surely commit more crimes, and I can empathize with the police in such cases. Too often, procedural requirements specified in the law seem unrealistic, abstruse, and downright obstructionistic.

In Sacramento, California, the police department has established the position of juvenile court police liaison, a specialist in juvenile law who is on hand to assist other officers in understanding the unique nature of the juvenile court. The liaison officer also cooperates in assisting the general public by, for example, directing a family to the proper courtroom, answering any questions they might have, and just being available to serve them in any way he can. In Great Britain, liaison officers fill a larger purpose by establishing a continuing relationship with juvenile offenders. This follow-up action helps to impress upon youngsters that the police are not merely interested in dumping them in jail and that the authorities do care what becomes of them.

To better uphold the purposes of the juvenile court, it would be useful to give police officers seminars on the over-all objectives of the juvenile justice system as well as of the constitutional principles relating to due process, especially those that have been specifically upheld by the U.S. Supreme Court. It is crucial for all police officers to understand that locking up juvenile offenders is not the only answer to juvenile crime—that, in fact, it often aggravates the problem by reinforcing the negative influences on the minor. Unless the aim of the juvenile justice system is to reinforce the *good* qualities of the children who come before it, the whole procedure becomes one of self-fulfilling prophecy: all kids are bad, are treated as bad, and come out worse. The police officer, as the man on the front line in the fight against juvenile crime, must be the first to change his attitudes toward the kids he deals with.

22 • Television's Future: Dr. Jekyll or Mr. Hyde?

We have already extended our senses and our nerves by the various media. Any extension, whether of skin, hand, or foot, affects the whole psychic and social complex.
–Marshall McLuhan,
Understanding Media: The Extensions of Man

When we speak of "the media," we tend to think of television to the exclusion of other forms of communication. Tentatively, for the present discussion, we will accept this oversimplification because television is by far the most prominent means of mass communication in this country. This is not meant to imply that the print media cannot be helpful in attacking juvenile crime. Dedicated journalists are still influential, as their role in digging out the facts about Watergate confirms. More relevant to the problem of delinquency, in 1974 the *Los Angeles Times* ran a series of stories and editorials uncovering degrading conditions in the Los Angeles Central Juvenile Hall. These reports led directly and swiftly to what seemed to be improvements in the medical facilities at the hall. This is only one instance of how vigorous efforts by the press can have an impact on juvenile justice.

But whatever contribution crusading journalism can make, it is likely to be local in scope. Television alone has the range and impact to be able to affect delinquency on a nationwide basis, since it has the greatest direct contact with America's youth. On any given evening far more youngsters are glued to the television screen than to the theater screen, and on any given morning far more children are watching their favorite shows than are reading the newspapers. Indeed, television is the only window on the world for many American youngsters, serving as babysitter, conversation partner, and even parental surrogate. Moreover, it is one of the major means of socialization available to young people. Through television they learn what society expects of them, how they are supposed to act, to feel, and to think.

Properly used, television could have a most sweeping and constructive influence on America's youth. In recent years the industry has made improvements in its programing. Television is no longer predominantly a "vast wasteland" excoriated and ridiculed by the intelligentsia. But there is plenty of room for improvement before the desert comes into full bloom. Part of that improvement should include creative programing that could significantly help to combat juvenile crime.

Is televised violence really necessary?

It is in programing that television can make its major contribution. To begin with, volence for its own sake must be deleted from the screen. In the words of the President's Commission on Law Enforcement, "The broadcasting industry should recognize the strong probability that a high incidence of violence in entertainment is contributing to undesirable attitudes and even to violence in American society." Reacting to such criticism, in the sixties television made an effort to tone down the bloodletting, but according to a 1975 statement by the Los Angeles Probation Department, more than 62.5 per cent of today's shows feature aspects of violence, making 1975 the bloodiest year in television history. In its March 1975 issue, *McCall's* magazine listed the ten most violent shows on the air: *Mannix, Cannon, Kojak, Police Woman, Police Story, Streets of San Francisco, The Rookies, Get Christie Love, Kung Fu,* and *Hawaii Five-O.* When it compared these ten programs with the first ten in the Nielsen listings, *McCall's* made the interesting discovery that they were not the most popular shows.

Renewed efforts must be made to reduce the excess gore. While it is safe to say that violence will never be excised from American life, it should be depicted on television only to the extent necessary to make the dramatic point in a story. Senseless violence whose only purpose is to stun, shock, or thrill the audience is dangerously unnecessary. Violence begets violence, and when it is portrayed as a positive force, as something to be admired, it can be very harmful to impressionable youngsters.

Proposals for reform are easy to make but difficult to implement, since television is such a leviathan industry, comprised of the three huge networks, a loosely-knit public education network, and innumerable independent stations. Thus proposals for any kind of uniform national policy must be handled carefully and with imagination. Television is not an arm of the government, nor should it be. But the laissez-faire dimension of free enterprise can only go so far in achieving reform. At some point, some kind of regulation is mandatory.

Self-regulation by the media

The federal government should provide some regulation, and indeed does so through the Federal Communications Commission's power to revoke broadcasting licenses for a station's failure to abide by legal and ethical canons, but it emphatically should not be allowed to establish or impose national standards of taste. To do so could lead to the "governmentalization" of television, which would mock the First Amendment guarantees of free speech and free press. To be effective as well as constitutional, regulation should be done voluntarily by the industry itself.

Industry self-regulation, however, is hampered by three major factors: the inertia bred by competition, the quest for profits, and the anti-trust laws of the United States. The latter poses the most manageable problem. If and when Congress recognizes that the national interest requires the television industry to cooperate internally in setting programing standards, it could within limits exempt the networks from the confines of anti-trust legislation. This would clear the way for the commercial networks to work together—along with the public network and independent stations—in forging a national policy for the industry.

The other two obstacles are more difficult to overcome. Since the networks and independent stations are in fierce competition for the finite viewing audience, they will not willingly reveal to one another their future programing plans, traditionally kept fanatically secret until they are unveiled with spectacular fanfare each season. But the leaders of the industry must realize that the welfare of America's youth takes precedence over such practices. In any case, program standards could be formulated without revealing too many precious secrets, if half as much effort were invested in cooperation as in selling commercial time.

The trickiest obstacle in bringing about changes in television is the profit motive. Incessantly maneuvering to attract the largest audience for their advertisers, the networks' overriding criterion for program selection is potential popularity. Conventional wisdom holds that violence appeals to the viewing masses—just look at all the programs featuring police and detective exploits. Assuming the popularity of violence, the networks try to outdo each other in slinging gore. All of this, however, overlooks the possibility that the industry may be creating an appetite for what it insists on feeding the public: if violence is the only game in town, then it is the game that will get the play. Conditioned to bruising TV action for years, it may prove impossible for us to give up "cops and robbers" entertainment. But if the networks adopt a no-violence or minimal-violence policy, they might find that it is not the audience which insists on watching prime-time death rattling and calamity. According to the Nielsen ratings, the most popular shows are *not* the gung-ho violent series. The overwhelming public approval of such basically intelligent series as *All in the Family, The Waltons,* the *Mary Tyler Moore Show,*

*M*A*S*H*, *Rhoda*, and *Sanford and Son*, as well as the growing acceptance of Public Education Network programing, demonstrates that mass audiences can respond to high-quality, low-violence television content.

Can public television show the way?

At present public television is a moderately important force, pioneering an alternative to commercial TV that is simultaneously interesting on its own terms and a needed goad to the commercial networks. As time goes on, however, public television could become a truly vital cultural influence. Whether this potential will be realized or not is largely up to the government.

Television is an exorbitantly expensive proposition, and if educational TV is ever to be able to compete with commercial television, it must have adequate public funding without strings attached. The quasi-governmental Corporation for Public Broadcasting must be guaranteed independence from political interference of the kind seen in the Nixon administration's attempt to manipulate the commercial networks. If government funding, which at present is reduced to a trickle, is substantially increased—as it must be—the money should be allocated unconditionally so that public television can serve as a powerful catalyst for social reform. If too many government strings are attached, public television could degenerate into little more than a propaganda mouthpiece for whatever administration is in office. It is up to the public to be vigilant and to make sure that government money is used to provide the widest latitude of creative freedom.

Commercial television could, of course, also be instrumental in fostering social betterment. One idea worth exploring is to induce the major networks to offer prime-time cultural and educational programs on a rotating basis. The networks presently shy away from such programing, with some notable exceptions, primarily because it is so difficult to find sponsors for them. The standard rationale is that cultural programs do not sell products because mass audiences are not interested in mind-expanding challenges. Quite clearly, public television is demonstrating that this premise is not necessarily valid.

The major networks should provide edifying programs in prime time for at least three hours a week. The overwhelming acceptance of their rotating coverage of the Senate Watergate committee hearings should reassure them that the audience will not completely disappear. No one network would have to assume the brunt of the supposed lower audience ratings, and all of them would be involved in improving the quality of life for Americans all across the country. Balanced programing is not too much to ask of an industry whose major occupation is that of keeping us entertained and informed.

If Rosemary's babysitter were ever caught telling her grotesque and gruesome tales, surely her parents would fire the sitter; yet her parents tolerate quite blithely an electronic babysitter that regularly spins tales full of blood and gore. Electronic babysitters must also be held accountable.

23 • Gun Control

Every twenty-one minutes, an American dies by the gun—more than eight hundred thousand persons since the turn of the century, more deaths than in all our wars from the Revolution through Vietnam.
—Dee Helfgott, Coalition for Handgun Control

The main question to be explored with respect to firearms is whether federal gun-control legislation can serve as an effective solution—in whole or in part—to the problem of juvenile crime in America.

Most, if not all, of the states have enacted statutes which attempt to limit the use of firearms. State registration of weapons is one obvious example. Requiring hunting licenses works to "control" firearms to some degree, if only to prescribe criminal penalties for those who hunt without the proper license. It seems evident, however, that state control lacks the purview necessary to affect gun ownership on a national level.

At present a torrential flow of illegal firearms moves across state lines with impunity because there is no barrier to the importation of firearms. Even a state with comparatively strict regulatory laws can do nothing to stop interstate gun traffic because of the constitutional division of power between the federal and state governments. For example, New York State, whose regulations are bitingly stiff, has no power to examine the mails to determine whether firearms are entering from

Texas, whose regulations–in the Wild West Shoot 'Em Up tradition–tend to be permissive on firearms. Nor do the states have dominion to regulate interstate commerce, since the Constitution has invested this power in the federal government, leaving the states in a condition of regulatory impotence.

The arguments for and against

Thus if gun control is to be effective the effort must emanate from the federal government. Gun control conjures up different images for different people. Generally speaking, there are four basic kinds of gun control: registration of firearms, prohibition of ownership, increased penalties for criminal possession, and restrictive licensing. Each has its own requirements, and truly effective gun control would doubtless combine features from all of them.

Registration of firearms means simply that records are kept of all firearms sold. Prohibition of ownership assumes that certain classes of people are poor risks as gun owners–convicted felons and known drug addicts, for example–and they would not be legally permitted to obtain weapons. By necessity, all prospective purchasers of firearms would be subject to investigation and licensing. Licensing is also required under the third type of gun control, but the main emphasis is placed on heavier penalties for armed crimes on the premise that a potential criminal will think twice before bringing a gun along. Finally, restrictive licensing would require prospective purchasers to demonstrate an affirmative need before they would be allowed to buy a weapon, and the need would be defined by statute to limit the discretion of gun dealers.

The subject of gun control always sparks a controversy. To a vehement gun lobbyist the notion is an abomination. Proponents are equally impassioned on the other side. It will be useful to summarize the arguments, pro and con.

Champions of gun control–especially of handguns–assert that handguns are little used except in the commission of crimes. They cite statistics such as those compiled by the President's Commission on Law Enforcement that 63 per cent of all homicides in America in 1967 were committed with firearms, with handguns responsible for 92 per cent of them. In England and Wales, which have restrictive licensing, only 18 per cent of the homicides were committed with firearms. Senator Edward Kennedy argues that guns generate a national sense of fear because of the rising rate of armed offenses. The profusion of handguns menaces civilized life, he says, and unless the spread of weapons is stemmed, we will regress to the predatory perils of the wilds where, in the Hobbesian phrase, "life is nasty, brutish, and short." Only a vigorous assault on guns will repel the rising tide of juvenile crime.

Opponents of gun control tersely remind us with bumper stickers that people, not guns, kill. They contend that to impose mandatory restrictions on gun ownership is a violation of two of the most fundamental tenets of our constitutional democracy. First, under our Constitution, the police power resides in the states, and since gun control is indivisible from that authority, only the states have jurisdiction over firearms. Secondly, the Second Amendment to the Constitution states that "a well-regulated militia being necessary to the security of a free state, the right of the people to keep and bear arms shall not be infringed." Therefore, the federal government is prohibited from placing any restraints on who may own weapons. This language supports the deduction that it was the framers' conviction that, in the words of Representative John Rarick of Louisiana, "the citizen soldier—not the military—is the strength and the defense of this country from foreign or domestic take-over."

Representative Rarick argues further that the American people need weapons for self-protection in the face of an elevating crime rate. The National Rifle Association (NRA) maintains that the vast majority of firearms in America are held for legitimate purposes, not for criminal use, and cites figures showing that the handguns used in murders in 1970 represent far less than 1 per cent of the total number of handguns owned by Americans.

The heated debate on gun laws engenders conflicting conclusions as to specific strategies. Those in favor of a registration plan claim, for example, that it would both help police in tracing weapons and deter a registered owner from using his own gun for crime and from transferring his registered weapon illegally. Opponents of this plan reply that criminals would simply choose not to register their firearms, and therefore the program would be futile since the only persons complying would be law-abiding citizens.

As for a strategy of restricting certain classes of people from owning guns, proponents claim it would reduce the use of firearms for criminal purposes. Unconvinced, the NRA declares that such a plan, while inconveniencing legitimate gun users, would not keep criminals from obtaining weapons illegally. Believers in the method of harsher sanctions say the smart criminal is simply not going to risk getting caught with a gun. The fallacy of this belief is seen in the fact that gun-related crimes already carry stiff sentences, and do not seem to be much of a deterrent.

The issue of restrictive licensing arouses the most acrid debate. Opponents argue that such a plan would require the surrender of lawfully held firearms, amounting to illegal confiscation. Advocates insist that such licensing would substantially diminish the number of handguns in circulation.

The President's Commission on Law Enforcement recommended a wide-ranging national firearms policy, including public-education programs, research, and legislation. At the heart of the program, however, is the restrictive licensing of handguns, a policy that seems both reasonable and necessary. There is ample evidence in statistics and in daily headlines that violence with firearms is near the top of the list of America's problems. Too long have we nebulously procrastinated and faintly faced the issue. Decisive steps to implement gun control should proceed immediately, regardless of how modest the initial stride. Only qualified, responsible citizens should be entitled to hold weapons or to purchase ammunition, and society should have a computerized record of who these people are. A strictly enforced restrictive licensing and restrictive ammunition sales policy would slam the brakes on accelerating gun crimes.

Can gun control reduce juvenile crime?

The question remains whether this type of gun-control plan would have any effect on the rate of juvenile crime in America. The answer must be substantially yes for the same basic reasons that it would help to reduce adult crimes. The key to the solution lies in the limited availability of weapons. A potential juvenile offender who is considering using a gun in his crime must first obtain a weapon, and his options are the same as his adult counterpart's. He can steal one, borrow one from a friend, buy one, or, if he's clever enough, manufacture one. Because of his age, a juvenile cannot buy a weapon from a legitimate source. His purchase will be on the street at the same underground supermarket in which the adult criminal shops for his hardware.

Irate gun lobbyists say that restrictive licensing would be ineffective precisely because it would fail to stop illegal gun traffic. Initially this might be true, because of necessity such legislation would be directed at the legitimate sales of firearms and ammunition. Gradually, however, street sales of guns should decline because severe penalties for the possession of unlicensed handguns are integral to a restrictive licensing plan. All unauthorized guns and ammunition retrieved by the police would be destroyed. Faced with more severe penalties for unauthorized weapons, a good number of juveniles would be deterred from using them in crime. Over time, as the police continue destroying unauthorized weapons and ammunition becomes increasingly scarce, the number of loaded weapons in circulation will decrease and thereby make the acquisition of handguns progressively more difficult for minors.

No overnight miracle will be wrought by any form of gun control. Only after many years will the attrition rate make a palpable dent in the gun supply. But we are not dealing with a problem that bubbled into existence overnight. For a long time, Americans have had a fondness for and fascination with handguns. At one time in our history their use was thought to be necessary, if not entirely justifiable. But handguns are no longer necessities of life in our society. When is America going to catch up to the rest of the civilized world? There are no tantrums or petulance in Japan or England because weapons are regulated.

Public education should be concentrated on the young, and should debunk and demythify our Wild West heritage and macho traditions. Such education, along with a reduction in the number of handguns circulating on the streets, might lead to a new mood in American youth in which guns are not a symbol of manhood. Guns in American culture should represent a sportsman's instrument or a collector's prize. By the twenty-first century, everyone should begin laughing if anyone tries to resurrect the rusty anachronism that guns are associated with manhood.

24 • Private-Sector Commitment

If unemployment and recession continue to mount, crime will also climb, and in the end our cities may fall into jungles
—Brendan Byrne, Governor of New Jersey

Business and private organizations must accept responsibility by demonstrating initiative in improving social welfare and helping to solve our social ills. Such initiatives are particularly important because the creation of employment opportunities is the most direct, effective, and lasting economic measure possible to upgrade the economic level of a community.

IBM grows in Brooklyn

In 1974 I visited a manufacturing plant of a major corporation. The board of directors do not see anything special about their plant. As far as they are concerned, it is one of the several hundred manufacturing facilities the company owns across the country, a plant that meets its production goals well and operates with a great deal of efficiency in its day-to-day operations. The people who work there enjoy their work and they work well together, in large measure because most of them live near the plant. All in all, the plant—International Business Machines' Systems Manufacturing Division in Brooklyn, New

York—appears to be a well-oiled, efficient cog in IBM's corporate machinery.

What makes this plant different from IBM's other manufacturing facilities, and different from any other large factory in the nation, is that it is located in the Bedford-Stuyvesant section of Brooklyn, one of the most destitute ghettos in America. "Bed-Stuy's" population is greater than Louisville's and is almost as large as that of Minneapolis. The unemployment rate is higher and the average income lower than that of Harlem or Watts. Rats, drug addicts, and litter abound, and crime festers in the streets like a fungus. Beneath all this social rubble, however, the community has potential. IBM recognized this potential and felt a responsibility to do something about it.

From the outside, IBM's Bedford-Stuyvesant plant is not strikingly impressive except that it is the only building in the area untainted by graffiti, a sign of genuine respect in the community. The building used to be a warehouse, and converting it to manufacturing was not easy, but the fact that the physical configuration is not ideal for production has not kept the plant from competing on an even footing with IBM's other plants around the nation. When it first opened in 1968, the plant did not meet its production goals, but by the end of 1970 it was running more than 11 per cent above its goals, spewing out 25 per cent of the cables and 33 per cent of the power units for IBM's System/370 and System/3 computers. In 1974 the Bedford Stuyvesant plant was among the most efficiently productive operations in IBM's vast international galaxy.

Production figures alone do not tell the story of IBM Brooklyn. The real story is in the people who work in the plant. When company executives decided to open it, they also resolved to hire predominantly from the neighborhood, which was defined as that area within a three-mile radius of the factory. As a result, more than 90 per cent of the people on the payroll are black or Puerto Rican, and, reflecting the extensive training programs carried on in the plant, over 80 per cent of the managerial personnel is made up from minority groups. Halvan J. Lieteau, the able and amiable general manager of the plant, is black. He replaced the previous manager—a white man—in 1970. Mr. Lieteau showed me around the plant when I visited, obviously proud of the smooth operation.

"This is a business entity operating with standard measures," he told me. "This is no case of charity and it never has been. What we've done is constantly uplift the skills of our employees. We're always looking for new products to make here, and we hope that soon we'll be building a complete terminal display unit." The plant runs with gliding efficiency, despite the logistical problems of moving materials and personnel around a five-story manufacturing structure. IBM's tradition is one of quiet precision and perfectionism, and that tradition is mirrored in the Bedford-Stuyvesant operation. "It's a good place to work," I was told by a neatly dressed assembly-line employee. She went on to say, "When I came to work here I didn't know anything about electronics or wiring boards. I had big toes for fingers. But the company patiently taught me. Now I got a skill I can use for the rest of my life." Or, as another worker said, "I been here for going on three years now, and I think I'm going to stay for a long time. At first my family and my neighbors thought this place was some kind of rip-off—you know, white dudes come in to exploit the community. But now we see how the place works and how they run it, and nobody feels that way any more. Matter of fact, my brother and my uncle applied for jobs here too and they might get hired some day, if the waiting list ever gets short enough."

Hyland Gear, who manages the cable-assembly segment of the operation, was previously the assistant manager of a chain book store. "I felt I had gone as far as a black man could go in that other company," he said. "I took the job here because I liked what I heard in the interview. It meant a cut in salary, but I was told that if I proved myself, I would get ahead. No promises. No time frame. I liked the fact that the people I talked to seemed relaxed and confident working for IBM. And I have gotten ahead."

The early days in building a production capacity at "Bed-Stuy" were troublesome. Absenteeism was an unshakable problem for a long time, running as high as 12 per cent during the first eighteen months in business. The rate has since dropped to around 5 per cent and continues to hover about that figure, which is a bit higher than the average at IBM's other manufacturing facilities in America, but executives are confident of improvement. "I expect by the end of 1975 our rate will be about the same as, say, our San Jose plant," Mr. Lieteau told me.

Annual employee turnover at the beginning was high, about 25 per cent, of which about half were dismissals. But now that rate too has dropped as a result of the plant's steadfast commitment to the area and the emergence of a loyal, permanent work force. "Our turnover rate is still higher than we'd like it to be," Mr. Lieteau noted. "But it's a lot lower than the rates of other employers of blacks in this area. I think that's because of IBM's education and training programs, and salary levels which are much higher than other manufacturers, and because we encourage our employees to train and advance into management. And our turnover rate is way down, just like our absenteeism rate. Our production figures show this," he added. "Our dollar volume is always going up. In 1971, for instance, our dollar volume doubled from 1970."

All in all, the Bedford-Stuyvesant plant is impressive. The only saddening thing about my visit, as a matter of fact, was that when I walked out of the plant's front door I was back in the ghetto. Bedford-Stuyvesant's face has changed very little, in spite of the fact that the plant pumps about $350,000 annually into the neighborhood's economy. The problem does not lie with IBM, but rather in the failure of other corporations to follow IBM's lead and establish branches in Bedford-Stuyvesant. IBM had hoped that such a move would take place, and its board chairman, Vincent Learson, continues to hope it will. This was one of the company's three original goals in its decision to open the plant in the first place, he says, and since the first two—manufacturing computer components and creating employment opportunities in a neighborhood clearly in need of them—have not only been met but surpassed, perhaps the third will follow. I hope so. My visit confirmed that this kind of economic booster shot is what areas such as Bedford-Stuyvesant desperately need, and as far as I'm concerned IBM is the kind of enlightened corporation that that can help to restore pride in America.

The example of IBM's plant in Bedford-Stuyvesant is an affirmation of how private enterprise can function to improve conditions in the slums. Business and industry leaders have been averse to investing in the ghetto, afraid of being torn to shreds by crime. The untouchable status of IBM, because of respect in the community, and the stellar record of measured profits achieved by the Bed-Stuy plant, should convince the skeptics that a capital investment in the ghetto is sound, safe, and rewarding. From the perspective of social responsibility, the IBM test has proven that hard-core youthful offenders, once branded unregenerate and unemployable, *can* be hired, trained, and helped to become mature citizens. The young men I talked to at the IBM plant exuded pride, a sense of dignity, and the serenity that comes from comfortable security, knowing they would have a paycheck at the end of the week. There was not a hint that they would ever be interested in crime.

IBM's commitment to dealing with social problems goes beyond its magnificent undertaking in Bedford-Stuyvesant. As a regular feature of its organization, IBM offers its employees social-service sabbaticals to enable them to serve the community during working hours. The eligible community services span a spectrum of health, medicine, education, social welfare, civic and cultural affairs, and science. The time given ranges from a few hours a week to a full year or more. During the period away from his job, an IBM employee may be serving as a teacher or probation officer, for example, and continues to receive his normal salary from the company.

Also commendable is IBM's Fund for Community Service program, designed to stimulate employee involvement in local service projects by providing financial backing. All regular, retired, and part-time employees are eligible to participate. Decisions on which efforts to support are made on a case-by-case basis, with consideration given to the value of the specific project, the availability of other funding resources, and the participation of other employees in other projects. In this way, IBM is donating funds to better the community in a wide variety of projects by, for example, furnishing a school library with books, constructing a hospital in a ghetto, or building a recreation center in a low-income neighborhood.

Other concerned business and citizens' groups

Many groups within the community are actively showing that the responsibility for juvenile delinquency does not rest in the hands of a few trained specialists. Complaints about the shortage of staff to control and rehabilitate offenders have been rebutted by the accomplishments of groups of individuals who volunteer their time, service, equipment, and money to reach out and involve themselves in the work of restoring the youth to the community. An examination of these efforts will provide guidelines for similar projects that might be carried out throughout the nation.

The community serves as an important resource in making rehabilitation more individualized and sensitive to needs of youthful offenders or potential offenders. "Big brother" programs offer opportunities for delinquents to have friendship and guidance in "going straight." In Memphis, Tennessee, insurance salesmen participate in a man-to-teen program to counsel minors. In Israel, soldiers serve as big brothers to delinquents; a similar program in this country would provide servicemen with a way to use their free time constructively during peacetime.

The community can also help by participating in administrative duties and law enforcement. College students from Mars Hill, North Carolina, for example, serve as voluntary part-time probation officers, dealing with less serious cases. In Brooklyn, the pressure on police officers is lessened by auxiliary neighborhood task forces, with private citizens assisting on patrol and performing crime-control duties. The school system can be helped by the active involvement of parents, as is being done in some Los Angeles schools, where parents are working closely with teachers in shaping their children's education. In Peoria, Illinois, local doctors, lawyers, and psychiatrists used their skills working with juvenile offenders in the reformatory.

Teenagers can also be helpful to delinquents, as has been proven by the effectiveness of the Nova Halfway House in Pittsburgh, Pennsylvania.

The National Center for Youth Outreach Workers in Chicago conducts week-long training sessions for people who want to work with youth in such agencies as the YMCA, United Way, settlement houses, and other community-service programs. Instruction is offered in handling drug abuse, alcoholism, pregnancy, and gangs, and the curriculum is adapted to the needs of each enrolling group.

The New York Life Insurance Company contributed a mortgage loan of $530,000 to finance a reception center for young people in Bedford-Stuyvesant. The center will provide temporary housing, counseling, and educational services for delinquent youth. Marion Laboratories of Kansas City has taken drug abuse as its particular area of social responsibility by providing pamphlets outlining the types and causes of drug abuse and dispatching a mobile unit to teach parents how to recognize drug-abuse symptoms and what to do when they spot them. Literature and labor materials for the mobile unit were donated by fifty local businessmen. In line with these efforts the company has distributed over two thousand Drug Awareness Speakers Kits to police departments, schools, and churches across the nation.

The CNA Financial Corporation of the Midwest provided money for a special rehabilitation and job-training program conducted by Pace Institute for the inmates of the Cook County jail in Illinois. Before the program was begun 75 per cent of the first-termers at the jail eventually returned. The recidivism rate for those who have participated in the program is only 15 per cent.

The Association of Business and Commerce of Detroit, Michigan, donated $27,000 to the school system to purchase machinery and equipment for a special program of occupational education, creating enthusiasm among the students and motivating forty dropouts to return. The Johnson Shoe Company in Endicott, New York, has purchased the books used by virtually all the public schools in the community and has built low-cost housing for its employees as well as supporting hospital and recreational services.

Private groups have also been instrumental in providing employment for youth. The Chamber of Commerce in El Monte, California, decided it was time to do more than merely talk about how bad the juvenile crime problem was getting. These concerned businessmen decided to try to find jobs for every gang member in the community. Manpower, Inc., an international organization based in Milwaukee, is a temporary-service firm whose activities include a nonprofit foundation, Youthpower, which recruits young people from sixteen to twenty-one for summer jobs through a free referral service. The entire Youthpower program is operated by volunteers, including training clinics operated by volunteer experts. A summer work-study program linking inner-city high school youths and the Hartford Insurance Group gives young people on the job training through its Skills Training Adjustment Group, which offers students who have successfully completed the summer program part-time employment during the year while they are still in high school. STAG participants can then move directly to full-time employment with the firm after graduation. Project JOVE of Pasadena, California, says it is dedicated to quality assistance for the juvenile ex-offender in motivating him or her to become a productive citizen. Administrator Paul Jones says, "We believe that our clients should become taxpayers rather than tax-users. We seek to give hope to the lost, and a new direction to those who are misdirected." During the first eighteen months of JOVE's existence, nearly eight hundred ex-offenders were referred from its office for employment, and more than five hundred were placed on jobs and are still at work, as evidenced from follow-up studies. In the initial eighteen-month period the city of Pasadena reported a 22.4 per cent drop in crime; JOVE believes, with some justification, that it has contributed to this reduction. Of those ex-offenders who have become clients of this organization, about 85 per cent remain free and productive. It has helped to save the State of California in excess of $150,000 in terms of the minimum of $6,000 per inmate it costs each year to keep a person behind bars. In terms of loss of life and property and the disruption of families and society, the value of JOVE to the community is invaluable. America needs more JOVEs.

Sports programs: a constructive outlet

The first time I saw Sugar Ray Robinson he was dressed in a canary-yellow suit, getting out of his outer-space styled fuschia Cadillac, in New York City. The next time I saw him, twenty years later, he was dressed in slacks and sneakers, getting out of a nondescript white Ford, and about to enter a repainted frame building that housed the California offices of his Sugar Ray Youth Foundation. I climbed the rickety steps behind him and we went into his office, where he told me about his plans to help ghetto youth through recreation.

Still trim but bulkier through the chest and shoulders, the man called the greatest fighter, pound for pound, in ring history told me: "Boxing did a lot for me. If it wasn't for sports I know I would have ended up in prison. What I'm trying to do here is bring kids in off the streets. Black kids, white kids, Chicano kids, don't make no difference. I put gloves on them, teach them how to box. We have a basketball league, a football league. We take a hundred kids out to the country in the summer. But it isn't enough, you know? What I'd really like to see is a Junior Olympics. We get all these kids from different neighborhoods to compete in athletic events. Instead of cutting each other up or shooting each other to prove something, they can prove it in sports. Sports can be a substitute for gang wars, you see? I believe that's what we need to do: take the knives and guns out of their hands and give them boxing gloves and footballs."

His plan made sense to me. It reminded me of the political theorists who said that we must find a moral substitute for warfare. If teenagers could be organized into athletic groups competing in sports, I believe—with Sugar Ray Robinson—that the juvenile crime problem in our cities would be reduced.

It is normal and healthy for kids to want to have fun, make friends, acquire skills, engage in sports and hobbies, and meet with members of the opposite sex. The plain fact is that opportunities to do so are rare, and this is a prime factor in juvenile delinquency in our cities. Statistically, high delinquency areas are very likely to lack sufficient recreational facilities. I can recall that when I was growing up in Brooklyn—where some three million working-class and low-income families live in an area of extremely high population density—there was only one golf course for that entire huge population. You couldn't find a tennis court for love or money in the ghettos of Williamsburg, Bedford-Stuyvesant, or Red Hook. A number of the high schools did not even have playing fields, and schoolyards were often locked up after three o'clock in the afternoon. Stickball in the streets was the chief athletic outlet in Brooklyn.

Physical-education programs in ghetto schools often serve only a very small minority of the students—those who excel in sports. There is often a policy of punishing delinquents and troublemakers by not allowing them to try out for sports teams. I remember being a serious contender for McKinley Junior High School's Hall of Champions, but after I was involved in a fight down in the schoolyard, I received a letter from my gym teacher telling me that I was disqualified from the contest because of "conduct unbecoming the human race."

Nor do delinquency-prone youngsters have much access to well-rounded sports programs outside of school. Little League types of sports programs, which are so much a part of childhood for most middle-class youngsters, are almost completely nonexistent in the slums. And youth groups such as Scouts, the YMCA, and Boys' Clubs tend to attract only "good" boys and girls and are thus not prepared to serve maladjusted kids. Consequently, as statistics indicate, delinquents seldom participate in sports or recreational programs, not because they don't want to, but rather because they simply have no access to such things. They are alienated from a normal and healthy aspect of the growing-up process.

It makes intuitive sense that active and restless delinquency-prone youngsters need an outlet for their energy. Athletics are not only a safety valve, but an activity to which youngsters can easily relate. A study titled *Perceptual Charac-*

teristics of Juvenile Delinquents, for instance, notes that young offenders see similarities between themselves and athletes in combative sports—football, wrestling, and boxing. Both groups appear to need stimulation and movement instead of more relaxed forms of recreation. Programs of emphasizing energetic, competitive activity might provide socially acceptable means of relieving monotony and curb the need for less desirable kinds of activity.

What society must do seems reasonably clear-cut. First, existing recreational facilities and programs must be expanded to recruit delinquency-prone youngsters. Such programs not only provide a wholesome and supervised environment for youngsters to have fun and meet friends, they also offer model situations in which kids can learn the basics of socialization. Sports can supply the matrix for leadership and teammate roles, which delinquents often specifically lack, thus leading them to rebel at authority.

In addition, schools must revamp and revitalize their physical-education programs so that participation in athletics is not used as a reward but rather is an integral part of the educational process. Logic decrees that a child's development is not helped by barring him from the gym or the classroom. A student struggling to succeed in school because of emotional problems should not be denied a source of personal satisfaction—athletic competition—which might be the very release he needs to overcome his disability. Physical education classes and affiliated sports programs should be the one school experience that youngsters can participate in with gusto and verve, whatever their level of ability. The fun of sports can potentially serve as a bridge between these kids and the more formal facets of education.

Youth groups such as the Scouts and the YMCA must be encouraged to undertake an active effort to enlist lower-class kids, particularly delinquents. As in the Jewish enclaves of Brooklyn, where the crime rate is minuscule, ghetto communities elsewhere should have several socializing and recreational centers for teenagers. Even before they acquire funds to establish such centers, the YMCA and Scouts could make an effort to enlarge existing programs so that children from the inner cities and suburbs would have an opportunity to interact with each other. Slum and suburb dwellers alike would benefit. Society can help by supporting efforts financially and by extending the full cooperation of concerned governmental agencies.

Other private organizations—business firms, churches, and service or fraternal clubs—can do their share by sponsoring Little League types of programs and by financing centers and playgrounds in poorer neighborhoods. Of course, a few organizations already exist for the purpose of helping kids through sports and athletic programs. Sugar Ray Robinson's Youth Foundation is one example. Another is Direction Sports, a privately endowed, nonprofit organization working to cut the disparity between the number of sports programs available in the suburbs and the ghetto.

In addition to offering a cornucopia of exciting sports, Direction Sports provides an opportunity for meaningful interaction between youngsters and adults by means of field trips. The imaginative leadership of Direction Sports has also conceived of a program to stir interest in basic learning skills through sports-related curricula. Arithmetic is learned, for example, by computing batting averages or yardage gains on the football field.

Both Direction Sports and the Sugar Ray Youth Foundation try to utilize the magnetism and personal satisfaction of athletic competition to provide a motivational breakthrough for disadvantaged youngsters. Both are precisely the type of programs that can be significant in preventing juvenile delinquency in America. What is important about these programs is that they *work*. They are valid and viable methods of combating juvenile delinquency, and that is what we need now.

As the above examples demonstrate, citizen groups can do a great deal to counteract the tide of juvenile crime. Everything helps, from donating basketball equipment to erecting a plant that employs thousands of persons. But such involvement cannot alone possibly solve the enormous problems spawned by the economically depressed conditions in America's ghettos.

They must be met by society and government as a whole if there is any hope of success. Up to now the emphasis has been on reaction rather than prevention, calling for more police protection and harsher penalties for crime. Rather, we must strike pre-emptively, before juvenile crime has a chance to develop.

25 • Rehabilitating the Cities

Too often we think of crime control exclusively in terms of the criminal justice system. This is a dangerously narrow view. . . . Merely to contain the effects of conditions that breed crime is to engage in an endless and losing battle.
—Ramsey Clark, Crime in America

Despite a recent eruption of juvenile crime in the suburbs, the main source of the problem remains in the overcrowded low-income areas of our cities. The obvious conclusion to be drawn is that if we were to ameliorate unemployment, destitution, and squalor in the slums we would reduce delinquency. The National Commission on the Causes and Prevention of Violence stated in 1967 that "violent crimes are committed mainly by the young, poor, male inhabitants of the ghetto slums." The January 20, 1975, issue of *Newsweek* placed unemployment for teenagers in general at 18.9 per cent, and by February it had climbed to over 20 per cent. For ghetto teenagers it ranges as high as 50 per cent in such cities as Detroit. Economist Belton Fleisher goes so far as to suggest that for a typical high-delinquency city area, a 10 per cent rise in income would mean a 20 per cent decline in juvenile crime.

Every move to improve life in America's inner cities is also a move against juvenile crime. Money for schools is money against crime. Programs for job training are programs to end crime training. When young citizens are assured of a decent living, enough to eat, and a good place to live, we will have taken the single most important step toward diminishing juvenile crime. The most highly touted scientific methods of therapy in juvenile institutions will be meaningless if when the boy returns to his community he is faced with unemployment and frustrating idleness. The ghettos and slums must be rehabilitated before the young persons who are driven to crime can be fully rehabilitated.

National urban policy

Paramount to rehabilitating our cities is the development of a coherent and comprehensive urban policy aimed at intelligent, unrelenting urban renewal. No private business would undertake a multimillion-dollar investment program without first preparing a detailed, long-range plan, yet this is exactly the federal government's approach. Funds are budgeted for a smorgasbord of fast-moving programs–uncoordinated, and unmindful of the total effect. The task at hand, then, is how to make better use of the resources already at our disposal.

As a first step the federal government should re-examine the national urban policy proposed by Patrick Moynihan to the Commission on the Causes and Prevention of Violence. Moynihan says a primary object of federal urban policy must be to restore the fiscal vitality of the cities. In trying to meet their responsibilities local governments often end up lurching from one fiscal crisis to another, and they rarely have enough resources to make local initiatives in public affairs a reality. Cities that are most in need of financial help are often denied their fair share of federal money by state government. Federal aid programs should have built-in guarantees for a fair allocation of funds among city, state, and local municipal governments.

Part of the typical city's inability to cope with urban problems is due to the obsolescent structure of government. Since metropolitan areas are governed by an orbit of satellite departments, often fragmented in different jurisdictions, effective government action on many critical problems is frustrated by red tape and conflicting priorities. Responsibility for municipal services must be centralized and efforts must be coordinated to better meet the needs of citizens, particularly the poor. The President might profitably convene an "urban convention" with delegates from all the major cities to advise the national administration on the best means of enhancing urban efficiency and accountability through structural changes in local governments.

A restructuring of area-development programs is well within the present range of our economic commitment. The current strategy was pioneered over thirty years ago in the Chicago Area Development Project, which was concerned mainly with offering supportive-agency services to a specific high-crime area with very low income and high population density. Today several of these area development programs still flourish, offering a vast array of welfare services. Even though these programs may be worthwhile, they are still essentially package deals to dispense federal aid and do not affect the basic economic and social structures of the communities being serviced. All efforts should be comprehensively reorganized to treat the community as an organic unit and to deal with basic problems.

The most compelling argument for long-range planning is that piecemeal approaches to improving slums often merely aggravate the problem. Urban-renewal programs, for example, commonly tear down old, unsightly housing and replace it with new high-rise dwellings that do not have as many units as the old, thereby forcing displaced residents to move into other old buildings, further exacerbating housing conditions. Similarly, new highway construction usually means that housing must be torn down and businesses dislocated, unbalancing the social ecology and altering the real property-tax base of the neighborhood. Synchronized planning considers renewal as a whole and coordinates all social and economic factors, developing the total community.

The remnants of President Johnson's war on poverty, which was waged with an arsenal of fly swatters, are limping along, not making any real impact on the economic base of ghetto communities. What is desperately needed are perpetual sources of income within these communities. The federal government, in cooperation with banks, could grant special low-interest loans to individuals who want to start small businesses or form food cooperatives, for example, on the same basis as relief is given to disaster areas. Special tax provisions could be established as incentives for slum development.

Youth employment

More directly related to the problem of juvenile delinquency is finding jobs for ghetto youth. In our society, employment is more than a means of earning a living; it is also important in achieving self-improvement, social mobility, and a sense of personal worth. Ghetto youngsters are faced with herculean obstacles in that they are not only discriminated against because of race, nationality, and age, but also because they lack basic marketable skills and the "social graces" that are necessary to be employable by middle-class standards. Training ghetto youths for available and fulfilling employment requires a government effort crackling with dynamic vision and spirited drive.

Currently government, public institutions, and many private employers have joined in an affirmative-action recruitment program directed toward the employment of minorities and women. These programs can be extended to inner-city youth, with the government providing tax breaks or contract preferences to those companies which participate. Neither unions nor business should feel threatened by the opening of youth opportunities. It is ultimately to their benefit, since young people commit 86 per cent of the crimes against personal property.

In the long run, however, what is most needed is the creation of new jobs for youth. The most natural approach would be to adopt the spirit and ideals of the New Deal—the Civil Conservation Corps and the National Youth Administration. The AFL-CIO, for instance, has proposed the establishment of a public-works acceleration program. Financed by either government or private organizations, or both, various programs could be created to provide jobs in medicine, health, education, sanitation, child day-care centers, and especially conservation, an area where masses of unemployed youth could furnish a vitally needed service. Given the rapid diminishing of natural resources, young people could serve for a period in a new version of the Conservation Corps in, for example, reclaiming all the precious recyclable metals, glass, paper, and wood from a community's garbage. Other young people could serve in forestry, agriculture, and law enforcement, among other areas. Besides reducing delinquency, this constructive use of youthful energy would have the net effect of greatly improving community life.

The creation of government-sponsored service organizations should not be seen as interfering with private business because any solution to the problem of juvenile crime helps the businessman too. If our system is to survive it must be flexible and effective in dealing with the needs of all the people. Capitalism and social responsibility can be compatible; in fact, they *must* be compatible. If private enterprise responds to the problem of spiraling youth unemployment, if industry finds positions for the hundreds of thousands of new young people coming into the labor market each year, they will be doing a great deal to open up new areas of human potential—and, incidentally, to reduce juvenile crime.

By far the best effort government can make to help provide jobs is to give significant tax breaks to those who employ youths and to give larger tax incentives and contract preferences to corporations like IBM, who go into the ghetto and build a factory, thereby creating thousands of jobs and pumping real money into the local economy, thereby uplifting national productivity and helping drive down unemployment and crime.

A number of political figures realize the urgency of moving on tax incentives to create jobs for youth, among them James Hayes, Yvonne Braithwaite Burke, Jacob Javits, and Alan Sieroty. Governor Edmund G. Brown of California represents the kind of state leader best able to confront the urban youth crisis, a man of shrewd political instincts who is philosophically idealistic and progressive yet tempered by a strong sense of pragmatism and historical realism. He is willing to venture into creative innovation, is incisively attuned with the times, and is ultimately morally responsive to the demands of social justice.

26 • Charting New Cultural Directions

I have an unfailing faith that there is a treasure in the heart of every young person if we can only bring it out.
—Winston Churchill

Juvenile crime in America, like any other national problem, has no one single cause. Countless threads come together to form a tapestry of social deviation. Some of these threads can be isolated and examined by means of statistical analysis; others, however, are harder to pin down, since they run through the fabric of society in no predictable pattern.

Nearly all of these tangled threads have been discussed in this book: our inverted sense of cultural and economic priorities; the fact that as a nation we are steeped in violence; that the strong sense of family that helped mold earlier generations has been weakened; that we seem to be more interested in day-to-day comforts than in solving our long-range problems; that we place much too great an emphasis on winning to the exclusion of taking pride in a job well done, win or lose; the inadequacy of too many of our laws; the lack of true moral leadership at the highest levels.

But these are only symptoms of an underlying sense of

malaise and alienation, which is most clearly revealed in our children. While we as adults may have our roots in a seemingly more stable era, our youth have never known anything but what they have seen around them for the past ten or fifteen years: a growing ecological disaster; a war in a remote country in which many of their friends were killed or maimed, a war that seemed misguided and perniciously wasteful to the point of absurdity; assassinations of respected, forceful leaders; a looking away from the pressing needs of the elderly and the poor; bitter struggles for the rights of minorities and women; and, finally, the open sore of Watergate. Small wonder there is aimless drug use, an apparent moral vacuum, and an increase in violent crime among our young people.

The mood in the fifties and sixties

One mood seems to dominate the youth of the seventies, pervading all activity and unifying all segments of a generation—the mood of disillusionment. Today's youth is floundering in a stunned emptiness, coming down from the drug-high euphoria of the sixties, in a desperate search for a renewed confidence in the future. To understand the mood of the seventies—and to understand something about the nature of juvenile crime today—it is necessary to review recent history.

America in the fifties was a country consumed by anti-communist paranoia, by the cold-war rhetoric of brinksmanship, by McCarthy's inquisition against political heretics. It was a decade in which a conformist culture predominated: the emphasis was on loyalty oaths, the organization man, being well adjusted, "fitting in." The fifties' ripple of "beatnik" protest generated more curiosity than substantial social change. Americans were smugly satisfied with their bland, TV-dinner lives. Playwright John Osborne lamented that "nobody thinks, nobody cares." It was a time of Howdy Doody happiness, of the move to suburban life styles, of Detroit's fascination with whale-sized cars, of teenage joyriding, blaring jukeboxes, and beer-drinking frat parties. The fifties, in short, was an era distinguished by a crew-cut economy of feelings, a complacent brutality of attitude, a time of numbing apathy.

And then came the sixties, and the mood of the country began to change. It was a change that could be seen virtually everywhere; it could be felt, almost, in the air. There was a rousing stir of activism, of idealism, a renaissance of vision. We began to feel that we could finally bring about rational order on earth. "Peace" became the greeting on a generation's lips. We believed in our ability to go to the stars. The dreams of the Enlightenment were resurrected, and a seismic rumble of creative energy lifted our national spirit. If the fifties was a decade of moral stupor, the sixties ushered in a decade of spiritual awakening—the dawning of the Age of Aquarius.

The composers of *Hair* could scarcely have anticipated the uses the phrase "Age of Aquarius" would spawn. The period's chief medium of expression—music—underwent a spontaneous transformation, commencing with the youthful rock groups in San Francisco, carried forward by the personal and musical charisma of the Beatles, nurtured by ever-larger electronic amplifiers, and coming to full maturity on the fields of Woodstock. The music of the sixties was full of raunchy, sweaty sexuality, potent energy, and a declaration of revolutionary fervor. One of Bob Dylan's most popular compositions—"The Times They Are a-Changin' "—captured the generation's mood.

The literature of the sixties echoed the hopeful themes of the decade's music. In *The Greening of America* Charles Reich proclaimed: "Today we are witnesses to a great moment of history: a turn from the pessimism that has closed in our modern industrial society; the rebirth of a future." Students interpreted Albert Camus' *The Myth of Sisyphus* to mean that attempts to attain economic success could no longer supply the needed existential challenge; instead they emphasized non-materialistic priorities. Kenneth Keniston's book describing the fifties was called *The Uncommitted;* his major work of the sixties was *Young Radicals: Notes on Committed Youth*. This surge of passionate concern was sudden and sweeping, manifested in the love ethic, in the spread of psychedelic drugs, and—most conspicuously—in the rise of political activism.

When the Free Speech Movement was unleashed at the Berkeley campus of the University of California, Sproul Plaza was choked with a chanting, crying sea of lovingly entangled humanity. Eight hundred policemen were needed to clear the area. In 1968 the contagion spread to Columbia University when Mark Rudd and his followers seized an administration building. Students who took part reported that it was a communal experience like nothing they had ever known. Even Harvard—seemingly aloof and remote from such flamboyance—was touched by this moving energy. Describing the campus strikes in 1969, the *Harvard Bulletin* noted: "Seldom if ever in the history of Harvard has such a rush of events been packed into so short a period."

Nor was this new spirit of supercharged activism confined to college campuses. High school students too, a group previously unheard from in such a context, began asserting their rights—and their lives—as never before. They became interested in politics and social change; high school students were "on the lines" next to their collegiate counterparts in virtually every mass demonstration. "Underground" high school newspapers appeared across America, in the face of official condemnation. High school students began to stop acquiescing in the arbitrary administrative actions handed down to them by their principals, deans, and assorted assistants; they began to demand, and strive for, their rights as students and as human beings.

And America was not alone in this new spirit of youthful idealism and activism. In France the energetic fury of the young spilled into the streets at the urging of Danny the Red, and exploded in other European nations under other young leaders such as Germany's Rudi Dutschke. Admittedly this activism contained elements of destructive anarchy and violence, but for the most part the civil rights marches, the ecology protests, and the Vietnam sit-ins were constructive acts of dynamic commitment, expressions of a real desire for change from the apathetic past. Thus, as the sixties unfolded, the country seemed to be changing for the better, and although the Age of Aquarius was not yet here, it certainly appeared to be waiting in the wings.

There was no single underlying cause for this seeming metamorphosis, and although its true flowering did not come until the mid-sixties, its roots—perhaps surprisingly—were in the fifties. Certainly the unconsciously nourishing years of the Eisenhower administrations, a time of relative peace and prosperity, helped turn the nation's face toward the new mood of the sixties. Youth free from material cares can aspire to loftier goals of idealism. The systematic defense of the disadvantaged by the Supreme Court under Earl Warren helped raise the nation's social consciousness. Khrushchev's de-Stalinization helped ease international tensions, and foreshadowed a new liberalization in Soviet policies. Pope John XXIII tilted the axis of ecumenism in the Roman Catholic Church, and in the United States other religious denominations appeared to be shifting away from fossilized dogma.

The economic climate of the sixties was also a major factor. The job market was wide open. Employers made extensive, occasionally lavish efforts to recruit college graduates. More than a hundred Harvard Law School graduates, for example, were flown to the west coast to be wined and dined by a law firm that had jobs for only a few of them. Employment ads for the aerospace industry took up page after page in newspapers. Teaching positions were plentiful. Thus comfortably cushioned, college students did not fret about jobs. Instead, they clamored for an end to the superfluous ritual of grades.

Perhaps most symbolic of America's optimistic mood in the sixties was the magnificent resolve to put men on the moon. The Apollo program, the ultimate demonstration of the incredible magic of science, captured the nation's imagination from its inception. Technology, it seemed, would provide the solutions to whatever problems America might face through the decade and beyond. As the space program advanced, the country became mesmerized by the myth that science could rise to any challenge, for mere mortals had finally been able to steal the heavens from the gods.

Although there was no single cause for the dramatic changes in the national psyche during the sixties, there was one predominant catalyst: John F. Kennedy, who almost singlehandedly rekindled America's vision of itself and of the world. Such innovative social programs as the Peace Corps demonstrated to young Americans that idealism could be translated into tangible results. Kennedy was able to make America's youth share his belief that the world could be bettered.

Kennedy's impact was most evident on the college campuses, where a new vitality was churning in students. As Dr. George A. Kateb of Amherst recalls, "The average student was far more giving, more open, more responsive. The brightest were more sophisticated, they were voracious in their intellectual appetites, politically and socially more aware and sensitive." Students called each other "sisters" and "brothers" unself-consciously. They were idealistic, convinced it was their mission to forge a new destiny. And they were united, the sons and daughters of the working class side by side with the elite of the Ivy League, on college and high school campuses all across America.

Youthful cynicism in the seventies

But as America moved into the seventies, the idealism of the sixties began to be tempered with a worldly-wise cynicism. Enthusiasm was overwhelmed by weariness; optimism was supplanted by skepticism. "When I asked the class what it was they wanted me to say for them," says Hillary Rodman, Wellesley College's valedictorian in 1969, "everyone came up to me and said, 'Talk about trust. Talk about the trust bust.' " In 1970 James Clark, the valedictorian at Georgetown University, said, "In our explorations we looked about us in frozen horror at what we beheld. . . . We are afraid, for ourselves, for our people, for our world." Or again, in the words of UCLA commencement speaker Tom Normington in 1970: "How much like helpless toys we have been: wooden students, numbered by computers, painted with bright clothes, harmlessly intoning protests heard long before our year." The joy of Woodstock had degenerated into the horror of Altamont.

On the UCLA campus students are now busy, cold, aloof. They have little interest in issues that would have spurred lively debate during the sixties. Says UCLA senior Nina Weinstein, "Students are lethargic. They have been pushed down and down and down so far that they now believe in the total futility of all action." At Berkeley, interest in penal reform—among other things—has fallen off. Fay Stendar, former attorney for the Soledad Brothers and firebrand founder of the Penal Law Institute, claims that students are no longer rallying to the cause. The situation has become so demoralizing that Fay herself has given up the fight. "I'm tired of beating my head against a stone wall," she sighs.

A former McGovern campaign leader, Dean Rolstead, told me: "I'm now totally apolitical. The system is so massive we can't really participate. The overwhelming sentiment of my generation is a sense of powerlessness in the face of corporate power. Emphasis on the individual has been lost. Tennis was once a calm, reflective game. Now it's like football, with crowds cheering and stomping. During the sixties I was swept up in the sense of changing the country. Now it's somewhat like crashing after a powerful drug trip. I don't like the bread-and-circus atmosphere in this country, but I realize the futility of trying to change things. My plans right now are to go to Paris and open up a little ice cream shop."

A midwestern graduate student, reflecting on her days as an activist, said bitterly, "What did I get out of it all except an ulcer?"

This mood of disillusionment is not limited to the college campuses; it can be seen at all levels of American society, from top to bottom, from coast to coast. Disillusionment pervades our high schools; it infuses the working class; it poisons ghetto youth. People's expectations, so high during the sixties, have given way to the growing national mood of disillusionment and cynicism. No longer is it the average working man's goal to buy a house of his own; if he finds one he can afford, he probably won't be able to find a loan at any price. With unemployment growing every day, he worries more about holding onto his job than about making the down payment on a home.

In the ghetto, where conditions are the worst of all, disillusionment runs through the streets like a noxious fog. A recurrent dream among ghetto youth is to get out, to find a better life—but when life *outside* the ghetto seems little better than life *in* the ghetto, that dream is dashed and broken. Unable to find work, less able each day to afford even the minimal necessities, their illusions shattered through no fault of their own, is it any wonder that ghetto youth turn to crime?

Controversial speakers are no longer sought by colleges and universities. During the sixties, the radical Jerry Rubin commanded a $3,000 speaking fee, and he was in demand on campuses all across the country. Today he probably couldn't speak on the commune circuit in exchange for food stamps. Bob Walker, president of the American Program Bureau—the nation's largest lecture agency—says, "Students are not buying social causes any more. What I get asked for now is stand-up comics. And nostalgia is big. I get a lot of dates for Buffalo Bob. The New Left still gets publicity, but the majority of students are security-minded. I think that feeling mirrors the general mood in America."

Almost a decade ago, just as student activism was catching fire, the American Council on Education began to poll college freshmen on a wide range of subjects, from their personal goals to their views on political reform. In January of 1975, the ACE released its findings on current freshmen, the class of '78. The results reveal a striking contrast between contemporary freshmen and their predecessors.

Based on responses from 311,950 freshmen at 576 colleges and universities, this year's survey shows a new caution and conservatism among entering students. More than half the freshmen think there is too much concern in the courts for the rights of criminals. Only 25.9 per cent place ecology high among their personal interests, a drop of nearly 10 per cent since last year. They are far less interested in either keeping up with or influencing political affairs. In the past year alone, the proportion who said it was important to keep abreast of current politics has dropped from 42.4 per cent to 36.6 per cent.

In California's 1974 gubernatorial primary election, voter turnout was the lowest since 1942, and young people stayed away from the polls in even larger numbers than their parents.

What has caused this massive disillusionment in the seventies? Why have young Americans lost the Aquarian sense of themselves and their world that blossomed just a few years ago? Again, there is no single cause, nor are there any easy answers. The end of the Vietnam war is one obvious factor. Just as the war provided a rallying point for protest, its lingering agony eroded faith and its termination defused the protest movement's ardor, leaving millions with an unfocused anger that was soon dissipated into disillusionment. The rash of assassinations–John F. Kennedy, Malcolm X, Martin Luther King, Robert Kennedy–extinguished the hopes of millions, and were especially traumatic to the young. And the mass of allegations, proven crimes, and loose ends called Watergate was the final stroke. These revelations tell a story of our highest officials flouting the Constitution, making dishonesty operative, and placing government in the service of special interest groups. Youth's faith has been shaken, if not shattered, and they have retreated into a shell of cynicism.

With the energy crisis and dependence upon Arab oil, Americans suddenly discovered that they were not the masters of nature. Everyone must be aware of alarming shortages ahead in basic metals, fuel, and food; our belief in technology's omnipotence has crumbled. Many young people are fleeing from science and the professions into the occult and mysticism. Our dream of conquering the universe has been deflated: we reached the moon in a blaze of glory, and in the eyes of many found only an inglorious rockpile; then the space program, like everything else, ran out of money.

In economics, the classical theories are proving to be inadequate. The international monetary system is skidding closer to the edge of chaos, the aerospace and teaching markets have dried up, and Ph.D.'s are working as waiters and barmaids. As the American economy appears to list toward depression, a creeping feeling of panic engulfs some, while disillusionment settles in all over America. Our hopes, so high in the sixties, have been dashed back to earth. The bright dawn of the Age of Aquarius has been dimmed for America.

The rising tide of juvenile crime is a cause as well as a manifestation of America's disillusionment. As youth becomes more disillusioned, as young people realize that the American dream may never come alive for them, more and more of them turn to crime—to lash out, perhaps, at a society they see as having gone bad virtually overnight, or perhaps just to make some kind of living for themselves. Thus juvenile crime reflects America's disillusionment. At the same time, the fact that ever-greater numbers of young people are turning to crime only deepens the nation's sense of disillusionment. It is a vicious cycle, far easier to describe and comprehend than to break—but it *is* breakable, and it can and must be broken.

The question on the bottom line, then, is: Must we resign ourselves to a pessimistic verdict? Reeling from the aftershock of crisis upon crisis, it may seem illogical to continue to hope—but it is intolerable to live without hope. A crucial dimension of the human condition resides in our collective spiritual consciousness. If the world were to totter into material ruin, it would only be a mild calamity compared to the day the human spirit went bankrupt. If people are *hopeful* about future possibilities, the psychological consequences of present tragedies may be diminished. If we cannot have faith in the future, though, our lives will reflect Clarence Darrow's description of a barren life: "An oppressive burden that no thinking humane person would wantonly inflict upon someone else." History is a continuing process of walking away from failures and building anew upon the rubble.

My own personal experience in overcoming my childhood in the streets of New York's Little Italy has imbued me with the philosophy of "try again and again, this way, that way, around or over, through no-man's-land via never-never land, up past outer borders, ever searching for the light." The pathways to perfection are limitless, and humanity has barely glimpsed the infinitesimal.

Restructuring society from the bottom up

In terms of long-range planning to eliminate crime—both juvenile and adult—we might look to ecology, the study of the interaction between living systems in nature, for guidance. When ecosystems get too large, they often topple of their own weight. There is a persuasive argument to be made that our social ecosystem, as it grows larger and larger, is in danger of such a catastrophe. One way to avert this kind of cataclysm is to restructure society into smaller, more self-contained units.

In Tokyo, where gore and violence glut the TV screens as much as they do here, and where there is as much or more crowding, poverty, and inflation, the crime rate remains comparatively low. This is due, apparently, to the fact that the city is divided into small, localized administrative jurisdictions that are more responsive to the wants and needs of the residents—and of course to the fact that family authority and respect are integral parts of the Japanese culture. Insofar as it has been able to contain crime, then, Japan is a good model, but in other ways it too is in peril of collapse.

We *can* take steps to prevent our social ecosystem from crashing around us. If we act out of enlightened self-interest and rekindle some of the spirit that helped our forefathers and mothers build this country, perhaps we can change our direction before it is too late.

The concept of community control and community involvement—of thinking small—can work. It is a way of regenerating in Americans a pride of place and a sense of belonging. Government today is so big and remote that the average person feels helpless. Nothing seems to work; the tax monies go out, but the taxpayers seldom see any return on their investment, at least any that they can relate to in their daily lives. If government were restructured from the bottom up, with the major emphasis being placed on the local area, the neighborhood, citizens *could* control the quality of their environment to a greater extent.

If a neighborhood bands together, whether for a block party or a town-hall type of meeting to discuss issues that affect them every day, they will start to get to know each other, and care for each other. And when they start to care for each other they will begin to be actively concerned with what is happening to their young people. Too many drugs, too much crime? At a local level the citizens can address themselves to these problems. They can plan and carry out their own programs, and they can exert real pressure on their state and local legislators to provide funds and programs on a higher level—the results of which they will expect to see back in their neighborhood. In any case, they will, after thrashing out their differences, reaching compromises, and coming up, usually, with plans they can agree on, express themselves on social issues in a coherent way.

If this kind of grass-roots caring and action were going on in every city and town across the country, the quality of our life would surely change. Rather than thinking in cosmic terms of millions of dollars and thousands of people, we would be thinking in concrete terms of what is needed *here* and *now* to solve our problems.

Along with all the other reforms suggested in this book, this kind of local activism could be a real deterrent to youthful crime. Children who see their parents actively involved in trying to get better education, employment, improved recreational facilities, and more effective law enforcement will be less likely to rip off their neighbors out of boredom or a sense of malaise. In the ghettos, the children would have models other than pimps and drug dealers to look up to—and might even benefit by the programs planned and put into action. Either way, the motivation for a lot of juvenile crime will have disappeared.

Building on the hope of the sixties

The children of the affluent sixties, their whims easily indulged and awash in affluence, were perhaps unprepared for the scarring hardship and unceasing struggle which are natural elements in humanity's eternal striving for perfection. When we evaluate the legacy of the sixties generation, however, we realize that considerable social progress was achieved and solidified, and that it will have a lasting impact. Thanks largely to their efforts, advances have been made in civil rights, due process and equal protection of the law, sexual freedom, women's liberation, and ecology. A new, broad variety of life styles, growing interpersonal openness, and a sensitive masculinity were indelibly imprinted on our national consciousness.

How much of our greatest resource—the faith of our young—we have irretrievably lost only history will be able to tell us. But the seeds of idealism sown in the sixties have not been destroyed. They are only dormant, and can be awakened by a new catalyst to high purpose. As John F. Kennedy observed: "The American by nature is optimistic; he is experimental, an inventor and a builder who builds best when called upon to build greatly. Arouse his will to believe in himself, give him a great goal to believe in, and he will create the means to reach it."

It would be a tragic loss if the potential for progress found in today's youth were to continue to be dissipated in disillusionment, cynicism, and—worst of all—apathy. But Author Mark Gerzon, a 1970 Harvard graduate, says that only his generation can "furnish the enthusiasm, manpower, and idealism that could mean the difference between a cooperative free world and disaster." The youth of the seventies may be disillusioned, but out of their disillusionment a new American idealism—an idealism that may ultimately be our salvation—may, like the phoenix, spring up anew. A cynic looks back on the historical follies and failures of humanity and is reconciled to this record as the permanent human condition, but someone who has faith in life believes in humanity's potential to grow, and that person remains unreconciled.

Bibliography

American Friends Service Committee, *Struggle for Justice*, New York: Hill & Wang, 1971.

American Psychiatric Association, *Training Schools for Delinquent Children*. Washington, D.C.: A.P.A. Mental Hospital Service, 1952.

Amos, William E., and Manella, Raymond L. (Eds.), *Delinquent Children in Juvenile Correctional Institutions*. Illinois: Charles C. Thomas, 1966.

——, *Readings in the Administration of Institutions for Delinquent Youth*. Illinois: Charles C. Thomas, 1965.

——, Manella, Raymond L., and Southwell, Marilyn A., *Action Programs for Delinquency Prevention*. Illinois: Charles C. Thomas, 1965.

Ariessohn, R. M., "Offense v. Offender in Juvenile Court," *Juvenile Justice*, August, 1972.

Arnold, William R., *Juveniles on Parole*. New York: Random House, 1970.

Babcock, Richard F. and Bosselman, Fred, "Citizen Participation: A Suburban Suggestion for the Central City," *Law and Contemporary Problems*, Spring, 1967.

Barron, Milton L., *The Juvenile in Delinquent Society*. New York: Alfred A. Knopf, 1954.

Bassiouni, M., *Justice in America: Youth and the Law*. Boston: Houghton Mifflin, 1970.

Bayh, Burch, "Toward Juvenile Justice." *American Scholar*, August, 1971.

Bazelon, David L., "Beyond Control of the Juvenile Court," *Juvenile Court Judges Journal*, Summer, 1970.

——, "Implementing the Right to Treatment," *University of Chicago Law Review*, Summer, 1969.

——, "The Law and the Mentally Ill," *American Journal of Psychiatry,* November, 1968.

Becker, Howard, *Outsiders.* New York: Free Press, 1963.

Bellush, Jewel, *Urban Renewal: People, Politics and Planning.* Garden City: Doubleday, 1967.

Benson, Charles M., "Impartial Trial," *SCJOA,* August, 1971.

Bloomquist, E. R., *Marijuana.* Beverly Hills: Glencoe Press, 1969.

——, *Marijuana, the Second Trip.* Beverly Hills: Glencoe Press, 1971.

Briar, S. and Piliaven, I., "Police Encounters with Juveniles," *American Journal of Sociology,* September, 1964.

Brown, Claude, *Manchild in the Promised Land.* New York: New American Library, 1965.

Bullock, Paul, *Watts: The Aftermath.* New York: Grove Press, 1969.

California Laws Relating to Youthful Offenders. California: Department of the Youth Authority, 1969.

Cannon, J. A., "Federal Court Intervention in Juvenile Court Proceedings," *Denver Law Journal,* 1972.

Carducci, Catherine, *What Can They Do—Lock Me Up?* Fort Worth: M. E. McAdam, 1974.

Carpenter, Mary, *Juvenile Delinquents.* Montclair, N.J.: Patterson Smith, 1970.

Casper, Jonathon, *American Criminal Justice.* Englewood Cliffs, N.J.: Prentice-Hall, 1972.

Cavan, Ruth, and Jordan, *Delinquency and Crime: Cross-Cultural Perspectives.* New York: Lippincott, 1968.

Cayton, C. E., "Emerging Patterns in the Administration of Juvenile Justice," *Journal of Urban Law,* November, 1971.

Chambliss, William J., *Crime and the Legal Process.* New York: McGraw-Hill, 1969.

Chayet, Neil L., "Legal Neglect of the Mentally Ill," *Mental Hygiene,* January, 1969.

——, "Your Child and the Law," *Today's Education,* March, 1972.

"Child Neglect: Due Process for the Parent," *Columbia Law Review,* March, 1970.

Cicourel, Aaron V., *The Social Organization of Juvenile Justice.* New York: John Wiley and Sons, 1968.

Clark, Kenneth B., *Dark Ghetto.* New York: Harper & Row, 1965.

Clark, Ramsey, *Crime in America.* New York: Simon & Schuster, 1970.

Cloward, Richard, and Ohlin, Floyd, *Delinquency and Opportunity.* New York: Free Press, 1960.

Coffee, J., "Privacy versus Parens Patriae," *Cornell Law Review,* April, 1972.

Cohen, Albert K., *Delinquent Boys.* Glencoe, Ill.: Free Press, 1955.

Cohn, Jerry, and Murphy, William, *Burn, Baby, Burn!* New York: E. P. Dutton, 1966.

Coles, R., Brenner, J., and Meagher, D., *Drugs and Youth*. New York: Liveright, 1970

Conrad, John P., *Crime and Its Correction*. Berkeley: University of California Press, 1965.

Corrigan, M., "Juvenile Court and Community Involvement," *Osgoode Hall Law Journal*, August, 1972.

Criner, Jane, *Use of Authority in the Treatment of Deviant Youth*. Los Angeles: University of Southern California, 1961.

"Crisis in Juvenile Courts," *U.S. News & World Report*, March 24, 1969.

Davidson, Henry A., "Mental Hospitals and the Civil Liberties Dilemma," *Mental Hygiene*, July, 1967.

——, "The Double Life of a Psychiatric Hospital," *Mental Hygiene*, January, 1969.

Davis, S. M., "Jurisdictional Dilemma of Juvenile Court," *North Carolina Law Review*, December, 1972.

——, "Justice for the Juvenile," *Duke Law Journal*, December, 1971.

"Delinquency and Middle Class Goals," *Journal of Criminal Law, Criminology, and Police Science*, LXI, 1965.

DeRopp, Robert S., *Drugs and the Mind*. New York: Grove Press, 1960.

Donnelly, Richard C., Goldstein, Joseph, and Schwartz, Richard, *Criminal Law*. New York: Free Press, 1962.

Echols, A. E., "Deadline, Vengeance and Tribute: A Prescription for Black Juvenile Delinquency," *Crime and Delinquency*, October, 1970.

Eldefonzo, Edward, *Law Enforcement and the Youthful Offender: Juvenile Procedures*. New York: John Wiley and Sons, 1967.

Faber, Dianne, "Dependent-Neglect Proceedings: A Case for Procedural Due Process," *Dusquene Law Review*, IX, 1971.

Feiss, Carl, "Progress and Poverty," *Law and Contemporary Problems*, Winter, 1965.

Ferman, Louis A., *Poverty in America*. Ann Arbor: University of Michigan Press, 1965.

Ferster, E. Z., "Juvenile Justice System: In Search of the Role of Counsel," *Fordham Law Review*, March, 1971.

—— and Courtless, T. F., "Post-Disposition Treatment and Recidivism in the Juvenile Court," *Journal of Family Law*, 1972.

Forer, Lois G., *"No One Will Listen."* New York: Grosset & Dunlap, 1971.

——, "Rights of Children: The Legal Vacuum," *American Bar Association Journal*, December, 1969.

Fort, Joel, *The Pleasure Seekers*. New York: Grove Press, 1969.

Freud, Sigmund, *Civilization and Its Discontents*. New York: W. W. Norton, 1962.

Frey, M. A., "Criminal Responsibility of the Juvenile Murderer," *Washington University Law Quarterly,* Spring, 1970.

Galvin, Ruth, "Breaking the American Stereotypes," *Time,* February 14, 1972.

Gandy, J. M., "Exercise of Discretion by the Police as a Decision-making Process in the Disposition of Juvenile Offenders," *Osgoode Hall Law Journal,* November, 1970.

Gebhard, Paul; Gagnon, John; Pomeroy, Wardell; and Christenson, Cornelia, *Sex Offenders.* New York: Grosset & Dunlap, 1967.

Geller, Allen, and Boos, Maxwell, *The Drug Beat.* New York: Cowles, 1969.

Gemignani, R. J., "Relating the Roles and Objectives of Delinquency Prevention," *Juvenile Court Judges Journal,* Summer, 1970.

George, Alexander, "Political Leadership and Social Change," *Daedelus,* Fall, 1968.

Gillers, Stephen, *Getting Justice: The Rights of the People.* New York: Basic Books, 1971.

Glazer, Nathan, "A Sociologist's View of Poverty," in *Poverty in America,* Margaret Gordon, ed. San Francisco: Chandler, 1965.

Glen, Jeffrey, "The Coming Juvenile Justice System," *American Bar Association Journal,* December, 1969.

Goffman, Erving, *Stigma.* Englewood Cliffs, N.J.: Prentice-Hall, 1963.

Goldberg, Harriet L., and Sheridan, William, *Family Courts—An Urgent Need.* Washington, D.C.: U.S. Department of Health, Education, and Welfare, 1960.

Golden Anniversary White House Conference on Children and Youth (March 27–April 2, 1960). Washington, D.C.: U.S. Government Printing Office, 1960.

Goldstein, Abraham S. and Joseph, eds., *Crime, Law, and Society.* New York: Free Press, 1971.

Governor's Commission on the Los Angeles Riots, *Violence in the City—An End or a Beginning?* Los Angeles: December, 1965.

Graham, Hugh, and Gurr, Ted, *The History of Violence in America.* New York: Bantam Books, 1969.

Green, B., "Disposition of Juvenile Offenders," *Criminal Law Quarterly,* June, 1971.

Green, Gary K., "California's New Mental Commitment Legislation: Is It Legally Sufficient?" *California Western Law Review,* Fall, 1969.

Griffin, C. W. Jr., "City Slums and Segregated Suburbs," *Saturday Review,* January 8, 1966.

Grilli, Mary Ann, "The MDSO-Uncivil Civil Commitment," *The Santa Clara Lawyer,* Fall, 1970.

Guttentag, Marcia, ed., *The Poor: Impact on Research and Theory.* Ann Arbor: Edwards Brothers, 1970.

Harrington, Michael, *The Other America.* New York: Macmillan, 1962.

Hart, H. L. A., *Law, Liberty, and Morality*. New York: Vintage Books, 1963.

Hechinger, Grace and Fred, *Teenage Tyranny*. New York: William Morrow, 1962.

Herzog, Elizabeth, *Identifying Potential Delinquents*. Washington, D.C.: U.S. Department of Health, Education, and Welfare, 1960.

Hindelang, M. J., and Weis, J. G., "Personality and Self-Reported Delinquency," *Criminology*, November, 1972.

Hood, Roger, and Sparks, Richard, *Key Issues in Criminology*. New York: McGraw-Hill, 1970.

Isenberg, Irwin, *The City in Crisis*. New York: H. W. Wilson, 1968.

Jacob, Herbert, *Justice in America*. Boston: Little, Brown, 1965.

Kaplan, John, *Marijuana–The New Prohibition*. New York: World Publishing, 1970.

Ketcham, O. W., "*McKeiver v Pennsylvania:* The Last Word on Juvenile Court Adjudications?" *Cornell Law Review*, April, 1972.

Leeper, Robert, and Madison, Peter, *Toward Understanding Human Personalities*. New York: Appleton-Century-Crofts, 1959.

Leinwand, Gerald, ed., *Crime and Juvenile Delinquency*. New York: Washington Square Press, 1968.

——, *The Police*. New York: Washington Square Press, 1968.

Lenon, H. F., "On Re-examining *Gault*–Again and Again," *Family Law Quarterly*, December, 1970.

Lewin, Stephen, *Crime and Its Prevention*. New York: H. W. Wilson, 1968.

Libarle, Marc, and Seligson, Tom, eds., *The High School Revolutionaries*. New York: Vintage Books, 1970.

Lieberman, Mark, *The Dope Book*. New York: Praeger, 1971.

Little, W. T., "The Need for Reform in the Juvenile Courts," *Osgoode Hall Law Journal*, August, 1972.

Lowe, Jeanne R., *Cities in a Race with Time*. New York: Random House, 1967.

MacFaden, W. E., "Changing Concepts of Juvenile Justice," *Crime and Delinquency*, April, 1971.

Mathias, C. M., "Everything Begins at Home: Problem of Juvenile Crime," *Judicature*, December, 1972.

Matza, David, *Delinquency and Drift*. New York: John Wiley and Sons, 1964.

Mays, John Barron, *On the Threshold of Delinquency*. Liverpool: Liverpool University Press, 1959.

Menninger, Karl, *The Crime of Punishment*. New York: Viking, 1968.

Meyer, Edward J., "Lawyer in a Mental Hospital–the New York Experiment," *Mental Hygiene*, January, 1969.

Meyerson, Martin, "Urban Policy: Reforming Reform," *Daedelus*, Fall, 1968.

Miller, Frank W., Dawson, Robert O., and Parnas, Raymond I., *The Juvenile Justice Process*. New York: Foundation Press, 1971.

Mogilner, J. J., "Admissibility of Evidence in Juvenile Court—A Double Standard or No Standard?" *California State Bar Journal*, May–June, 1971.

Morris, Norval, and Hawkins, Gordon, *The Honest Politician's Guide to Crime Control*. Chicago: University of Chicago Press, 1969.

Mulligan, W., "Dyslexia, Specific Learning Disability and Delinquency," *Juvenile Justice*, November, 1972.

Murphy, Raymond, and Watson, James, *The Structure of Discontent*. Los Angeles: Department of Sociology, UCLA, 1967.

Nelson, R. O., "Clinical Psychologist in Juvenile Court," *Juvenile Justice*, November, 1972.

Neumeyer, Martin, *Juvenile Delinquency in Modern Society*. Princeton: Van Nostrand, 1961.

Norman, Sherwood, *Detention Practice*. New York: National Probation and Parole Association, 1960.

Nelson, E. K., *Community Approaches to the Prevention of Crime and Delinquency—Some Research Leads*. Los Angeles: University of Southern California, 1961.

Oursler, Will, *Marijuana, the Facts, the Truth*. New York: Paul S. Erikson, 1968.

Palmai, G., "Crime and Social Class in Juvenile Delinquency," *Juvenile Court Judges Journal*, Spring, 1971.

Paulson, Monrad, *Equal Justice for the Poor Man*, Public Affairs Committee No. 367. New York: Public Affairs Pamphlets, 1964.

Penn, Nolan, Sindberg, Ronald, and Roberts, Allyn, "The Dilemma of Involuntary Commitment: Suggestions for a Measurable Alternative," *Mental Hygiene*, January, 1969.

Platt, Anthony M., *The Child Savers: The Invention of Delinquency*. Chicago: University of Chicago Press, 1969.

Popkin, A. B., Lippert, F. J., and Keiter, J. A., "Another Look at the Role of Due Process in Juvenile Court," *Family Law Quarterly*, Fall, 1972.

Potter, G., " 'Hotline' for Troubled Youth," *Federal Probation*, December, 1971.

President's Commission on Law Enforcement and Administration ot Justice, *Challenge of Crime in a Free Society*. Washington, D.C.: U.S. Government Printing Office, 1967.

——, *Task Force Report: Crime and Its Impact—An Assessment*. Washington, D.C.: U.S. Government Printing Office, 1967.

——, *Task Force on Juvenile Delinquency: Juvenile Delinquency and Youth Crime*. Washington, D.C.: U.S. Government Printing Office, 1967.

Pusateri, L. X., and Scott, R. K., "Illinois' New Unified Code of Corrections," *Illinois Bar Journal*, October, 1972.

Radzinowicz, Leon, and Wolfgang, Marvin, eds., *Crime and Justice.* New York: Basic Books, 1971.

Ragulsky, F., "Innovative Peer Group Program that Works," *Juvenile Court Judges Journal,* Summer, 1971.

Raven, Bertram, "Conflict and Power," in *The Structure of Conflict,* Swingle, Paul, ed. New York: Academic Press, 1970.

Reckless, Walter, *The Crime Problem.* New York: Meredith Publishing, 1961.

Reich, Charles, *The Greening of America.* New York: Bantam Books, 1971.

Rubin, Sol, *Crime and Juvenile Delinquency.* Dobbs Ferry: Oceana Publications, 1970.

Rubington, Earl, and Weinberg, Martin, *Deviance/The Interactionist Perspective.* London: Macmillan, 1968.

Rudstein, David, "Double Jeopardy in Juvenile Proceedings," *William and Mary Law Review,* Winter, 1972.

Sander, Stanley, "The Language of Watts," *The Nation,* December 20, 1965.

Scheuer, James, *To Walk the Streets Safely.* Garden City: Doubleday, 1969.

Schur, Edwin, *Our Criminal Society.* Englewood Cliffs, N.J.: Prentice-Hall, 1969.

Seligman, Daniel, "The Enduring Slums," in *The Exploding Metropolis.* Garden City: Doubleday, 1957.

Shaw, Otto, *Youth in Crisis.* New York: Hart Publishing, 1966.

Sheridan, William, and Freer, Alice, *Delinquent Children in Penal Institutions.* Washington, D.C.: U.S. Department of Health, Education, and Welfare, 1964.

Silberman, Charles, *Crisis in Black and White.* Clinton, Mass.: Colonial Press, 1964.

Smart, Frances, in *Neurosis and Crime,* B. Curtis Brown, ed. New York: Barnes and Noble, 1970.

Sorrentino, Joseph, *The Moral Revolution.* Los Angeles: Nash Publications, 1972.

——, *Up From Never.* Englewood Cliffs: Prentice-Hall, Inc., 1971.

Spergel, Irving, *Community Problem Solving, the Delinquency Example.* Chicago: University of Chicago Press, 1969.

Steel, Ronald, *New Light on Juvenile Delinquency.* New York: H. W. Wilson, 1967.

Strouse, Jean, *Up Against the Law.* New York: New American Library, 1970.

Struggle for Justice, prepared for the American Friends Service Committee. New York: Hill & Wang, 1971.

Sumner, H., "Locking Them Up," *Crime and Delinquency,* April, 1971.

Toffler, Alvin, *Future Shock.* New York: Bantam Books, 1971.

U.S. Department of Health, Education, and Welfare, *Better Ways to*

Help Youth. Washington, D.C.: U.S. Government Printing Office 1973.
——, *Delinquency Prevention Through Youth Development.* Washington, D.C.: U.S. Government Printing Office, 1973.
U.S. Department of Labor, *A Study of Successful Persons from Seriously Disadvantaged Backgrounds.* Washington, D.C.: U.S. Government Printing Office, 1970.
Wasserstrom, Richard, ed., *Morality and the Law.* Belmont, Calif.: Wadsworth Publishing, 1971.
White, Theodore, "A Call for New Thinking about Race Relations in the Big City," *Los Angeles Times,* August 22, 1965.
Whitlatch, W. G., "Toward Understanding the Juvenile Court Process," *Juvenile Justice,* November, 1972.
Winslow, Robert W., *Juvenile Delinquency in a Free Society.* Belmont, Calif.: Dickenson Publishing, 1968.
Witmer, Helen, *Delinquency and the Adolescent Crisis.* Washington D.C.: U.S. Department of Health, Education, and Welfare, 1960.
Yablonsky, Lewis, *The Violent Gang.* Baltimore: Penguin Books, 1970